WRITERS IN PARIS

Writers in Paris

LITERARY LIVES IN THE CITY OF LIGHT

DAVID BURKE

COUNTERPOINT

BERKELEY

Front cover image of Eiffel Tower courtesy of the Library of Congress, LC-USZ62-106561

Back cover photo of the Dôme and the Boulevard Montparnasse courtesy of Rue des Archives, Collection PVDE

Writer photos on front cover, top to bottom: Jean Rhys, Ernest Hemingway, George Sand, Charles Baudelaire, Jean-Paul Sartre and Simone de Beauvoir, Marcel Proust.

Library of Congress Cataloging-in-Publication Data

Burke, David, 1936–
    Writers in Paris / David Burke.
        p. cm.
    ISBN 978-1-59376-157-8
    1. Paris (France)—Intellectual life. 2. Paris (France)—
    Social life and customs. 3. Creative writing. I. Title.

DC715.B92 2008
914.4'3610484—dc22

                                    2007043548

Book design by McGuire Barber Design
Printed in the United States of America

Counterpoint
2117 Fourth Street
Suite D
Berkeley, CA 94710
www.counterpointpress.com

Distributed by Publishers Group West

10 9 8 7 6 5 4 3 2 1

For my wife, the marvelous Joanne

Contents

WRITERS IN PARIS

Introduction

A "MAGNET," a "Mecca," an "incubator," a "hothouse" for writers—all these things Paris has been called, and rightly so. No other city has attracted so much literary talent, launched so many illustrious careers, or produced such a wealth of enduring literature.

From the medieval poet-thief François Villon to his twentieth-century counterpart Jean Genet, from Rabelais to Henry Miller, from Molière to Samuel Beckett, from Madame de La Fayette to George Sand, from Colette and Gertrude Stein to Simone de Beauvoir and Marguerite Duras, Paris has nurtured countless poets, novelists, and playwrights who were among the finest writers and most intriguing personalities of their times.

In the eighteenth century Dr. Johnson noted "the uncommon regard paid in France to persons eminent in literature." For evidence of that, all we need do is take a stroll, and we are practically sure to come upon some of the more than four hundred streets, squares, or promenades honoring them. Even the naughty boys and girls of French literature have one: There's a Rue François-Villon, Rue Charles-Baudelaire, Place Paul-Verlaine, Allée Arthur-Rimbaud, and a Place Colette. Foreigners, too, are celebrated: Dante (Italian); Jean-Jacques Rousseau (Swiss); Heinrich Heine (German); Lord Byron and Charles Dickens (English); George Bernard Shaw, James Joyce, and Samuel Beckett (Irish); Edgar Allen Poe and Ernest Hemingway (American). Compare that to any other city in the world.

French adulation of literary talent has surely been part of the attraction, but writers really came to Paris for excitement, for stimulation, and for the promise—based on ever-growing evidence—of creative inspiration. Goethe raved about "the Paris of the nineteenth century, which, after three generations of men like Molière, Voltaire, Diderot and others, has kept up such a current of intellect as cannot be found twice in a single spot in the whole world."

The mystique of Paris as the navel of literary and artistic creation emerged in the Romantic era of the 1820s and 1830s and grew as the century went on, embellished by Henri Mürger's *Scènes de la vie de bohème*, George du Maurier's *Trilby*, and other works glamorizing the life of the struggling young artist on the Left Bank. Hemingway was still mining that mother lode in the 1950s with *A Moveable Feast*.

The University of Paris, founded in the thirteenth century, has long been an important attraction for French writers, and in the seventeenth century—*le grand siècle*, when literature became a passion—residence in Paris became *de rigueur*. Sartre and Beauvoir, teaching in provincial *lycées* in the 1930s, could not wait to get back to Paris to pursue their true callings. The intellectual stimulation, the competition, the business of literature, the life of the cafés—everything was in *la capitale*.

Just as our writers were enriched by living in Paris, our appreciation of their lives and their work—and indeed of the city itself—is heightened by following them from place to place in our imaginations or, even better, in our walking shoes.

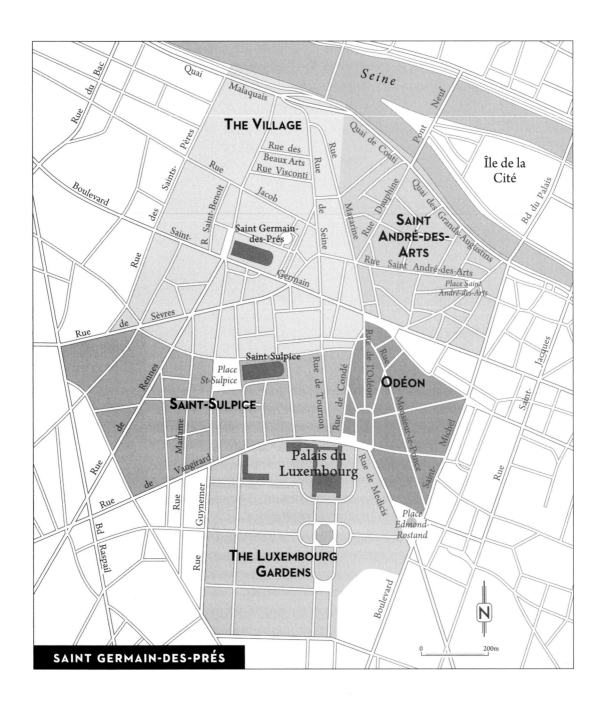

THE VILLAGE

Quai Malaquais

Rue des Beaux Arts
Rue Visconti

Rue Jacob

Saint Germain-
des-Prés

Germain

Seine

Quai de Conti

Pont Neuf

Île de la
Cité

Bd du Palais

**SAINT
ANDRÉ-DES-
ARTS**

Rue Saint André-des-Arts

Place Saint
André-des-Arts

Rue de Sèvres

Rue de

Saint-Sulpice

Place
St-Sulpice

SAINT-SULPICE

Rue de Tournon

ODÉON

Rue de Condé

Rue de l'Odéon

Palais du
Luxembourg

Rue de Médicis

Monsieur-le-Prince

Saint

Michel

Rue

Saint-

Jacques

Place
Edmond-
Rostand

**THE LUXEMBOURG
GARDENS**

Boulevard

Rue de Rennes

de

Vaugirard

de

Rue

Rue Guynemer

Bd Raspail

Rue

Madame

N

0   200m

SAINT GERMAIN-DES-PRÉS

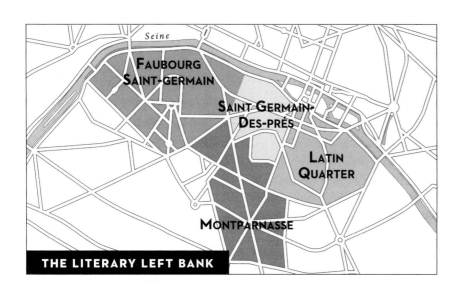

FAUBOURG SAINT-GERMAIN

SAINT GERMAIN-DES-PRÉS

LATIN QUARTER

MONTPARNASSE

THE LITERARY LEFT BANK

The Literary Left Bank

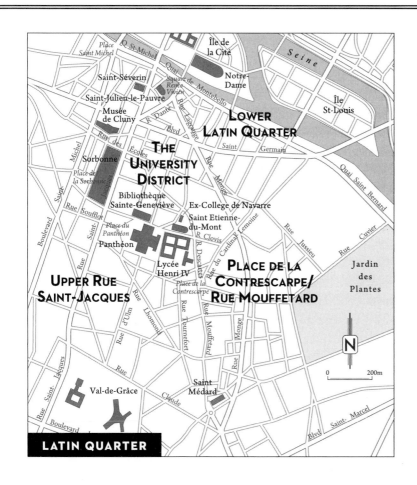

Place St Michel
Q. St-Michel
Île de la Cité
Seine

Saint-Séverin
Notre-Dame
Square de Renée Viviani
Quai de Montebello
Île St-Louis

Saint-Julien-le-Pauvre
Musée de Cluny
R. Dante
Rue Lagrange

LOWER LATIN QUARTER

Rue des Écoles
Saint
Germain
Quai Saint Bernard

Sorbonne
THE UNIVERSITY DISTRICT

Place de la Sorbonne

Bibliothèque Sainte-Geneviève
Ex-Collège de Navarre
Rue Soufflot

Saint Etienne-du-Mont
Rue du Cardinal Lemoine
Rue Jussieu
Rue Cuvier

Place du Panthéon
Panthéon
R. Clovis
R. Descartes

Lycée Henri IV
Jardin des Plantes

Place de la Contrescarpe

UPPER RUE SAINT-JACQUES
PLACE DE LA CONTRESCARPE/ RUE MOUFFETARD

Rue d'Ulm
Rue Lhomond
Rue Tournefort
Rue Mouffetard
Rue Monge

N

0   200m

Rue Saint- Jacques

Val-de-Grâce
Saint Médard
Rue Claude

Boulevard
Blvd. Saint- Marcel

LATIN QUARTER

A Bird's-Eye View

WHEN we think of Rive Gauche, images of youth, art, and *la vie de bohème* leap to mind. These are hardly what Philippe Auguste envisioned at the start of the thirteenth century when he extended the city wall to the south bank of the Seine. His aim was to lure industrious burghers to settle this undeveloped area. Instead, rebel scholars from the cathedral school of Notre-Dame moved in and created the University of Paris. Within a century it was the most illustrious school of theology in Europe, "the oven in which the intellectual bread of the Church was baked," as one medieval Pope called it. The hoi polloi nicknamed the district the Latin Quarter, after the language the scholars spoke.

The university gave the Latin Quarter its *raison d'être*, but it was the freethinkers— including the mavericks, the subversives, the spectacularly politically incorrect—who gave it its verve. Take François Villon, for example: poet, thief, priest-killer, and Master of Arts in Theology. Or the scatological monk Rabelais: he could have been burned at the stake for ridiculing the university's teachings. Four hundred years later, Simone de Beauvoir was a "dutiful daughter" until she fell under the spell of the squat future guru of existentialism while they were studying for an exam.

Foreigners also made their mark—young Rilke, young Hemingway, young Orwell— attracted by rents they could afford.

Between Moliere's first theater, Racine, Mme de La Fayette, and the founding of the Comédie-Française, Saint Germain-des-Prés finally saw the literary light in the seventeenth century, supplanting the Latin Quarter as the Left Bank's premier literary terrain. It reached its apogee during the fervent years after World War II, when figures like Jean Genet, Marguerite Duras, Richard Wright, James Baldwin, and the trio of Sartre-Beauvoir-Camus made it the intellectual capital of the western world.

Next-door Faubourg Saint-Germain went literary in the eighteenth century and remained so to the end of the *belle époque*. This aristocratic district was especially prized by writers as a setting in novels, including Sterne's *A Sentimental Journey*, James's *The American*, and Proust's *The Guermantes Way*.

For Montparnasse, apotheosis arrived in the twentieth century, when, as editor Samuel Putnam put it, "for a decade or more, Paris was a good deal nearer than New York or Chicago to being the literary capital of the United States, as far as earnest and significant writing was concerned." This was the "Lost Generation" era of Gertrude Stein, who coined the label. Her protégé Ernest Hemingway and many other writers, lost or not, spent "earnest and significant" time in the district. F. Scott Fitzgerald, Djuna Barnes, Ezra Pound, Ford Madox Ford, and Jean Rhys were among them. In the 1930s Samuel Beckett decided to settle in Paris for good, and the failed forty-year-old novelist Henry Miller made his miraculous breakthrough with *Tropic of Cancer*, inspired by the "constant army of artists" he saw all around him:

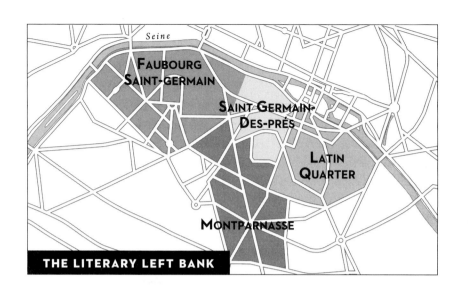

FAUBOURG SAINT-GERMAIN

SAINT GERMAIN-DES-PRÉS

LATIN QUARTER

MONTPARNASSE

THE LITERARY LEFT BANK

The Literary Left Bank

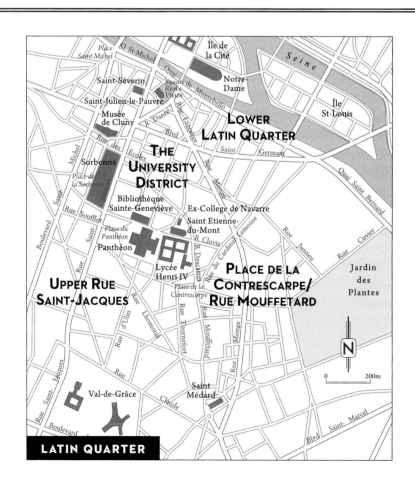

Place Saint Michel

Q. St-Michel

Île de la Cité

Seine

Saint-Séverin

Square de Rene Viviem

Notre-Dame

Saint-Julien-le-Pauvre

Île St-Louis

Musée de Cluny

R. Dante

Rue Lagrange

Quai de Montebello

LOWER LATIN QUARTER

Blvd

Saint

Germain

Quai Saint Bernard

Rue des Écoles

THE UNIVERSITY DISTRICT

Sorbonne

Place de la Sorbonne

Rue Monge

Bibliothèque Sainte-Geneviève

Ex-College de Navarre

Saint Etienne-du-Mont

R. Clovis

Rue du Cardinal Lemoine

Rue Jussieu

Rue Cuvier

Rue Souflot

Place du Panthéon

Panthéon

Rue Descartes

Jardin des Plantes

Boulevard

Lycée Henri IV

Place de la Contrescarpe

PLACE DE LA CONTRESCARPE/ RUE MOUFFETARD

UPPER RUE SAINT-JACQUES

Rue d'Ulm

Rue Lhomond

Rue Tournefort

Rue Mouffetard

Rue Monge

N

Rue Saint-Jacques

Val-de-Grâce

Rue Claude

Saint Médard

0   200m

Boulevard

Blvd Saint Marcel

LATIN QUARTER

A Bird's-Eye View

WHEN we think of Rive Gauche, images of youth, art, and *la vie de bohème* leap to mind. These are hardly what Philippe Auguste envisioned at the start of the thirteenth century when he extended the city wall to the south bank of the Seine. His aim was to lure industrious burghers to settle this undeveloped area. Instead, rebel scholars from the cathedral school of Notre-Dame moved in and created the University of Paris. Within a century it was the most illustrious school of theology in Europe, "the oven in which the intellectual bread of the Church was baked," as one medieval Pope called it. The hoi polloi nicknamed the district the Latin Quarter, after the language the scholars spoke.

The university gave the Latin Quarter its *raison d'être*, but it was the freethinkers—including the mavericks, the subversives, the spectacularly politically incorrect—who gave it its verve. Take François Villon, for example: poet, thief, priest-killer, and Master of Arts in Theology. Or the scatological monk Rabelais: he could have been burned at the stake for ridiculing the university's teachings. Four hundred years later, Simone de Beauvoir was a "dutiful daughter" until she fell under the spell of the squat future guru of existentialism while they were studying for an exam.

Foreigners also made their mark—young Rilke, young Hemingway, young Orwell—attracted by rents they could afford.

Between Moliere's first theater, Racine, Mme de La Fayette, and the founding of the Comédie-Française, Saint Germain-des-Prés finally saw the literary light in the seventeenth century, supplanting the Latin Quarter as the Left Bank's premier literary terrain. It reached its apogee during the fervent years after World War II, when figures like Jean Genet, Marguerite Duras, Richard Wright, James Baldwin, and the trio of Sartre-Beauvoir-Camus made it the intellectual capital of the western world.

Next-door Faubourg Saint-Germain went literary in the eighteenth century and remained so to the end of the *belle époque*. This aristocratic district was especially prized by writers as a setting in novels, including Sterne's *A Sentimental Journey*, James's *The American*, and Proust's *The Guermantes Way*.

For Montparnasse, apotheosis arrived in the twentieth century, when, as editor Samuel Putnam put it, "for a decade or more, Paris was a good deal nearer than New York or Chicago to being the literary capital of the United States, as far as earnest and significant writing was concerned." This was the "Lost Generation" era of Gertrude Stein, who coined the label. Her protégé Ernest Hemingway and many other writers, lost or not, spent "earnest and significant" time in the district. F. Scott Fitzgerald, Djuna Barnes, Ezra Pound, Ford Madox Ford, and Jean Rhys were among them. In the 1930s Samuel Beckett decided to settle in Paris for good, and the failed forty-year-old novelist Henry Miller made his miraculous breakthrough with *Tropic of Cancer*, inspired by the "constant army of artists" he saw all around him:

This is what makes Paris, the vast group of men and women devoted to the things of the spirit. This is what animates the city, makes it the magnet of the cultural world.

THE LATIN QUARTER

THE CHURCH OF SAINT-JULIEN-LE-PAUVRE

Consecrated in 1220, Saint-Julien-le-Pauvre was just nearing completion when the newly established University of Paris began setting up shop next door. And as the university had no buildings, this little gem of a church became its chapel and assembly hall. Over the centuries, it's where Petrarch, François Villon, and Rabelais prayed and attended gatherings. But in the 1520s students rioted and trashed the church. The clergy banned further assemblies.

Saint-Julien-le-Pauvre fell into decay, the Revolution closed the church, and Haussmann's successors scheduled it for demolition. But in 1877, public outcry saved the loveable old wreck. A decade later it came back to life as a Greek Orthodox house of worship, glowing with gilded icons.

In Jean Rhys's 1928 novel *Quartet*, the middle-aged writer Heidler, based on Rhys's lover Ford Madox Ford, takes his mistress to the church:

> Marya turned to watch Heidler go down on one knee and cross himself as he passed the altar. He glanced quickly sideways at her as he did it, and she thought: "I'll never be able to pray again now that I've seen him do that. Never!"

RUE DU FOUARRE

All that remains of the medieval Left Bank's most influential street is a sad little connector between Rue Lagrange and Rue Dante. Yet this was where, in 1215, the rebel intellectuals from the cathedral school of Notre-Dame founded the University of Paris. Because no classrooms were available, lessons were taught outdoors, with the students sitting on bundles of straw—*fouarre*. Young men flocked from all parts of Europe to literally sit at the feet of such theological giants as Albertus Magnus and Thomas Aquinas. By Dante's time, only a century after the university's founding, the street was so famous that he could write about it in the *The Divine Comedy* without even calling it by name, in a stanza about a star teacher:

> . . . the eternal light of Sigebert
> Who escaped not envy, when of the truth he argued,
> Reading in the straw-littered street.

LEFT François Rabelais

RIGHT Joris-Karl Huysmans

Starting with Boccaccio, in a lecture in Florence during the 1370s, many people have claimed that the father of Italian poetry lived in Paris, but no solid evidence has ever come to light. All the same, the city likes to think he did, and it gave Dante a street.

Boccaccio, the illegitimate son of a Florentine gentleman and a French lady, was almost certainly born in Paris. Oddly, he gets no street.

RABELAIS

By the early sixteenth century, over forty colleges, including the Sorbonne, were in operation, but Rabelais, then a graduate student, found their living conditions deplorable:

> The prisoners of the Moors are treated better, murderers in prison, even the
> dogs in your house. If I were the King of Paris, the Devil take me if I wouldn't
> start a fire in there and have the principal and the regent burned, who toler-
> ate such inhumanity before their eyes.

Lectures were still being held in Rue du Fouarre, where Rabelais's young giant Pantagruel takes on the cream of the Parisian intelligentsia, arguing the 9,764 most hotly debated issues of the day, and "notwithstanding their egos and sophistries, he made fools of them all, and conclusively proved to them that they were just calves in petticoats."

Pantagruel's sidekick Panurge—"a mischievous rogue, a cheat, a boozer, a roisterer"—bests the calves in a less cerebral way:

One day, when all the theologians were summoned to meet in the Rue du Fuerre, he made a mud pie composed of garlic, galbanum, asafetida, and castoreum in quantity and of turds that were still warm. This he steeped in the runnings from sores. Then, very early in the morning, he smeared and anointed the pavement, so that the devil himself could not have endured it. Three or four of them brought up the complete contents of their stomachs, there before everyone, as if they had flayed the fox; ten or twelve of them died of the plague, fourteen caught leprosy; eighteen got the gout, and more than twenty-seven contracted pox; but he did not care a fig.

In his two boisterous masterpieces, *Pantagruel* and *Gargantua*, published in the 1530s under the pseudonym of Alcofribas Naiser (an anagram of François Rabelais), the free-thinking Benedictine monk mocked the university's narrow scholastic education—a dangerous thing to do at the dawn of the Protestant Reformation. Several printers, including Rabelais's own, Étienne Dolet, were burned at the stake for publishing books casting doubt on the Sorbonne's teachings. Rabelais was also condemned, but he had well-placed protectors.

Saint-Séverin

In the Middle Ages the maze of streets that grew in the shadow of the church of Saint-Séverin was the honky-tonk and cheap eats district of the Latin Quarter, as it remains today. With narrow Rue de la Parcheminerie, once home to scribes and parchment sellers, ten-foot wide Rue Xavier-Privas, where Ronsard and fellow poets used to meet at the Cabaret de la Rose Rouge, and most buildings two or three centuries old, Saint-Séverin is the Latin Quarter's best-preserved area. It was also a key district in the strange life of Joris-Karl Huysmans, torn between his desire for loose women in the prostitute-infested neighborhood and the spiritual solace he craved at the church.

THE CHURCH OF SAINT-SÉVERIN

One of the most brilliant novelists of the late nineteenth century, Huysmans was baptized on February 6, 1848 in this moody Gothic church. It remained linked to his anguished vision, expressed in four novels tracing the spiritual journey of his alter ego, the writer Durtal. In *Là-bas*, a book so shocking that it could not be published in English for thirty years, and then in a sanitized version, Huysmans explores his fascination with Satanic practices. But in 1892, the year after its publication, a vision of Christ brought him back to the Catholic faith. Three years later he exorcised the "black book" *Là-bas* with the "white book" *En route*, in which this very church, "delicate and petite, muffled shiveringly in the rags of cabarets and hovels," becomes Durtal's sanctuary:

Saint-Séverin enraptured him, helped him better than any of the others to inspire in himself, on some days, an indefinable feeling of lightness and pity, and sometimes even, while reflecting on the rubbish bin of his senses, to wring regrets and dread out of his soul.

At the end of *En route*, Durtal retires to a Trappist monastery, presaging Huysmans's own retreats at Benedictine abbeys over the coming years.

MAURICE GIRODIAS AND THE OLYMPIA PRESS

Maurice Girodias—like his father Jack Kahane, Henry Miller's first publisher—specialized in English-language novels that could not be published in Britain or America because of obscenity laws. His books ranged from Rabelaisian erotica to out-and-out "DBs," dirty books churned out by pseudonymous hired hands. *Until She Screams*, *Tender Was My Flesh*, and *The Whipping Club* were a few of Olympia Press's top sellers. But Girodias also had genuine literary triumphs.

Early in 1957, flush with his profits from Nabokov's *Lolita*, he moved to the seventeenth-century building at No. 7 rue Saint-Séverin, where Allen Ginsberg appeared that September carrying a manuscript by his friend William Burroughs:

Naked Lunch seemed a natural for him, not from the point of view of being a porn novel—which it wasn't anyway—but because he'd published Durrell, Miller, Nabokov, Genet, Beckett.

Girodias hated the look of the manuscript—a bundle of tattered pages with scraps pasted together—and its total lack of "novelistic structure." He turned it down flat. But his divining rod began vibrating a year and a half later when the United States Postal Service cracked down on a Chicago magazine for publishing sections of the book it deemed obscene. He tracked Burroughs down at the Beat Hotel on nearby Rue Gît-le-Coeur, signed him to a contract, and gave him two weeks to get his manuscript typed. Ten thousand copies were in print by the end of July 1959. *Naked Lunch* was an immediate sensation.

A FRESH LOOK AT ENGLISH

In its first production in 1950, Eugène Ionesco's comedy *La Cantatrice chauve* (*The Bald Soprano*) closed after only twenty-five performances; however, tastemakers like André Breton and Raymond Queneau loved it, and *bouche à oreille*—"mouth to ear," as the French say—eventually got it back on the boards. The play reopened at the Théâtre de la Huchette at No. 23 rue de la Huchette in 1957 and has been there ever since.

The idea for the play came from the Rumanian-born author's struggle to learn English from a book called *L'anglais sans peine*, famed for its opening practice example: "My tailor is rich." While all France guffawed at the inane dialogue in the book, Ionesco imagined a world filled with such talk, and ended up writing one of the funniest plays of the twentieth century. Its success made Ionesco a star of the most influential non-realistic theatrical movement of the postwar period, the Theater of the Absurd.

Place Saint-Michel

A HOME AWAY FROM HOME

During the winter of 1922–1923, the weather turned too sharp for Hemingway to work in his garret near Place de la Contrescarpe. So, as he says in *A Moveable Feast*, he escaped to "a pleasant café, warm and clean and friendly" on the Place Saint-Michel. If he worked well he would reward himself with oysters and white wine, because "after writing a story I always felt empty and both sad and happy, as though I had made love."

While writing stories set in the Michigan woods, Hemingway hit upon one of his key convictions: transplanting could be "as necessary with people as with other sorts of growing things." It's a principle he would embrace for the rest of his life.

Quai Saint-Michel

JEAN GENET, *BOUQUINISTE*

If Jean Genet had been half as good a thief as he was a writer, he would have been one of the greatest criminals in France. Luckily, he wasn't, because for a number of years the only

Jean Genet, 1948
photograph by Brassaï

place he could get any writing done was in a jail cell. An illegitimate child abandoned at seven months by his mother, he was a juvenile delinquent, vagabond, thief, jailbird, homosexual, Foreign Legion deserter, and the twentieth-century heir to François Villon.

In December 1940 Genet was sentenced to his tenth term in prison for stealing books, this time from the big Gibert Jeune shop on Place Saint-Michel. Over the next few years he served his eleventh, twelfth, and thirteenth terms behind bars, and there wrote *Notre-Dame des fleurs* (*Our Lady of the Flowers*) and some of his best poetry. Between stretches, he supported himself by thieving and tending a friend's *bouquiniste* stall on the Quai Saint-Michel, across the street from his usual digs, the Hôtel de Suède.

In April 1942, thirty-one years old and yet to be published, Genet met two well-connected young browsers who offered to read his work. But before that could happen, he was arrested again and locked up for another six months. When the two men finally got the manuscript the following year, everything about *Our Lady of the Flowers* floored them, and they set up a meeting for him with Jean Cocteau. Ever on the lookout for new talent, Cocteau knew Genet was the real thing. Despite the severe paper rationing during the war, Cocteau arranged to have the novel published. Initially, *Our Lady of the Flowers* was sold under the counter as high-priced erotica, but it caught on in literary circles. "Saint Genet," as Sartre called him, and his book became a nationwide sensation.

BECOMING GEORGE SAND

On July 15, 1831, Aurore Dupin, the Baroness Dudevant, moved into a fifth-floor apartment in a house which probably stood at No. 29 quai Saint-Michel. She was twenty-seven years old, in the second year of her affair with Jules Sandeau, and working with him on a novel called *Rose et Blanche*. It appeared under the *nom de plume* of J. Sand at the end of the year, to generally favorable reviews. But by then she was writing her own novel about a young woman's quest for ideal love in a world where men no longer deny women their freedom. *Indiana*, the first book to be published under the name of George Sand, was a huge success the following spring. When Victor Hugo scoffed at the praise being heaped on the novel, a much-publicized feud developed—the best break an unknown writer could hope for—jumpstarting her illustrious career.

From her windows overlooking the Seine, Sand witnessed the brutal crushing of a workers' revolt in June 1832. Saber-wielding National Guardsmen shot or hacked down dozens of men, and their bodies were thrown into the river. "The June 6th revolt . . . has thrust me brutally into real life," she wrote a friend.

> . . . to see the straw lightly sprinkled on a cart pushed back to reveal twenty or thirty corpses, some in black suits, others in velvet waistcoats, but all torn, mutilated, blackened by powder, mud-splattered and bloodied; to hear the cries of women who recognize their husbands or their children is horrible. Yet even that is perhaps less awful than to see a poor fugitive being put to death beneath one's window, despite his pleas for mercy, and to hear the death rattle of the wounded man whom no one is allowed to comfort and who is condemned by thirty bayonets.

Quai de Montebello and Rue de la Bûcherie

GEORGE WHITMAN'S SHAKESPEARE AND COMPANY

With books spilling from every nook and cranny, Shakespeare and Company at No. 37 rue de la Bûcherie is the most colorful bookshop in Paris. George Whitman called it the Librairie Mistral when he opened in 1951, but switched to its current name in 1964, two years after the death of his friend Sylvia Beach, whose Shakespeare and Company in Rue de l'Odéon was the bookstore at the heart of the anglophone literary explosion of the 1920s.

Richard Wright, James Baldwin, Peter Matthiessen, J. P. Donleavy, Lawrence Ferlinghetti, Lawrence Durrell, Allen Ginsberg, Gregory Corso, and William Burroughs frequented the shop in the 1950s and gave readings. Shakespeare and Company still hosts frequent poetry and fiction readings, gives literary teas, and maintains a crash pad upstairs for aspiring writers. Whitman's daughter, Sylvia Beach Whitman, now runs the business.

PARIS AT NIGHT

The venerable house at No. 16 rue de la Bûcherie is where Nicolas-Edmé Restif de la Bretonne spent his last years and died, as a wall plaque on it notes. An obsessive nightwalker (the owl was his emblem), "Monsieur Nicolas" was the first writer to see ordinary Parisians as worthy subjects for literature, launching a genre. *Les Nuits de Paris*, the vibrant, acutely observed multi-volume chronicle of his prowls in pre-Revolutionary and Revolutionary Paris, was wildly successful. The books detail lively accounts of erotic happenings, but, unlike his contemporary the Marquis de Sade, whom he despised, Restif was no pornographer or libertine. Nor was he a revolutionist. Though he gave lip service to the Revolution to survive the Terror, he regretted the demise of the old ways, which were being swept away.

Restif de la Bretonne published some two hundred and fifty volumes of novels, plays, chronicles, memoirs, and an eight-volume, Rousseau-style confessional autobiography, *Monsieur Nicolas*, but financial setbacks during his final decade reduced him to taking a day job with the Ministry of Police. Forced into retirement by ill health, he ended his days in poverty. Nevertheless, two thousand admirers, from streetwalkers to duchesses, followed the cortege of the self-styled "perverted peasant" to the cemetery after his death on February 3, 1806.

BEAUVOIR HOTEL

By 1948 Simone de Beauvoir was sick of hotels. She had been living in them for almost two decades, and she wanted a place of her own. That October, as her fortieth birthday approached, she moved from the Hôtel La Louisiane to No. 11 rue de la Bûcherie: three tiny rooms in a fifth-floor walk-up, with a toilet down the hall, redeemed by a view of the river and Notre-Dame. "This will be our place . . . No man but you will ever sleep here" she wrote Nelson Algren, the tall, handsome American novelist she had fallen in love with in Chicago the previous year. He called it the "Beauvoir Hotel."

Algren arrived in May 1949, laden with so many presents they had to make several trips up the stairs. Beauvoir called him her "crocodile husband." Algren called her his "frog wife." *Le Deuxième sexe* (*The Second Sex*), her pioneering study of women's role in society, appeared the next month to ferocious hostility and wild acclaim, selling twenty thousand copies the first week. Algren became so incensed by the more vicious attacks

that he threatened to punch out the perpetrators. From then on, when anyone crossed the Sartre-Beauvoir "family," the response was "Send Algren."

It was a happy time, but it led them both to face the truth: Beauvoir's need for the supercharged intellectual life of Paris—with Sartre at the heart of it—and Algren's need for boxers, hoods, and poker-playing buddies made marriage impossible.

When Algren's plane made a refueling stop in Newfoundland on his return home in September, he learned that *The Man with the Golden Arm* had won the National Book Award.

Beauvoir began working on her novel *The Mandarins* right away, telling Algren, "I am going to dedicate the book to you, since I am yours and my work is yours in so many ways." But when he finally read it in English, he was outraged. The book contained details of their relationship that he considered private, and soul-searching conversations between them had been reproduced verbatim in the dialogue of the American writer Lewis Brogan (a near anagram of his name) and the French psychologist Anne. Algren broke with Beauvoir for several years, and though limited communication was reestablished, the bitterness on his part could never be bridged.

When *The Mandarins* won the Prix Goncourt in 1954, after a lifetime of pinching her *sous*, Beauvoir suddenly found herself a woman of means. She bought a place of her own in Montparnasse.

Quai de la Tournelle

Named for the tower at the eastern end of the Latin Quarter's medieval ramparts, this quay was the embarcadero for the *coche d'eau*, the horse-drawn passenger barge between

Paris and points south, and a popular spot for boat rides. The Tour d'Argent opened at its current site as a *guinguette* in 1582, but quickly evolved into a prestigious restaurant.

In the nineteenth century many literary celebrities graced the penthouse dining room, including the lovers George Sand and Alfred Musset, Victor Hugo and Juliette Drouet, and Alexandre Dumas *père* with his long line of mistresses.

In Henry James's *The Ambassadors*, Lambert Strether invites Mme de Vionnet to lunch at "a wonderful, delightful house of entertainment on the left bank" where the compulsively rational New Englander finds himself losing his intellectual grip:

> How could he wish it to be lucid for others, for anyone, that he, for the hour, saw reasons enough in the mere way the bright, clean, ordered water-side life came in at the open window?—the mere way Mme de Vionnet, opposite him over their intensely white table-linen, their *omelette aux tomates*, their bottle of straw-colored Chablis, thanked him for everything almost with the smile of a child, while her gray eyes moved in and out of their talk, back to the quarter of the warm spring air, in which early summer had already begun to throb, and then back again to his face and their human questions.

PAUL VERLAINE, BOURGEOIS

Before becoming the scandalous homosexual, absinthe abuser, and *poète maudit*, Paul Verlaine was a young married man with a pretty wife, the author of two well-received volumes of verse, and a civil servant at the Hôtel de Ville. He was a short, skinny man, half-bald with a bulbous forehead, but Mathilde didn't care. He was a poet. He was twenty-six, she seventeen, when they married on August 11, 1870. They settled down in a fourth-floor apartment in the building at No. 2 rue du Cardinal-Lemoine. Mathilde recalled in her memoirs:

> Oh, those sweet little *déjeuners*! How happy they were! They were like little dinners, with the new china, the shining silver, and the white linen embroidered with our monogram. After lunch we would have coffee on the balcony, with that fine panorama before us. Then we would send the maid out for tobacco or something, so that we could kiss as much as we liked.

But it was not quite that idyllic. The Franco-Prussian War had broken out three weeks before their wedding, and Verlaine rushed her to the altar in order to qualify for a married man's deferment. After Napoléon III was defeated a month later, Verlaine managed to weasel out of National Guard duty while the Third Republic continued fighting, and he kept a very low profile while the Commune controlled Paris. After crushing the Communards in May 1871, the Republicans gave Verlaine the sack, assuming he had been sympathetic to the Reds (as he was). So Verlaine and the pregnant Mathilde had to move in with her parents in Montmartre, where he received some astonishingly good verses from an unknown poet in a town near the Belgian frontier. Arthur Rimbaud was sent an invitation to visit.

Place Maubert

This little square's name is most likely a corruption of "Maître Albert," the title given to *Doctorus Universalis* Albertus Magnus by his students, who included the young scholar Thomas Aquinas. People thronged to this spot at the foot of Rue de la Montagne-Sainte-Geneviève to attend his theological discourses. In succeeding centuries the area degenerated into a hangout for rowdy students and thugs ("the cesspit of la Maube," Erasmus called it), and a place for public executions. In the summer of 1546, when the Catholic reaction to Calvinism reached the point of hysteria, four printers were strangled and burned at the stake, including Rabelais's publisher Etienne Dolet, for printing books deemed heretical by the Sorbonne.

The University District

THE SORBONNE

After its early days on Rue du Fouarre, the University of Paris expanded up the slopes of the Montagne Sainte-Geneviève, topped at that time by the massive abbey of Sainte-Geneviève, now by the dome of the Panthéon. In 1253, Saint Louis's confessor Robert de Sorbon created the first residential college for a small number of secular students who intended to work toward a doctorate in theology. Other residential colleges quickly sprang up in the area, but all recognized the Sorbonne as the sole body authorized to issue degrees. Villon, Rabelais, Ronsard, du Bellay, Molière, Racine, Cyrano de Bergerac, Voltaire, Diderot, and the Marquis de Sade were students in the pre-revolutionary years.

In 1468, the Sorbonne hired the Gering brothers from Basel to set up Paris's first printing press. Five years later the Gerings opened France's first commercial printing company, Le Soleil d'Or, on lower Rue Saint-Jacques. From then to the end of the *ancien régime*, Rue Saint-Jacques maintained a near-monopoly on printing, book publishing, and book sales in Paris, strengthening the Latin Quarter's already tight grip on the literary and intellectual life of France.

FRANÇOIS VILLON

The original bad boy of French poetry was born François de Montcorbier (or François des Losges) in Paris in 1431, the year Joan of Arc was burned at the stake. His father died when he was a little boy, and Guillaume de Villon, the chaplain of the church of Saint

149 ANCIEN PARIS — L'ÉGLISE DE LA SORBONNE À LA FIN DU XVIIIᵉ S — ND

Benoît-le-Bétourné on Rue Saint-Jacques, adopted him, gave him his name, and eventually sent him to study for the priesthood at the Collège de Navarre. Villon earned his Master of Arts in Theology degree in 1452, but carousing in taverns was more to his liking.

Three years later, for reasons unknown, a fight broke out between Villon and a priest named Philippe Chermoye by the tower of Saint-Benoît, which stood at the corner of Rue Saint-Jacques and today's Rue des Écoles. The priest pulled a knife and slashed Villon's face; Villon responded with a knife to the groin. Chermoye died in the Hôtel Dieu hospital a few days later. Villon got his first taste of prison—six months in the Grand-Châtelet—but after a long inquest he was pardoned by Charles VII.

In 1456 he published his first book of poetry, *Lais*, also known as *Le Petit Testament*. On Christmas night of the same year, he took part in a robbery at his old college for which he was banished from Paris. While living among brigands in the Touraine, he was arrested for theft and imprisoned in the castle of Meung-sur-Loire, where he wrote *Le Grand Testament*, a long poem in the form of a will with humorous bequests to family, friends, and enemies, interspersed with ballads. Thanks to a general amnesty declared for the coronation of Louis XI, he returned to Paris in 1461.

The following year, Villon was arrested for robbery but quickly cleared. Soon after, he was arrested again, this time for his involvement in a brawl in which a pontifical notary was stabbed to death. He was subjected to *la question de l'eau* (water torture), convicted of murder, and condemned to be hanged. While awaiting execution, he wrote perhaps his most famous poem, "La Ballade des pendus" ("The Ballad of the Hanged Men").

On appeal, his sentence was reduced to ten years of exile. He left Paris in January 1463 and was never heard from again.

PLACE DE LA SORBONNE

The Baroque chapel of Sainte-Ursule-de-la-Sorbonne on Place de la Sorbonne, commissioned by Cardinal Richelieu and completed in 1635, is the sole remaining building of the pre-revolutionary Sorbonne; everything else was replaced by the *belle époque* behemoth La Nouvelle Sorbonne. Today, cafés scatter their tables onto the tree-shaded square, and Place de la Sorbonne remains the student gathering place *par excellence*.

After being dumped by Mme de Bargeton, Balzac's twenty-year-old hero in *Lost Illusions*, Lucien de Rubempré, moves to a cheap furnished room on Rue de Cluny. Nevertheless, he writes his sister, "I dine quite well for twenty-two *sous* at the restaurant of a man called Flicoteaux, right in the square in front of the Sorbonne."

Flicoteaux's big, bustling refectory-style eating house at No. 8 served potatoes, whatever else was cheapest in the market, and—as a sign on the wall proclaimed—BREAD AT YOUR DISCRETION. Flicoteaux kept countless students, writers, and artists alive, and the combination of youth, dreams, and poverty made finding kindred souls easy:

> Opposite Lucien sat a thin, pale young man, seemingly as poor as he was, whose handsome but already ravaged face announced that shattered hopes had seared his brow and left furrows in his soul in which sown seed had not germinated. Lucien felt drawn to this stranger by these lingering signs of idealism, also by an irresistible urge of sympathy.

Etienne Lousteau came to Paris to become a serious writer, like Lucien, but instead he's drifted into the sordid world of journalism where bribes, kickbacks, and lies are a way of life. Despite Lousteau's warnings, Lucien—the "great man in embryo"—puts his poetry and novel aside, and enters that other, sordid world. With splendid and miserable results.

Boul' Mich'

In the waning years of the nineteenth century, the Boul' Mich', as students have always called the Boulevard Saint-Michel, was home to a score of bookshops, several big literary cafés, and a very special tourist attraction: Paul Verlaine. Waiters would point out the down-at-the-heels drunk to their customers. When admirers approached and told him how much they loved his poetry, he would tell them, "In that case you might oblige me with five francs." That went for absinthe at one of his favorite cafés. Nonetheless, so respected was the fifty-year-old bad boy of French letters that his fellow poets elected him Prince des Poètes. Paul Fort, a later Prince of Poets, wrote about Verlaine's funeral procession in 1896: "The descent down the Boulevard Saint-Michel of the whole of French or at least Parisian literature was a vision not to be effaced from any memory."

In *The Notebooks of Malte Laurids Brigge*, Rilke's death-obsessed Danish poet lives a few steps from the Boulevard Saint-Michel, and roams the streets of the area, perceiving a sinister reality lurking behind appearances. One day, Brigge becomes fascinated with the strange, hopping gait of an emaciated man with a cane, and follows him down to the Pont Saint-Michel:

> He turned his head slightly, and his gaze wobbled over sky, houses, and water, without grasping a thing. And then he gave in. The cane was gone, he stretched out his arms as if he were trying to fly, and some kind of elemental force exploded from him and bent him forward and dragged him back and made him keep nodding and bowing and flung a horrible dance out of him into the midst of the crowd. For he was already surrounded by people, and I could no longer see him.
>
> What sense would there have been in going anywhere now; I was empty. Like a blank piece of paper, I drifted along past the houses, up the boulevard again.

Rue de la Montagne-Sainte-Geneviève

Twisty old Rue de La Montagne-Sainte-Geneviève climbs the hill of that name from Place Maubert to Place du Panthéon. For five hundred years a large swath of the left side of the street was home to the Collège de Navarre, a fashionable school founded in 1304 by Philip the Fair's wife, Jeanne de Navarre. In the sixteenth century it was known as "le collège des trois Henris," when two future kings—Henri III and Henri IV—and Henri, duc de Guise, the third Henri, were fellow students and, legend has it, shared the same mistress.

François Villon earned two degrees at Collège de Navarre. Four years later he came back to burglarize his alma mater.

In Rabelais's *Pantagruel*, Panurge pulls one of his pranks in the locality:

> At one time he collected three or four good yokels, made them drink like Templars all the evening, and afterwards took them under the walls of Sainte-Geneviève, or to a spot by the Collège de Navarre just when the watch was coming up that way—and to discover the moment, he rested his sword on the pavement and put his ear to it. For when he heard his sword quiver, it was an infallible sign that the watch was at hand. At that moment, then, he and his companions took a dung-cart and pushed it off, so that it rushed with all its force down the hill and knocked all the watch over like so many pigs. Then he and his yokels ran away in the other direction.

Place du Panthéon

The transfer of Voltaire's body to the Panthéon in 1791

THE PANTHÉON

This vast, pompous, lofty-domed neoclassic temple atop the Montagne-Sainte-Geneviève, the highest point of the Latin Quarter, was built in fulfillment of a vow made by Louis XV in 1744. He promised to thank Saint Geneviève if she helped him recover from a wicked attack of the pox. Architect Jacques Soufflot's church took three decades to build, and was finally consecrated in 1789, on the eve of the Revolution. Two years later, the Assembly stripped it of its religious functions and converted it to a secular necropolis. Of the sixty or so *grandes hommes* entombed within the church (two of whom are women, Marie Curie and Sophie Berthelot), only six are writers: Voltaire, Rousseau, Victor Hugo, Alexandre Dumas, Émile Zola, and André Malraux. Entry for writers is based more on political symbolism than literary merit.

Voltaire and Rousseau, those bugbears of the *ancien régime*, were voted in as ideological precursors of the Revolution. Voltaire entered during the euphoric early years of the Revolution, on July 11, 1791; Rousseau entered on October 11, 1794, after the Revolution's bloodiest period—the Terror—had ended.

Despite Hugo's wish for a simple burial, the Third Republic installed him in the Panthéon in a grand public ceremony to honor his eighteen years of self-imposed exile in opposition to Napoléon III's regime, which had helped keep the vision of democracy alive. On June 1, 1885, more than two million Frenchmen followed his funeral cortege from the Arc de Triomphe.

Zola, a hero of the Left because of his courageous accusation of the army in the Dreyfus Affair, was voted in by a Socialist government in 1908. At the induction ceremony, a zealot shot Captain Dreyfus, who was in attendance. Luckily, the bullet only grazed his arm. The would-be assassin was arrested, smoking gun in hand. The jury found him not guilty.

Malraux was *panthéonisé* by Jacques Chirac's Gaullist government in 1996. A committed Leftist in the 1920s and 1930s, and the leader of a Left-leaning Résistance unit during World War II, Malraux converted to *gaullisme* when he met the General in 1945, became a key figure in de Gaulle's inner circle, and was a minister in both of his governments.

Inducted in 2002, Dumas became the first person of African descent to be enshrined. His father was a mulatto general in Napoléon's army.

The descent to the necropolis's crypt leads to a disconcerting environment, rather like an abandoned underground parking garage. The tombs of Voltaire and Rousseau, enemies in life, face each other at the entrance. A life-size statue of the *"prince de l'esprit"* strikes a pose beside Voltaire's imposing marble sepulcher. Rousseau's tomb is in striking contrast: A rustic wood cabin covers the coffin. Hugo, Dumas, and Zola lie in simple white limestone funerary boxes in one small, vaulted chamber. Malraux rests in a separate chamber with three of his political contemporaries, including the martyred Résistance chief Jean Moulin.

SAINT-ETIENNE-DU-MONT

Built between 1527 and 1624 in a blend of flamboyant Gothic and Renaissance styles, the church of Saint-Etienne-du-Mont is loaded with surprises, including a shrine with relics of Sainte Geneviève, the patron saint of Paris. There is no body to entomb because a revolutionary mob burned her corpse on the Place de Grève, and dumped the ashes into the Seine. So much for the miracle worker who saved Paris from Attila the Hun.

A few steps from the saint's shrine are the tombs of Jean Racine (1639-1699), France's greatest dramatic poet, and Blaise Pascal (1623-1662), the mathematical prodigy and founder of the modern theory of probability, physicist, and philosopher. Published by friends after his untimely death, Pascal's luminous *Pensées*—notes for a work-in-progress—preach the need for mystical faith in understanding the universe.

Though Verlaine was a pauper when he died, several hundred mourners—Stéphane Mallarmé, François Coppée, and Paul Fort among them—packed the church on the day of his funeral, January 10, 1896. Gabriel Fauré, who had set *Clair de lune* and sixteen other Verlaine poems to music, was at the organ.

BIBLIOTHÈQUE SAINTE-GENEVIÈVE

This magnificent nineteenth century library at No. 10 place du Panthéon was built on the former site of the Collège de Montaigu, where, three centuries earlier, such incongruous thinkers as Erasmus, Rabelais, Ignatius Loyola, and Calvin studied. The library houses the Fonds Littéraire Jacques Doucet collection, open to accredited scholars and fabulously rich in manuscripts of Baudelaire, Verlaine, Rimbaud, Mallarmé, Gide, Paul Valéry, Tristan Tzara, André Breton, and other innovative nineteenth- and early twentieth-century writers. In the early 1920s, Breton and Louis Aragon worked for Doucet, a rich *couturier* with a passion for manuscripts and modern art. At Breton's urging Doucet bought what is arguably the most important painting of the twentieth century, Picasso's *Les Demoiselles d'Avignon*.

The airy cast-iron and glass reading room of the library was Simone de Beauvoir's favorite place to study when she was a student at the Sorbonne. It is here she earned her lifelong nickname of "*le castor*," "the beaver," because of her amazingly rigorous work habits.

THE CRADLE OF SURREALISM

"My point of departure will be the Hôtel des Grandes Hommes, Place du Panthéon, where I lived in 1918," writes André Breton in the Surrealist classic *Nadja*. If any place can be called "the cradle of Surrealism," it is this attractive hotel at No. 17, where Breton and Philippe Soupault invented automatic writing—prose texts without story, characters, or planned exposition that flowed automatically from their pens, or so they claimed, under the dictation of their subconscious minds. *Les Champs magnétiques* (*The Magnetic Fields*) was cowritten in 1919 and published the following year. The young Surrealists-to-be joined Tristan Tzara and the Dadaists in their anti-art pranks, but broke with them in 1922 and launched their own movement aimed at developing ways to tap the vast, creative reservoir of the subconscious. The founding members, all in their twenties, included Breton, Soupault, Louis Aragon, Benjamin Péret, Paul Éluard, and Robert Desnos. With the publication of his first *Surrealist Manifesto* in 1924, Breton became their acknowledged leader. Over the next few years, the increasingly authoritarian "Pope of Surrealism" would excommunicate almost all his early comrades for violating his arcane and oft-changing rules, while, paradoxically, the Surrealist vision was liberating the minds of writers and artists all over the world.

A ROUGH START

On his first stay in Paris during 1902 and 1903, Rainer Maria Rilke lived in a shabby student room at No. 11 rue Toullier, between Rue Soufflot and Rue Cujas. The house is still there, neat, cream-colored, with weathered shutters. The Prague-born poet was twenty-six years old when he arrived, unquestionably gifted, but emotionally and artistically immature. To him, Paris was a sinister place. He jotted down observations and elaborated on them in letters to his former mistress, Lou Andreas-Salomé, in Vienna. Those letters became the basis for his novel *The Notebooks of Malte Laurids Brigge*. It begins:

Rainer Maria Rilke, 1901
portrait by Helmut Westhoff

SEPTEMBER 11TH, RUE TOULLIER

So this is where people come to live; I would have thought
it is a city to die in.

Notebooks tells the story of a young Danish poet who comes to Paris
to study and write poetry. But as he prowls the city, he finds decay,
fear, and death lurking everywhere, even in that oasis of verdant tranquility—the Luxembourg Gardens. Rilke's purpose in coming was
to write an article about his wife Clara Westhoff's teacher, Auguste
Rodin, whose sculpture he admired intensely. Rodin, thirty-five
years Rilke's senior, befriended the young man, and a father-son
relationship developed. In 1905 Rodin hired Rilke as his secretary,
but fired him abruptly six months later. It was a devastating blow,
but it triggered in Rilke an explosion of new poetry, including the
famous "thing-poems" of 1907, which were influenced by Rodin's
approach to art.

Despite Rilke's early vilification of the city, Paris was the birthplace of the three major
works that turned the apprentice into an acknowledged master: the third part of *The Book
of Hours, New Poems*, published in 1907 and 1908, and *The Notebooks of Malte Laurids
Brigge*, completed in 1910 after almost eight years of creative anguish.

"POULOU" ON RUE LE GOFF

Every man has his natural place. Neither pride nor price determines its altitude:
childhood decides it. Mine is a Parisian sixth floor with a view over the roofs.
—Jean-Paul Sartre, *Les Mots* (*The Words*)

After the death of her husband in 1906, Anne-Marie Sartre, *née* Schweitzer, moved with
her year-old toddler, Jean-Paul, to the home of her parents in Meudon. Five years later
they all moved to the top floor of the Haussmann-style building at No. 1 rue Le Goff,
where "Poulou" grew up in the book-filled milieu of his grandfather, a noted linguist.
Like all members of the illustrious Alsatian family, Sartre was a talented musician. From
childhood on, he played four-handed Chopin waltzes and Schubert *lieder* with his "sister-
mother," who was only twenty-four years old when she became a widow. The idyll continued until he was twelve, when she remarried and her husband, Joseph Mancy, moved
them to La Rochelle. After two disgruntled years, Sartre was allowed to come back to
Paris as a boarder at the Lycée Henri IV. Following a brilliant career at *lycée* and the École
Normale Supérieure, Sartre met his "essential love" in 1929, when friends brought Simone
de Beauvoir into their study group for *l'agrégation*, the dreaded teacher's license exam.

Paul Verlaine in the Café François-Premier, photo by Dornac

Tall, attractive, and very serious, she was twenty-one years old and still "a dutiful daughter." He was an odd-looking young man, three years her elder, barely five feet tall, with a strabismic eye. Already known as a remarkably successful skirt-chaser, he would live up to the reputation for the rest of his life.

Sartre came in first in the *agrégation*, Beauvoir second. But by all accounts, it was a toss-up: their presentations were both dazzling. Sartre's age and the fact that he was a man seem to have tipped the judges' decision. Beauvoir never complained about that bit of sexism. To her, at least in public, nothing relating to Sartre could be wrong.

The Words, Sartre's story of his early years, is his only autobiographical work. Published in 1964, the year he refused the Nobel Prize, it is a trenchant look at his seductive, *grand bourgeois* Parisian upbringing, and the revolt he staged against it in order to become a free-thinking, politically *engagé* writer.

Upper Rue Saint-Jacques and Val-de-Grâce

A Ville de Paris plaque at No. 157 rue Saint-Jacques marks the site of the Porte Saint-Jacques, one of the main gates in the Philippe Auguste wall. Taverns sprang up outside the gate to lure travelers on their way to Saint-Jacques de Compostella and other points south. Non-travelers were lured by the cheap wine, untaxed outside the city limits. From the days of François Villon to the end of the nineteenth century, upper Rue Saint-Jacques was a paradise for literary bohemians. Before converting to a bistro in 1900, Le Perraudin at No. 157 was a *bougnat*, a low-class coal and booze shop, where Verlaine and Rimbaud used to "shoot" absinthe during their prodigious debauch of 1871 and 1872.

VERLAINE

Besides frolicking in this neighborhood with Rimbaud, Verlaine spent the better part of his final, booze-clouded decade here, punctuated by at least one lengthy hospitalization per year. But thanks to a penetrating critical study by Charles Morice in 1888, the public awakened to the greatness of his poetry.

From March to November 1888, he lived at the Hôtel Royer-Collard on the gently sloping street of that name, where the big, gloomy house at No. 14 still stands. Thanks to a publisher's advance, he began holding a Wednesday salon, welcoming up to forty visitors at a time. Just down the hill was his "oasis of tranquility," the Café François-Premier, at No. 69 boulevard Saint-Michel. It is gone now, but famous photos by Dornac and Harlingue show Verlaine in his "throne room" with a big glass of absinthe and an utterly blasted look on his face.

After blowing his advance, Verlaine moved to the Hôtel des Nations in a run-down six-story building, which still stands today, at No. 216 rue Saint-Jacques. Though his room was dark and cramped, his salon continued to draw a distinguished literary crowd until he gave it up six years later.

For much of 1893 and 1894, he lived with the prostitute Eugénie Krantz at No. 9 rue des Fossés-Saint-Jacques and No. 272 rue Saint-Jacques. During one of his hospital stays, in 1893, he decided to promote himself as a candidate for the Académie française. The doctors and nurses at the Hôpital Broussais, who had grown fond of the old reprobate, chipped in to buy him a top hat and tailcoat for the required calls on Academy members. He was so delighted with the outfit that he had himself photographed in it when he left the hospital. He sold it the following day. It seems that upon further reflection, a table at the Café François-Premier was more important than a chair at the Académie française.

LOVE'S EPIC

A plaque on the building at No. 218 rue Saint-Jacques honors the medieval alchemist, astrologer, and poet Jean de Meung. It was here in the 1270s that he completed *Le Roman de la Rose*, a 21,000-line poem whose first 4,000 lines had been composed by Guillaume de Lorris forty years earlier. This allegorical epic on the theme of erotic versus idealized love (the erotic side winning, which got de Meung in serious trouble with the Church) was hugely influential throughout Europe well into the sixteenth century. Chaucer translated at least part of the poem into English a hundred years after its composition, and used it as a model for his early works. *Le Roman de la Rose* is the oldest work in French still read today.

VAL-DE-GRÂCE

In 1637, childless after twenty-three years of marriage, Anne of Austria, Louis XIII's queen, made a vow to build a magnificent church for the Benedictine convent of Val-de-Grâce if her prayers for a child were answered. Louis XIV was born the following year. François Mansart, France's greatest neoclassic architect, was hired to design the splendid Roman-domed edifice we see today. The Revolution converted the convent into a military hospital. Its period of greatest literary interest was during World War I.

On October 27, 1914, a twenty-year-old corporal in the 12th Heavy Cavalry Regiment named Louis-Ferdinand Destouches was wounded in the arm in Flanders and sent to "that noble pot-bellied citadel" to recuperate. One of his fellow patients was a wily sergeant named Albert Million, who became the model for the "old hospital hand" Sergeant Branledore (a play on the slang term for wanking off) in *Voyage au bout de la nuit* (*Journey to the End of the Night*), published eighteen years later under Destouches's pen name,

Louis-Ferdinand Céline. In the novel, Branledore shows young Bardamu and his comrades how to win the hospital staff's sympathy:

> Between two choking fits, if a doctor or nurse was passing, Branledore would
> sing out: "Victory! Victory! Victory will be ours!" Or he'd murmur those
> same words with one corner or the whole of his lungs, as the circumstances
> required. Thus attuned to the ardently aggressive literature of the day by a
> well-calculated bit of histrionics, he enjoyed the highest moral standing. That
> man knew his stuff.

During his hospitalization, Destouches was awarded the *Médaille Militaire* for bravery under fire, pinned on his chest by General Joffre in person. In later accounts of his war injury, Céline upped its gravity from a serious, but far from life-threatening gash in the arm to a near-fatal head wound. That myth and the *Médaille Militaire* would become crucial after World War II when he had to defend himself against charges—all too true—of writing anti-Semitic material during the Occupation.

Two other young men at "the Val" during World War I were André Breton and Louis Aragon, exempted from front line duty to study medicine. They had first met in 1917 at Adrienne Monnier's legendary bookshop on Rue de l'Odéon, but their friendship developed while working as orderlies at the hospital. They became fascinated by the ravings of shell-shocked soldiers in the psychiatric ward. These miraculous revealers of the aesthetic cornucopia of the unconscious mind, as Breton and Aragon saw them, would become important stepping stones on the path to Surrealism.

Place de la Contrescarpe–Rue Mouffetard

Place de la Contrescarpe is the axis of a large, formerly working-class district, the ancient Faubourg Saint-Médard, gentrified, but still colorful, that spreads to the south on both sides of the market street Rue Mouffetard. In the Middle Ages the area lay outside the walls of the city. It has long been a haven for outsiders, real and fictional.

François Villon caroused at the taverns outside the Porte de la Bourdelle, the gate to the road to Lyon, in the fifteenth century, when the little plateau which is now Place de la Contrescarpe teemed with the activity of travelers, stable hands, traders, teamsters, and sedan chair porters. The most popular tavern was the Maison de la Pomme de Pin, where students and fellows came to drink cheap, untaxed wine. Rabelais drank at this tavern in the early sixteenth century, and a few years later Pierre Ronsard, Joachim du Bellay, and fellow poets formed the Pléiade to promote the controversial idea that French was as legitimate a language for poetry as Latin.

TOUT PARIS
1080 – Panorama du Vᵉ arrᵗ – La rue Mouffetard

The lower end of the Rue Mouffetard market street, the church of Saint-Médard on the right

MADAME VAUQUER AND COMPANY

Etched in bold letters into the ancient stone wall on the northwest corner of Rue du Pot-de-Fer and Rue Tournefort is the old name of a street sure to ring a bell with readers of Balzac:

> For the past forty years the elderly Madame Vauquer, *née* Conflans, has kept a boarding house in the Rue Neuve-Sainte-Geneviève between the Latin Quarter and the Faubourg Saint-Marcel.

Rue Neuve-Sainte-Geneviève is now Rue Tournefort, and the model for Mme Vauquer's *pension bourgeoise* in *Le Père Goriot* is down the hill. Most literary archaeologists agree it is the tall, plain, cream-colored house at No. 30.

By the time the novel came out in 1834, Balzac had been living nearby on Rue Cassini for five years, and insatiable *flâneur* that he was, he knew "the grimmest quarter of Paris," as he calls it, inside out.

Balzac took an intense interest in people's surroundings, not merely to use for colorful literary settings, but because he saw the environment both as a molding force and an extension of personality. The odious Mme Vauquer is a perfect example: "The unwholesome plumpness of this little woman is a product of the life she lives here, by the same process that breeds typhoid fever from the noxious vapors of a hospital."

Two of the most vital characters in Balzac's vast series of novels *La Comédie humaine* first appear in *Le Père Goriot*: the law student Eugène de Rastignac, the quintessential young man from the provinces come to make it big in *la capitale*; and the sinister Vautrin, strangely drawn to the handsome young Rastignac (Balzac giving the first hints of homosexuality in French fiction). Vautrin is eventually unmasked as a notorious criminal.

Everything revolves around money, which is another idea Balzac introduced to French fiction. During the Bourbon Restoration, when the story takes place (1819 is the year Balzac specifies), after the successive collapses of the aristocracy of the *ancien régime* and the new Napoleanic nobility, money emerged as the one source of real power. Rastignac sees this force cruelly at work in the fate of Goriot, an old fellow-boarder he befriends and tries to help, who is being bled dry of his retirement funds by his glamorous daughters. But despite the money-grubbing and social-climbing that Rastignac sees all around him and finds disgusting, he cynically plunges into the fray.

About Balzac's characters Baudelaire said:

> From the summit of the aristocracy to the lower depths of the plebian, all the
> actors of his *Comédie* are more greedy for life, more active and cunning in
> the struggle, more patient in misfortune, more gluttonous in pleasure, more
> angelic in devotion, than the comedy of the real world shows them. In short,
> in Balzac, even the door-keepers have genius. All his souls are loaded to the
> muzzle with will. Just like Balzac himself.

JEAN VALJEAN AT THE CHURCH OF SAINT-MÉDARD

Unlike Balzac, Victor Hugo could not roam the streets while he was writing *Les Misérables* in the 1860s. The giant of French letters was then living in self-imposed exile on the Isle of Guernsey. But he had explored every corner of the city during the period the story unfolds, from 1815 to the early 1830s, and a relief map was etched in his heart. Hugo follows his characters virtually block by block in this immense, sprawling novel, naming the streets they traverse, and the landmarks they come upon, including the moody fifteenth-century church of Saint-Médard at the foot of the Rue Mouffetard food market.

After escaping Thénardier's clutches, Jean Valjean and little Cosette are holed up in a hovel at No. 50–52 boulevard de l'Hôpital. Valjean often visits the church of Saint-Médard. He goes at dusk, when the area is almost deserted. His generous nature gets him into trouble, however, when the curiosity of the locals is aroused by the sight of this big man in a threadbare yellow coat and battered hat giving handouts to beggars. Inspector Javert, ever alert to possible sightings of his prey, disguises himself as a *clochard* and squats in front of the church to spy on "the beggar who gives alms." Emerging from the church and placing a coin in the disguised inspector's hand, Valjean gets a split-second glimpse of what he thinks is the "terrible and familiar countenance" of Javert. The resourceful ex-convict tracks Javert to the police station, then immediately sets out with Cosette on their night flight from the Left Bank, with Javert and his men at their heels.

HEMINGWAY'S FIRST HOME

When young Ernest Hemingway lived in the Place de la Contrescarpe area in the early 1920s, it was solidly lower class. In *The Snows of Kilimanjaro*, the writer Harry, dying of a wound in Africa, thinks back to his life in this neighborhood:

> . . . And in that poverty, and in that quarter across the street from a Boucherie Chevaline and a wine-cooperative he had written the start of all he was to do. There never was another part of Paris that he loved like that, the sprawling trees, the old white plastered houses painted brown below, the long green of the autobus in that round square, the sudden drop down the hill of the rue Cardinal Lemoine to the River, and the other way the narrow crowded world of the rue Mouffetard.

Hemingway was twenty-two, his wife Hadley twenty-six, when they moved to No. 74 rue du Cardinal-Lemoine, three weeks after arriving, on January 9, 1922. By then he was already cultivating his diamond-in-the-rough persona, and it suited him to be living among real people, rather than the eggheads in the Latin Quarter or the expatriate phonies in Montparnasse. The plain old apartment building is still there, with a plaque commemorating the stay of the future Nobel Prize winner. He and Hadley lived in a two-room cold-water flat on the fourth floor (*troisième étage*), WC down the hall.

"We could not afford a dog nor even a cat then," Hemingway writes in *A Moveable Feast*. But in fact, between his earnings as a correspondent for the *Toronto Star* and Hadley's revenue from her trust fund, their income was on a level with the French middle class ($5,000 a year, out of which they were paying $18 a month rent). Skiing vacations in the Alps, fishing and bullfighting trips to Spain, and outings to the racetrack were perfectly within their reach. They dined out often, though usually at cheap places because Hem was a tightwad.

Gertrude Stein and Alice B. Toklas paid them a visit in March 1922, and Hemingway gave Miss Stein all the fiction he had written up to this point. Stein objected to his use of dirty words in his story "Up in Michigan." She said they made the story "*inaccrochable*," a term art dealers use about paintings that cannot be hung in a show. The dirty words stayed put. But he took her advice about a novel he had begun: "Begin over and concentrate." He waited three years before starting *The Sun Also Rises*.

JAMES JOYCE AND VALERY LARBAUD

A plaque on the wall by the gateway at No. 71 rue du Cardinal Lemoine, one block downhill from the Hemingways' place, honors Valery Larbaud, who had an apartment here from 1919 to 1937. Larbaud was one of the leading French men of letters, a novelist (most notably of *The Diary of A. O. Barnabooth*), poet, critic, translator, and travel writer *extraordinaire*. This bear of man, wealthy and known for his generosity, was a close friends with Adrienne Monnier and Sylvia Beach. Beach introduced him to James Joyce on Christmas Eve, 1920. The following summer, Larbaud loaned his spacious apartment to Joyce and his family in order to provide the solitude Joyce desperately needed to finish *Ulysses*.

The house is in a leafy residential square at the end of a long driveway with ivy-covered walls. It faces the entrance to the square, slightly to the left, with Larbaud's apartment comprising the whole ground floor.

It was a crucial time for Joyce. After reaching a dead end with publishers in Britain and America because of the censorship laws, Sylvia Beach had stepped forward and offered to publish his masterpiece. Admitting nobody except his wife Nora and the housemaid, Joyce closed himself in his room for long periods of intense work. Struggling with a severe attack of glaucoma that hampered his progress, he worked on Molly Bloom's final monologue:

> ... and then I asked him with my eyes to ask again yes and then he asked me
> would I yes to say yes my mountain flower and first I put my arms around
> him yes and drew him down to me so he could feel my breasts all perfume
> yes and his heart was going like mad and yes I said yes I will Yes.

Joyce completed *Ulysses* in September 1921, and Larbaud began translating it into French, a labor almost as Homeric as Joyce's.

VERLAINE AND HEMINGWAY

In *A Moveable Feast*, Hemingway writes about "the hotel where Verlaine had died, where I had a room on the top floor where I worked." This is the house at No. 39 rue Descartes, where, as a plaque on it notes, the poet expired in 1896. Hemingway rented the garret in the fall of 1922 because the apartment on Rue du Cardinal-Lemoine was too cramped. The room put him in the right frame of mind when he was struggling to get a new story going:

> I would stand and look out over the roofs of Paris and think, "Do not worry.
> You have always written before and you will write now. All you have to do
> is write one true sentence. Write the truest sentence you know." So finally I
> would write one true sentence and go on from there.

GEORGE ORWELL

Rue Mouffetard was so-named because of the *mouffle*—Old French for *stink*—that came from the river Bièvre at the foot of the hill, where skinners, tanners, and tripe butchers plied their pungent trades until the city paved it over at the end of the nineteenth century. This is Orwell country, the area he wrote about in *Down and Out in Paris and London*. Whereas Hemingway romanticized his "very poor but very happy" life as a young writer among the colorful poor of the area, Orwell exaggerated the grimness of the place, and the futility of his and the denizens' struggles.

Down Rue Mouffetard from Place de la Contrescarpe is Rue du Pot-de-Fer. Restaurants with outdoor tables and cuisine from every nation line this narrow but cheerful walking street. In the book he calls it the Rue du Coq d'Or:

George Orwell in his
Down and Out days

> . . . a ravine of tall, leprous houses, lurching toward one another in queer attitudes, as though they had all been frozen in the act of collapse. All the houses were hotels and packed to the tiles with lodgers, mostly Poles, Arabs and Italians. At the foot of the hotels were tiny bistros, where you could be drunk for the equivalent of a shilling. On Saturday about a third of the male population of the quarter was drunk. There was fighting over women, and the Arab navvies who lived in the cheapest hotels used to conduct mysterious feuds, and fight them out with chairs and occasionally revolvers.

Eric Blair, Orwell's real name, was just short of twenty-five when he arrived in the spring of 1928. To his family's distress, he had resigned his commission with the Indian Imperial Police in Burma in order to become a writer, ending up in a squalid hotel at No. 6, the model for the bug-infested Hôtel des Trois Moineaux, which he describes with such loving disgust in *Down and Out*. The inspiration for the book came with his sudden plunge into poverty after most of his money was stolen. In the novel, "a young Italian who called himself a compositor" takes the money from his hotel room; in real life, it was a prostitute named Suzanne. Over the following three months, he went for as long as three days without eating, pawned all his clothes except what he was wearing, and scrounged for menial jobs, most unforgettably as a dishwasher in the none-too-sanitary bowels of a luxury hotel.

The poverty was largely voluntary. His Aunt Nellie lived in Paris and would gladly have come to his aid if he had asked. But he wanted to know what living in these depths was like. And though he was only a visitor, he gave a voice to those who had no escape.

To avoid embarrassing his father, a retired colonial administrator, Eric Blair decided to use a pseudonym when *Down and Out in Paris and London* was published in 1933, choosing the name of a small river near his parents' home in East Anglia. He intended to use "Orwell" only for this book, but the reviews were so good and the sales so unexpectedly healthy that the pseudonym became too valuable to abandon.

Jardin des Plantes

SANCTUARY

In Strindberg's *Inferno*, after the narrator flees from the Hôtel Orfila because he is convinced people there are plotting to kill him, he takes refuge in a hotel near the garden:

> That marvel in the heart of Paris, the Jardin des Plantes, unknown to
> Parisians, had become my private park. I wandered without peril in the midst
> of savage beasts, the entire creation gathered into that small space, a Noah's
> Ark, a Paradise regained.

But the persecutions resume: The manageress of the hotel is spying on him . . . the bumping in the room above starts again, probably those murderous electromagnetic ray guns being rolled into position. "I was condemned to death! But by whom?"

Convinced that he is about to be executed, he goes to the zoo "to say farewell to Creation. I brought some bread and cherries as a treat to my old friend Martin the bear who knew me personally . . ." But after evading his executioners by hiding all night in the hotel's garden, he escapes the next morning to Dieppe, and continues on to Sweden.

RILKE'S PANTHER

In July 1907, Rainer Maria Rilke wrote to his wife Clara that he had spent the whole morning at the Jardin des Plantes zoo watching three gazelles: "As women gaze out at you from pictures, so they gaze out with something, with a soundless, final turn." This observation became the inspiration for *The Gazelle*, one of Rilke's "thing-poems," heavily influenced by Rodin. Watching Rodin work, Rilke saw how he breathed vitality into clay, bronze, and stone, making inanimate figures come to life. Absorbing the spirit of his artistry and transforming it into his own, Rilke went the other way: He turned animate objects into things, sculpted from the words of his poems.

Animals in cages fascinated him, wild cats especially, their eyes and their lifelike movements constantly straining against their confinement, as in *The Panther*:

> His gaze has grown so tired from the passing
> of the bars that it can take in nothing more.

...

Then an image enters in,
passes through the limbs taut stillness
and in the heart ceases to be.

As they did in Rilke's time, gazelles still gaze out, and the bars still pass back and forth before the eyes of a black panther as he paces his cage.

LOLITA IN PARIS

After fleeing his native Russia after the Revolution, Vladimir Nabokov lived the shabbily genteel life of an impoverished aristocrat in exile for two decades in England, Germany, and France, alighting in Paris for the last few years. The Jardin des Plantes played a role in inspiring his most famous novel:

> The first little throb of *Lolita* went through me in late 1939 or early 1940, in Paris, at a time when I was laid up with a severe attack of intercostal neuralgia. As far as I can recall, the initial shiver of inspiration was somehow prompted by a newspaper story about an ape in the Jardin des Plantes who, after months of coaxing by a scientist, produced the first drawing ever charcoaled by an animal: this sketch showed the bars of the poor creature's cage. The impulse I recorded had no textual connection with the ensuing train of thought, which resulted, however in a prototype of my present novel, a short story some thirty pages long. . . . The man was a Central European, the anonymous nymphet was French, and the loci were Paris and Provence. I had him marry the little girl's sick mother who soon died, and after a thwarted attempt to take advantage of the orphan in a hotel room, Arthur (for that was his name) threw himself under the wheels of a truck. I read the story one blue-papered wartime night to a group of friends—Mark Aldanov, two social revolutionaries, and a woman doctor; but I was not pleased with the thing and destroyed it some time after moving to America in 1940.

But the "little throb" stayed with him anyway, and he finally had to write what turned into a novel. The Paris connection came full circle when, unable to find a publisher in the United States or England, Nabokov sent the manuscript to Maurice Girodias's racy Olympia Press, which published *Lolita* in 1955. It was another book in a long list of brilliant English-language novels—*Ulysses*, *Tropic of Cancer*, *The Ginger Man*, *Naked Lunch*—too hot to handle in London or New York.

SAINT GERMAIN-DES-PRÉS

The Village

The epicenter of the cultural explosion emerging from World War II—that fiery mix of "existentialist" philosophy, Cold War politics, literature, theater, and jazz—was the heart of Saint Germain-des-Prés, "the village," as its denizens call it. As the century moved on, more and more fashion boutiques moved into the district, and the ambiance shifted from "Sartre to the sartorial." Even so, this remains the sun of France's literary solar system. Most of the important publishers are here. Brasserie Lipp remains the clubhouse of writers and editors. Les Deux Magots and Café de Flore have their stalwarts. And with fanfare galore, all three cafés present annual literary prizes.

On Place Saint Germain-des-Prés

DEUX MAGOTS

In *Scènes de la vie de bohème*, Henri Mürger refers to the Deux Magots of the 1840s as "a famous drapery establishment, to the window of which Mimi's coquetry used very frequently to pay its devotions." In 1875 the fabric shop took on a new life as a café. It is named for the two little statues of Chinese dignitaries mounted on the wall, already there when the café opened. Nobody knows their history.

The most glamorous of the three establishments, with a spacious *terrasse* on Place Saint Germain-des-Prés, Deux Magots bills itself as "The Rendezvous of the Intellectual Elite." This is no empty boast. Few intellectuals in Paris have *not* rendezvoused here. Verlaine and Mallarmé came in the late nineteenth century. During his miserable last years, Oscar Wilde lifted his spirits with coffee in the morning and with absinthe at night. James Joyce favored the café in the 1920s, and Djuna Barnes often joined "Jim" (she was the only writer who had the temerity to call him by his first name) for a drink. Janet Flanner, a regular in the 1920s and '30s, used to meet with Hemingway at a quiet corner table to discuss their fathers' suicides.

The terrace of the café adjoins Place Jean-Paul Sartre–Simone de Beauvoir, a narrow slice of Place Saint Germain-des-Prés inaugurated in 2000 by a Gaullist mayor in honor of those chronic thorns in the side of Général de Gaulle. In the late 1940s, they would get together with Richard Wright at the Deux Magots to discuss existentialism and politics. Beauvoir, who was fluent in English, translated until Wright learned enough French to hold his own.

When James Baldwin disembarked in November 1948, he was taken directly from the Gare du Nord to the Deux Magots to meet with Wright. At forty, Wright was the most successful African-American writer of his time, thanks to *Native Son* and *Black Boy*. Baldwin was twenty-four, had $40 to his name, and had published next to nothing. They knew each other from New York, where Wright had helped Baldwin land a writing grant. Wright stood up from the table and gave him his hearty "Hey, boy!" greeting. "I took this meeting as a good omen," Baldwin would later recall, "and I could not possibly have been more wrong."

An essay published by Baldwin the following spring would trigger a bitter feud.

FLORE

Named for the little statue of the goddess of spring by the front door, the Café de Flore at No. 172 boulevard Saint-Germain opened in 1865. It launched its career as a literary café two decades later, however, when Joris-Karl Huysmans, Remy de Gourmont, and fellow *décadence* writers gathered around the tables. But in the 1890s, Flore went political. Writers Maurice Barrès and Jacques Bainville and their ultra-nationalist anti-Semitic *Ligue de la patrie française* made it their headquarters during the Dreyfus Affair, and were soon joined by *L'Action française*, another group of the same stripe. Four decades later, one of its founders, writer Charles Maurras, was tried for his role in the Vichy regime's anti-Semitic agenda. When the verdict of life imprisonment was read out in court, the old man shouted, "This is revenge for Dreyfus."

In 1917 Guillaume Apollinaire, the man who invented the word "surrealism," met André Breton at the café and introduced him to Philippe Soupault, who became Breton's writing partner on *Les Champs magnétiques*, the first Surrealist book. Jacques Prévert, another early Surrealist, made the café his local in the 1930s. André Malraux and poet and champion *flâneur* Léon-Paul Fargue were also regulars.

But during the Occupation, as Sartre recalled, the café was far more than a local for him and Simone de Beauvoir:

Jean-Paul Sartre and Simone de Beauvoir crossing Place Saint Germain-des-Prés, mid-1950s

> We worked from 9am until noon, when we went out to lunch. At 2 PM we came back and talked with our friends till 4 PM, when we got down to work again until 8 PM. And after dinner, people came by to see us by appointment. It may seem strange, all this, but the Flore was like home to us: even when the air-raid alarm went off,

we would merely feign leaving and then climb up to the first floor and go on working.

Beauvoir started working here in January 1941, while Sartre was in a German POW camp. She chose it because it was warm. Even during the worst shortages, the owner, Boubal, always managed to find fuel. And since the German officers preferred the ground floor and the *terrasse*, French customers went upstairs where they were left alone. After Sartre returned that April, he and Beauvoir did virtually all their work at the café. And 1943 was a breakthrough year for them both. He published *L'Être et le néant* (*Being and Nothingness*), and his first play, *Les Mouches* (*The Flies*), was produced; she published her first novel, *L'Invitée* (*She Came to Stay*). Sartre's *Huis-clos* (*No Exit*) was produced at the Théâtre du Vieux-Colombier the following year.

After the war they became celebrities. People would stare at them as they strode through Saint Germain-des-Prés, fascinated by their bohemian lifestyle and by Sartre's intriguing notion of "necessary" and "contingent" loves. Young men lugged around *Being and Nothingness*: In a district where *intellectuel* equalled *sexy*, it was a formidable tool for attracting girls. When Nelson Algren saw Sartre in action, he was amazed: "Despite the fact that he was undersized, wall-eyed, and shabbily dressed, he had no more trouble finding people to sleep with than did Cary Grant."

In the late 1940s, the café's upstairs room became a sanctuary at night for gay men, "*mes mignons*," as Boubal called them. This was a key place for young James Baldwin, who was struggling to come to terms with his sexuality. He later said, "In some deep, black, stony, and liberating way, my life, in my own eyes, began during that first year in Paris." His experience came to literary fruition eight years later with *Giovanni's Room*, a novel entirely set in Paris, about a gay love affair.

BRASSERIE LIPP

The Brasserie des Bords du Rhin, as it was originally called, was opened in 1880 by an Alsatian named Léonard Lipp, who could not bear to remain in his homeland while it was under German rule. But as people always called the brasserie "chez Lipp," he eventually put up a new sign. It is at No. 151 boulevard Saint-Germain.

Lipp has long attracted France's political elite. Presidents De Gaulle, Pompidou, Mitterrand, and Chirac lunched within its Art Nouveau tiled and mirrored walls. But its most important clientele are writers and editors, and Gallimard, Grasset, Hachette, Flammarion, Plon, Seuil, and Editions de Minuit are among the publishing houses nearby. "I go there as an Englishman to his club, sure to find a true friend," said Léon-Paul Fargue. Camus and Sartre lunched regularly during the early days of their friendship.

In the spring of 1949, Lipp became the scene of a showdown between Richard Wright and James Baldwin. On the very day Baldwin's essay "Everybody's Protest Novel" was published in the magazine *Zero*, he stopped by and was beckoned by Wright to his table. Wright accused Baldwin of trying to destroy his reputation and that of his novel *Native Son*. In the essay, Baldwin claimed that the "failure of the protest novel lies in its rejection of life, the human being, the denial of his beauty, dread, power, in its insistence that it is his categorization alone that is real." To illustrate such a stereotypical figure, he had singled out Bigger Thomas, the violence-prone black man who kills a white woman in *Native Son*, labeling him the twentieth-century heir of another stereotypical black fictional character (though a benign one rather than violent): Harriet Beecher Stowe's Uncle Tom.

"All literature is protest," insisted Wright. "All literature may be protest," replied his quick-witted protégé, "but all protest is not literature."

Though they would often meet over the coming years, the friendly feelings they once shared never revived. After Wright's sudden death in 1960, Baldwin was consumed by remorse. In his essay *Alas, Poor Richard*, published several months after Wright's death, Baldwin said:

> He saw clearly enough, far more clearly than I had dared to allow myself to
> see, what I had done: I had used his work as a kind of springboard into my
> own. His work was a road-block in my road, the sphinx, really, whose riddles
> I had to answer before I could become myself.

SARTRE AND MADAME MANCY ON RUE BONAPARTE

While right-wing newspapers continued to portray him as living amid "a penumbra of spilled ashtrays and scattered clothes in squalid hotels," Jean-Paul Sartre was living in *grand bourgeois* style with his widowed mother, Mme Mancy, in the large apartment they bought in October 1946, located on the fourth floor of the Haussmann-style building at No. 42 rue Bonaparte. Then forty-one, Sartre was at the height of his influence. Other than Voltaire and Victor Hugo, no writer in French history has held such sway over the intellectual climate of his time. Sartre's output of literary, philosophical, and theatrical works was prodigious—fueled, it must be said, by staggering quantities of alcohol, amphetamines, barbiturates, tobacco, and coffee. His championing of leftist political positions made him the paramount *intellectuel engagé*.

He and Beauvoir were no longer lovers, or only occasionally. But their intellectual passion never dimmed. "La Grande Sartreuse," as the wags called her, was the linchpin of the Sartrian machine, including his magazine *Les Temps Modernes*. She continued to critique every word he wrote, while at the same time writing her own works, most importantly *The Second Sex*.

In the early 1950s, when many intellectuals were starting to distance themselves from Communism, Sartre became a frequent guest star at rallies of the French Communist Party, and he and Beauvoir paid highly publicized visits to Castro, Tito, and Khruschchev.

Though they never joined the Party, they hewed to the Stalinist line until 1956, when the brutal crushing of the Hungarian uprising by the Red Army cooled their ardor.

In 1960 the Minister of the Interior wanted to arrest Sartre for his support of the Jeanson network—named for Francis Jeanson, Sartre's *Temps Modernes* colleague—which had been outlawed for its aid to the FLN rebels in Algeria. President de Gaulle overruled his minister, saying, "You don't arrest Voltaire."

In July 1961, and again in January 1962, the anti-Algerian independence OAS (Secret Army Organization) bombed Sartre's apartment. No one got hurt, but the second blast blew down the front door and did considerable damage. Sartre sold the apartment, and he and Mme Mancy moved to Montparnasse.

MARGUERITE DURAS ON RUE SAINT-BENOÎT

After Sartre and the Sartrians became tourist attractions at the Flore, one of the places they would hole up was the Montana Bar, still there at No. 28 on this block-long street, after the war the entertainment district of "the village." Sartre, a passionate jazz fan, was a regular at the Club Saint-Germain at No. 13, where he was introduced to Charlie Parker. "I dig your playing, man," the jazz great told him.

But the writer who owns this street is Marguerite Duras. Though she was born to a struggling French family in Indochina, where her best-known novels are set, her fiery and amazingly complicated literary, political, and amorous life took place during her long residence at No. 5 rue Saint-Benoît. She found her apartment though a chance encounter in 1940 with the wife of writer Ramon Fernandez, who lived in the building and who would soon become a leading collaborator of the Nazis.

In 1943, Duras, her husband Robert Antelme, and her lover Dionys Mascolo joined the Résistance network directed by François Mitterrand, alias Morland, and her apartment became one of its meeting places. Mitterrand actually lived here for a while, and it was a way station for Jews. Meanwhile, directly upstairs, Ramon and Betty Fernandez were entertaining Nazi officials and the cream of the collaborationist literati, Drieu la Rochelle, Céline, and Jacques Chardonne. While this risky cat and mouse game was going on, Duras and her lovers were leading sex lives straight out of a farce by Feydeau. She and Dionys were keeping their affair secret from Robert, who was his best friend. Meanwhile, Dionys was deeply involved with another woman, and Robert was in love with another woman as well. As for Marguerite, she rented a little flat because she was juggling so many other men.

On June 1, 1944, the Gestapo arrested Robert Antelme at his sister's home on Rue Dupin. In the chapter of Duras's memoir *La Douleur* (*The War*) entitled *Monsieur X, Here Called Pierre Rabier*, she describes a bizarre relationship that developed between herself and a French Gestapo agent from whom she was seeking information about her husband's fate.

During the war, Duras published her first novel, *Les Impudents* (signing it with the name of her family's village of origin in the Dordogne rather than her birth name of

Donnadieu), but her first book to arouse a critical stir was *Une Barrage contre le Pacifique* (*The Sea Wall*) in 1950, a powerful novel about an obsessive mother, based on Duras's childhood in Vietnam. One literary success followed another—*The Square, Moderato Cantabile*, her screenplay for Alain Resnais's *Hiroshima Mon Amour*, her Prix Goncourt-winning novel *The Lover*, and *The North China Lover* among them. Her only failures were with the many films she directed.

A passionate political idealist, Duras joined the French Communist Party in 1944, but she was too independent to last for long under its unswervingly Stalinist direction. It dumped her after five years.

Though ferociously opinionated and unable to accept contradiction, she could be funny and charming, and had many friends, almost all of them men.

Duras died here on Rue Saint-Benoît on February 28, 1996, at eighty-one densely packed years of age.

DIDEROT

Jean Gautherin's vigorous bronze of Denis Diderot is one of the finest statues of a writer in Paris. It stands at No. 245 boulevard Saint-Germain, a few steps from the house where Diderot lived from 1754 to 1784, later replaced by the Deux Magots's building. One of the big three of the Enlightenment, Diderot shared with Voltaire and Rousseau a passion for philosophy, literature, morality, and the betterment of the human race, but only he delved deeply into science and technology, making him the consummate "universal man."

Diderot is chiefly remembered for *L'Encyclopédie*. This project began as a job translating

Ephraim Chambers's pioneering English *Cyclopaedia*, but instead, Diderot and mathematician Jean Le Rond d'Alembert developed a plan for a vast new work. With seventeen volumes of text, eleven volumes of plates, and sixty thousand articles, it would become the very embodiment of the Age of Reason.

The first volume came out in 1751, and nine more followed until 1759, when the Conseil du Roi abruptly halted the project on the grounds that Diderot and his contributors (Voltaire and Rousseau among them) were lacing the books with challenges to church and state with ideas such as this:

> The good of the people must be the great purpose of government. By the laws of nature and reason, the governors are entrusted with power to that end. And the greatest good of the people is liberty. It is to the state what health is to the individual.

After Diderot threatened to publish the *Encyclopédie* in Holland—no idle threat, because the project was one of Paris's leading employers—the government allowed publication to resume. He agreed to let the censors review everything, but invented all sorts of cunning ruses to get around them.

Diderot's works of fiction, brilliant, often droll, and remarkably modern in tone, were written for his own enjoyment and that of select friends. Almost all were too scandalous to be published at the time he wrote them. They include *La Religieuse* (*The Nun*), *Jacques le fataliste et son maître* (*Jacques the Fatalist and his Master*), and *Le Neveu de Rameau* (*Rameau's Nephew*). Only one novel, *Les Bijoux indiscrets* (*The Indiscreet Jewels*), published in Holland, came out during his lifetime. In it, women talk "from the most sincere part of them and the best instructed in the things you desire to know . . . from their jewels." It was a version of *The Vagina Monologues* two and a half centuries before its time.

Rue de Seine and its Cross Streets

SARTRE AND BEAUVOIR AT THE LOUISIANE

Thanks to a contract Sartre landed to write screenplays, he and Beauvoir were able to move in the fall of 1943 from their shabby digs on Rue Dauphine to the Hôtel La Louisiane at No. 60 rue de Seine, in the Buci food market. Sartre had a tiny room whose "bareness surprised more than one visitor," Beauvoir notes in *La Force de l'âge* (*The Prime of Life*). "He did not even own any books." She took a large, circular room down the hall with a divan, big table, and stove, where she cooked for Sartre and "the family," and—when she could scrounge enough food to go around—old friends such as the Queneaus or Sartre's new friend Albert Camus. This "simple, cheerful soul," as she called him, was then editor-in-chief of *Combat*, the leading Résistance newspaper, and the author of *L'Étranger* (*The*

Stranger) and *Le Mythe de Sisyphe* (*The Myth of Sisyphus*), published the previous year. "The quality's not exactly brilliant, but the quantity is just right," he joked after his first time at her table.

Sartre lived at the Louisiane until he moved to Rue Bonaparte in 1946. Beauvoir left for Rue de la Bûcherie two years later.

LA PALETTE

This venerable bohemian haunt at No. 43 has the air of a Jean Rhys novel, and indeed, James Ivory shot scenes for his movie of *Quartet* in the café. Artists made up much of the clientele in the early days—the École des Beaux-Arts being steps away—but Jarry, Apollinaire, and André Salmon often got together to share poetry at the dawn of the twentieth century. In *La Force des choses* (*The Force of Circumstance*), Beauvoir recalls the fiery debates during the Algerian War. Jacques Prévert, another onetime Louisiane resident, also favored this café, as did Alberto Moravia whenever he was in Paris. He loved La Palette because he never failed to find people in passionate discussion.

THE BARONESS COMES TO TOWN

The Baroness Dudevant made an arrangement with the baron that she could spend three months a year in Paris for her writing career, while he would remain on their estate in Nohant with the children. For propriety's sake, she moved in with her half-brother Hippolyte when she arrived on January 4, 1831. A plaque on the townhouse at No. 31 rue de Seine marks the brief stay of the future George Sand. A month later she moved in with her "petit Jules," Jules Sandeau.

Rue Jacob

YOUNG RACINE

Jean Racine came to Paris at nineteen, in 1658, to study at the Collège d'Harcourt (now Lycée Saint-Louis), and fell in with group of tavern-loving poets, including Jean de La Fontaine, a distant relative eighteen years his senior. To extricate the youngster from such influences, the Racine family (his parents having died when he was a child) sent him to live with his cousin Nicolas Vitart—a fellow member of the puritanical Jansenist sect—at his home, the seventeenth-century house with the bulging belly at No. 7. To further distance him from temptation, the family sent him to live with an uncle, the vicar-general in Uzès, hoping Racine would forget about poetry and become a priest. After a year and a half in the south, he was back at No. 7 rue Jacob, writing poetry and plays, and carousing with La Fontaine. In 1663, Racine made a name for himself with an ode to Louis XIV, and the following year his new drinking companion, Moliere, gave Racine his first theatrical production with his tragedy *La Thébaïde, ou les Frères ennemis*.

THE AMAZON

Natalie Clifford Barney, known as "The Amazon" because of her quasi-military pursuit of other women, was a wealthy, attractive American socialite who, as a teenager, scandalized the right-thinkers of Cincinnati with her openly lesbian poetry and the conduct to match. Even before settling in Paris, at twenty-five, Barney was notorious in France thanks to *L'Idylle saphique*, a 1901 *roman à clef* by the courtesan Liane de Pougy, which graphically detailed her affair with the lusty *américaine*. In 1909, the year she moved to the house at No. 20 rue Jacob, Barney created her literary salon. Over the next thirty years, it attracted such luminaries as Gide, Apollinaire, Proust, Colette, Valéry, Cocteau, Stein, Joyce, Pound, T. S. Eliot, and Djuna Barnes.

At a little Greek *temple d'amitié* in the garden (built by George Sand's grandfather Marshal Maurice de Saxe for the actress Adrienne Lecouvreur), Sapphic dances were performed by Barney, her lover and fellow poetess Renée Vivien, and other young women, including Colette, who reportedly had a fling with the hostess.

One of her conquests, Barney claimed, was Djuna Barnes. Barnes later denied that, but she was an intimate of the house. In *Ladies Almanack*, her comic novel about the Left Bank lesbian world, the wench-chasing heroine Dame Evangeline Musset is Barney. Nip and Tuck, the messengers who alert her to the arrival of a new wench in town, are fictionalized versions of Janet Flanner and Solita Solano.

Despite Barney's fascist and anti-Semitic leanings, she remained friendly with Gertrude Stein and Alice B. Toklas, though they lost touch during World War II. Barney was living in Mussolini's Rome, while Stein and Toklas were hiding from the Nazis in Savoy.

Barney died at her home on Rue Jacob in 1972 at ninety-five years of age.

COLETTE À PARIS

In *Claudine à Paris*, published in 1901, the seventeen-year-old heroine, whose father has dragged her away from their village in Burgundy, starts to take a look at the city:

> I can't conceive why people live in Paris for their pleasure, without being forced to do so, no, but I'm beginning to understand that you can take an interest in what happens in these big six-story boxes.

The six-story house at No. 28 is where twenty-year-old Sidonie-Gabrielle Colette lived when she first arrived in 1893, shortly after her marriage to Henry Gauthier-Villars, an industrious jack-of-all-literary-trades who wrote under the name of Willy. He was thirteen years older than Colette. "It was marry Willy or become an old maid or teacher," she said.

They lived well. Colette had a cook and a maid, and Willy a valet. But they spent little time in the apartment: "We were always out—dinners, lunches, soirées, theater."

Willy squired his country girl to the liveliest salons, most importantly that of Mme Arman de Caillavet, who took her under her wing. She met Mme Arman's lover Anatole France, poetess Anna de Noailles, Maurice Ravel, Georges Clemenceau, and many other celebrities, and a youngster named Marcel Proust. She later repaid Mme Arman's kindness by satirizing her as old Ma Barman, the vulgar, bitchy Jewess with a hooked nose in the *Claudine* series. Anatole France, alias Gréveuille, comes off as a windbag, and Proust is a "pretty boy of letters" who presumes to analyze Claudine's soul.

Colette and Willy

Colette wrote her first novel, *Claudine à l'école* (*Claudine at School*) on Rue Jacob. According to Colette, Willy locked her in a room and made her write a fictionalized story of her school days. But when he read it, he said it was useless, and stuck it in a drawer. A few years later he came upon it by chance, reread it, liked it, and took it to a publisher—who accepted it. Otherwise, she said, "it is probable that I should never have produced another line."

It is true that Willy urged her to write the book—and encouraged her to work in a bit of schoolgirl lesbian flirtation—but Colette wrote it of her own volition: 656 handwritten pages between October 1895 and January 1896. Willy then took it to several publishers, but none was interested. Three years later, the success of another schoolgirl novel inspired him to show it around again. *Claudine at School* came out in 1900. It was a best seller.

Willy took sole credit as the author.

A NEST OF AMERICANS

The Hôtel d'Angleterre at No. 44 rue Jacob, so named because it once belonged to the English, holds far happier memories for Americans. It was here that Franklin, Adams, and Jay began negotiating the peace treaty granting America its independence.

In 1805, Washington Irving stayed in the building, already a commercial hotel: "60 livres per month room pleasantly situated on the ground floor with a cabinet etc., looks out on a handsome little garden," he noted in his journal. Then twenty-two, Irving was spending two years exploring Europe, mainly the Mediterranean, where he met Lord Nelson in Sicily shortly before Trafalgar. Fifteen years later his stories "Rip Van Winkle" and "The Legend of Sleepy Hollow" made him the first American fiction writer to become famous in Europe.

But the hotel's main claim to fame is the stay of another twenty-two-year-old American would-be writer, who checked in with his wife Hadley a few days before Christmas in 1921. Ernest Hemingway had heard of the hotel from Sherwood Anderson, who urged him to go to Paris, telling him he could live cheaply and write stories about America. Anderson also gave him letters of introduction to three friends: Sylvia Beach, Ezra Pound, and Gertrude Stein.

Djuna Barnes stayed at the hotel in the spring of 1921 and throughout much of 1922. Another guest that year was the novelist and *Broom* magazine editor Harold Loeb, an important friend of Hemingway's in the early years, until he read *The Sun Also Rises*.

STERNE AND YORICK

No. 46 rue Jacob is the site of the former Hôtel de Modene, where Parson Yorick is a guest in Lawrence Sterne's *A Sentimental Journey through France and Italy*. This comic novel, published in 1768, was loosely based on the author's travels on the continent—in search of treatment for a grave and worsening case of consumption—from 1762, the year he stayed at the hotel, until 1765.

Yorick, who first appeared in *Tristram Shandy*, the wildly digressive comic novel that made Sterne famous, is fascinated by a beggar who accosts fashionable ladies in front of the hotel and unfailingly gets them to dip into their purses. He approaches the beggar and worms out his secret: "Flattery, the more outrageous the better, will get you any-where with women in Paris." Yorick tests the theory on hostesses in the Faubourg Saint-Germain, with sterling results.

THE PLACE DE FURSTENBERG

This tiny square is one of the most elegantly proportioned in the city. In *Tropic of Cancer*, Henry Miller says:

> The other night when I passed by it was deserted, bleak, spectral. In the mid-
> dle of the square four black trees that have not begun to blossom. Intellectual
> trees, nourished by the paving stones. Like T. S. Eliot's verse. Here, by God,
> if Marie Laurencin ever brought her Lesbians out into the open, this would
> be the place for them to commune. *Très lesbienne ici.* Sterile, hybrid, dry as
> Boris's heart.

Fronting on the square at No. 6 is the Musée Delacroix, where the great painter moved in 1857 to be near the church of Saint-Sulpice for a commission. One of the murals Delacroix painted, *Jacob Wrestling with the Angel*, deeply moved August Strindberg when he was living through the spiritual nightmare described in *Inferno*. Named after the painting, the sequel, *Jacob Wrestles*, details his escape from the nightmare.

Baudelaire, who characterized Delacroix as "a volcanic crater artistically concealed beneath bouquets of flowers," visited him at the studio, as did George Sand. Letters and documents in the museum evoke the painter's close ties with them and other writers.

Rue Visconti

OLD RACINE

In 1692 Jean Racine moved to the house at No. 24, part of a much larger house built a century earlier at a time when this short, narrow street was a Calvinist stronghold known as "little Geneva," where much blood was shed in the Saint Bartholomew's Day Massacre. Racine lived here for his last seven years, dying at sixty in 1699, as the plaque on the house notes.

Racine was the greatest French poet of the seventeenth century, and France's greatest tragedian. *Andromaque*, *Britannicus*, *Bérénice*, and *Phèdre* remain the very core of the French tragic repertory. He wrote his most important plays between 1667 and 1677, but abandoned the theater for an appointment as Historiographer to the King.

Despite his Jansenist religious convictions, Racine was perfectly capable of stabbing a friend in the back, as he did to Molière in 1665, when he took a play already in rehearsal at Molière's theater and gave it to a rival company to put on. He could be a hypocrite as well. When Pierre Corneille was old and desperately poor, Racine—a wealthy man with a large house and numerous servants—did nothing to help him. Yet when the father of French tragedy died in 1685, Racine delivered a stirring funeral oration at the Académie-Française.

BALZAC'S PRINTING BUSINESS

After failing to make his mark early as a novelist, twenty-seven-year-old Honoré Balzac (no "de" yet) decided to go into business. In June 1826 he opened a printing shop in the house at No. 17 rue Visconti, with his shop on the ground floor and a tiny flat upstairs overlooking the street. The business was underwritten by loans from his mother and from Mme de Berny, his mistress. Balzac had the excellent idea of publishing the complete works of great authors of the past at affordable prices; however, a deep economic depression set in, and he went bankrupt two years later. His response was to plunge into the writing of *Les Chouans*, his first successful novel, published the following year. It was the first of many demonstrations of Balzac's astounding ability to shrug off a catastrophe and move on.

The shop's failure left him heavily in debt, a condition that would dog him almost to the end of his days, but his losing battle with capitalism made him a novelist acutely aware of the power of money. It helped him create characters who vividly reflect his belief that individuals can never be separated from their economic environment. Through David Séchard's struggle for survival in the printing business in *Lost Illusions*, Balzac paid himself back richly for the suffering he went through on Rue Visconti.

Rue des Beaux-Arts

A chic little street lined almost exclusively with art galleries, Rue des Beaux-Arts is also the site of a diminutive hotel with a large place in literary history, mainly because of the first writer to check in.

Oscar Wilde

WILDE'S LAST DAYS

"I am dying beyond my means," Oscar Wilde famously quipped as he lay on his deathbed. And it was perfectly true. Dirt cheap though the Hôtel d'Alsace was, if it hadn't been for the soft heart of the owner, Wilde would have been evicted for nonpayment.

After his release from Reading Gaol in 1898, Wilde fled England for France, penniless, and demoralized by the British public's crushing rejection because of his homosexuality. Even so, his genius for the devastating line never failed him. About the dreadful wallpaper in the hotel room he said, "One of us has to go."

He went, at forty-six, on November 30, 1900.

In *The Importance of Being Earnest*, when Jack Worthing tells his friends in Shropshire that his brother Earnest has died, Canon Chasuble asks, "Will the interment take place here?"

Jack: "No. He seems to have expressed a desire to be buried in Paris."
Canon Chasuble: "In Paris! (*Shakes his head*) I fear that hardly points to any very serious state of mind at the last."

To the last, Wilde remained true to the philosophy of the play: "We should treat all the trivial things of life seriously and all the serious things of life with sincere and studied triviality."

He is buried at Père-Lachaise Cemetery.

Now called simply L'Hôtel, the ex-Hôtel d'Alsace at No. 13 rue des Beaux-Arts is just the kind of place Wilde would have been delighted to die in: a chic little hostelry with a gleaming black marble lobby and luxurious rooms. His room, No. 16, has been decorated in the style of his London apartment, with everything as he would have had it, except for one thing: the unpaid hotel bill in a frame on the wall.

WOLFE

American novelist Thomas Wolfe stayed at the still modestly-priced Hôtel d'Alsace during the winter of 1924–1925, as does Wolfe's alter ego Eugene Gant in *Of Time and the River*:

It was a good hotel and was the place where Oscar Wilde had died. When he wanted to see the celebrated death room, he would ask to see "le chambre de Monsieur Veeld," and Monsieur Vely, the proprietor, or one of his buxom daughters, would willingly show it.

BORGES

Argentine poet, essayist, and short story writer Jorge Luis Borges stayed at L'Hôtel on several visits he made to France between 1977 and 1984, after the hotel had gone upscale. Though his tales of fantasy and multiple worlds would eventually become classics, he was unknown internationally until he was in his sixties. Borges was deeply grateful to France, the first non-Hispanic country to recognize his genius, for making him a commander of the Ordre des Arts et des Lettres in 1962. Twenty-one years later, France granted him the Légion d'honneur. He was eighty-four years old.

Plaques over the front door of L'Hôtel honor Wilde and Borges.

LEFT George Sand in men's clothing, 1836 engraving by Luigi Calamatta from an 1834 portrait by Delacroix

RIGHT Alfred de Musset at the time he met George Sand

Quai Malaquais

GEORGE SAND AT HER *MANSARDE BLEUE*

The four years George Sand lived in her "*mansarde bleue*," the top-floor apartment above the treetops and open to the sky, were among the wildest years in a life rarely lacking for excitement. During the first few months of 1833, she signed a contract for her new novel *Lélia*, became romantically involved with the actress Marie Dorval, ended her affair with Jules Sandeau, and had a disastrous fling with Prosper Mérimée. On June 19 she met Alfred de Musset, and six weeks later began her celebrated affair with the boy wonder of Romantic poetry. At twenty-one, he was seven years Sand's junior, as was the discarded Sandeau.

The first big disruption in their off-again, on-again relationship took place the following March when Musset fell ill with a fever in Venice. A young, handsome physician named Pagello came to the room. Sand fell for him immediately. As they were sitting at the patient's bedside one day, she wrote a love note and slipped it to the doctor. He naively asked whom it was for. She took it back and wrote, "*Au stupide Pagello.*"

When Musset recovered and saw what was going on, he left Venice in a fit of jealousy. Sand moved in with Pagello and proceeded to redecorate his apartment (there was a distinctly maternal side to all her affairs). After traveling through Europe that summer, they alighted in her love nest on the Quai Malaquais. But Pagello returned to Italy at the end of

October, and Sand and Musset resuscitated their amour. Five storm-tossed months later, on March 6, 1835, she cut off her hair, sent it to Musset, and fled to her estate in Nohant, breaking with him for good.

Despite and undoubtedly because of the suffering he went through with Sand, the emotionally fragile Musset wrote his most enduring works during their affair: his plays *Les Caprices de Marianne, Fantasio, On ne badine pas avec l'amour,* and *Lorenzaccio,* and wrote his novel about their relationship, *La Confession d'un enfant du siècle,* shortly after it had ended. As for Sand, she published *Lélia,* thirteen other novels, and three travel books during her *mansarde bleue* period.

A plaque on the building at No. 19 quai Malaquais notes her stay.

ANATOLE FRANCE

Jacques-Anatole-François Thibault, pen name Anatole France, was born in 1844 in a house in the rear courtyard of Sand's building, and he spent his childhood in the bookshops his father owned on Quai Malaquais and Quai Voltaire. There is a plaque in his honor on the École des Beaux-Arts building.

Though France may be remembered today mainly as Proust's model for Bergotte in *In Search of Lost Time,* and as the lover of the imperious Mme Arman de Caillavet, he was a graceful and subtle stylist who wrote with compassion for the downtrodden in his early novels, as did his contemporary Zola. But unlike Zola's books, France's are laced with irony. His most widely read novels are his biting, satirical political allegories *Penguin Island* and *The Revolt of the Angels* from the years leading up to World War I.

During the Dreyfus Affair, Anatole France became a strong supporter of the unjustly accused captain. When Zola was stripped of his membership in the Légion d'honneur for writing "*J'accuse,*" France publicly renounced his own membership.

France won the Nobel Prize in Literature in 1921. At his funeral procession three years later, the nation's most beloved writer drew 200,000 mourners, the largest turnout for a writer since Victor Hugo in 1885.

Place de l'Institut

THE BIBLIOTHÈQUE MAZARINE

In the east wing of the Institut de France building—the domed, crescent-winged landmark designed by Louis Le Vau—is the Bibliothèque Mazarine, a jewel of a seventeenth-century library created to house the book collection of Cardinal Mazarin, installed in 1668. It is both a museum of the history of books, with displays of illuminated manuscripts and rare volumes, and a working library, open to the public on weekdays.

In 1860 Baron Haussmann pushed through a resolution to demolish the Institut de France building, but Jules Sandeau saved it. Then Minister of Public Instruction, he went to Napoléon III and convinced him to visit the Bibliothèque. The Emperor was so enchanted that he overruled Haussmann and granted the library funds for renovation.

When Marcel Proust was in his late twenties, his father Dr. Proust, worrying that his son was becoming a dilettante, pulled strings to land him a prestigious volunteer position at the library. But Proust spent practically all his time on sick leave or vacation, and when the director of the library finally asked him to come in and do some work, he quit.

The Pont des Arts and the Institut de France

THE ACADÉMIE FRANÇAISE

Since 1805, when Napoléon installed the Institut de France in La Vau's landmark building, it has been the home of the Académie Française, France's most prestigious institution, established by Cardinal Richelieu in 1635 as the official guardian of the French language. The members, known as "immortals," are statesmen, generals, clergymen, academics, philosophers, and writers, though no more than a few writers occupy the forty *fauteuils* at any one time. The primary duty of the Academy is to prepare a dictionary of French language and usage. Work on the tenth edition, which began in 1985, should be completed by the 2030s.

The list of writers who became *académiciens* is impressive: Corneille, Racine, Boileau, La Fontaine, Saint-Amant, Voltaire, Chateaubriand, Hugo, Musset, Marivaux, Mérimée, Dumas *fils*, Rostand, Valéry, Mauriac, Claudel, Pagnol, Cocteau, Senghor, Julien Green, Ionesco, and Marguerite Yourcenar.

But the rejects and refuseniks are a lot more exciting: Molière, Diderot, Rousseau, Beaumarchais, Stendhal, Balzac, Dumas *père*, Sand, Flaubert, Baudelaire, Verlaine, Mallarmé, Zola, Huysmans, Maupassant, Apollinaire, Gide, Proust, Malraux, Breton, Aragon, Sartre, Beauvoir, Camus, Genet, Beckett, and Duras.

Before 1980, when Yourcenar was inducted (reluctantly on her part, she accepted only for the sake of women's rights), the Academy was all male. It now has a handful of *académiciennes*.

Rue Mazarine

THEATERS ON RUE MAZARINE

In the seventeenth century, theater companies would set up shop in abandoned courts where the original form of tennis was played—*le jeu de paume,* as it was called, because the players whacked the ball with the *paume* of their hand. These big, empty boxes were easily converted into playhouses. And as Molière once said (after he became successful), all he needed to create theater was "a platform and a passion or two."

ILLUSTRE THÉÂTRE

In December 1643, a new troupe called the Illustre Théâtre moved into the *jeu de paume* of Les Métayers at No. 12 rue Mazarine (then Rue des Fossés de Nesle), where a plaque on the present-day building notes its stay. The old pros of the company were the Béjarts, a family of actors whose star was the eldest daughter, Madeleine. She was a beautiful, supremely talented performer of twenty-six, who sang and danced well, could play all sorts of musical instruments, and had been on stage since she was twelve. Joining the company was her young boyfriend and theatrical novice Jean-Baptiste Poquelin, the goofy-looking son of a well-to-do cloth merchant who had rejected the safe bourgeois life of his father. It was here that young Poquelin first used the pseudonym of Molière. How he chose it nobody knows, but he would make it the greatest name in French theater. Not in this *jeu de paume*, however: The Illustre Théâtre only lasted a year. Molière's success would be a very long time coming.

THÉÂTRE GUÉNÉGAUD

Another converted tennis court with a troubled but truly illustrious theatrical history was the Théâtre Guénégaud at No. 42 rue Mazarine, where, as a plaque notes, the first French opera opened on March 3, 1671. *Pomone*, by Pierre Perrin and Robert Cambert, was a smash hit, running 146 performances. It would have run even longer if wily composer Jean-Baptiste Lully hadn't talked Louis XIV into granting him a monopoly on vocal music in theaters in Paris. He took over the theater and closed *Pomone*.

Lully was even more jealous of Molière. Only a few months after Molière died in 1673, Lully managed to get his troupe evicted from its theater in the Palais-Royal and moved his own company in. Molière's troupe, now homeless, merged with the company of the Théâtre du Marais to form a company called Les Comédiens du Roi. They moved into the Théâtre Guénégaud, opening that July with *Tartuffe*. In 1680 Louis XIV ordered the Comédiens du Roi to merge with the troupe of the Théâtre de l'Hôtel de Bourgogne, creating the Comédie-Française (the date is still boldly stamped on the company's logo). But nine years later, the troupe was forced to move from the Théâtre Guénégaud when the puritanical directors of the Collège des Quatre Nations, then housed in the Institut de France building, pulled strings to distance their innocent scholars from the theater's libertine men and painted women.

THE COMÉDIE-FRANÇAISE ON RUE DE L'ANCIENNE-COMÉDIE

The Comédie-Française decamped from the Théâtre Guénégaud to another *jeu de paume* a block and a half up the street at No. 14 rue de l'Ancienne-Comédie (a short stretch of

Rue Mazarine later renamed in the company's honor). On April 18, 1689, with Molière's widow Armande Béjart still in the troupe, the company opened with Molière's *Le Médecin malgré lui* and Racine's *Phèdre*. The company remained at this playhouse until 1770, when it embarked on a peripatetic existence, playing mainly at the Tuileries Palace, before settling into the Théâtre de l'Odéon in 1782.

A plaque on the facade of No. 14 commemorates the company's eight-decade stay.

LE PROCOPE

Paris's first coffee shop is still doing business at its original location, No. 13 rue de l'Ancienne-Comédie. Founded by Francisco Procopio dei Coltelli, a Sicilian nobleman who helped introduce the Oriental beverage called *café* at the Saint-Germain Fair, Le Procope opened in 1686. When the Comédie-Française moved directly across the street three years later, actors, theatergoers, and writers became hooked on the new beverage and the easy social atmosphere. The key figures of the Enlightenment later made it their local. Diderot and D'Alembert planned *L'Encyclopédie* at the café.

"Our office was a café," philosophers in Le Procope café in the 18th century

Among its many literary clients in the nineteenth century were Hugo, Balzac, George Sand, Musset, Gautier, Zola, Huysmans, and Maupassant. On July 10, 1894, two hundred leading men of letters gathered to elect a new Prince of Poets—a title first conferred on Ronsard in the sixteenth century—and chose Verlaine over Mallarmé by a two-to-one margin. By then a destitute alcoholic calamity, the new prince was deeply moved by the news. He gestured out of his hotel window toward the Luxembourg Gardens and said, "I have no palace, but this is my royal park."

In the twentieth century the Procope went into decline and closed for a while. But it reopened as a restaurant in 1988, ornately refurbished, even a bit kitschy, but filled with treasures: old prints, maps, manuscript pages, eighteenth-century portraits, busts of Voltaire and Franklin, and Voltaire's marble-top desk.

ZOLA AND THE PASSAGE DU PONT-NEUF

It takes quite an effort to picture today's cheery, art gallery-lined Rue Jacques-Callot as Émile Zola described it in his 1867 novel *Thérèse Raquin*, when the street was still known as the Passage du Pont-Neuf:

> At the end of Rue Guénégaud, as you come up from the river, you find the
> Passage Pont-Neuf, a sort of narrow, dark corridor connecting Rue Mazarine
> with Rue de Seine. This passage is thirty yards long and two in width at the

most; it is paved with yellowish flagstones, worn and loose, which always
exude a damp, pungent smell, and it is covered with a flat, glazed roofing
black with grime.

This is the setting for Zola's grisly tale of adultery, murder, and tortured conscience, a
roman noir with echoes of Poe. Some critics objected that Zola exaggerated the grimness
of the *passage*, and perhaps for the sake of his story he did. But Zola knew the area well.
As a young man he had lived nearby on Rue Monsieur-le-Prince in conditions almost as
squalid as those of the unfortunate Thérèse and her circle.

ROBERT DESNOS

From 1934 to 1944 Robert Desnos, the most playful of the early Surrealists, lived in the
house at No.19 rue Mazarine. He joined the movement in 1924, the year André Breton
published his first *Surrealist Manifesto*. Desnos was the champion at relating dreams while
under hypnosis. In his friend Man Ray's 1928 film *L'Etoile de mer*, based on Desnos's poem,
the poet is seen asleep and dreaming. Desnos lasted six years in the group before being
excommunicated by Breton; however, he remains among the most widely read of the
Surrealists, thanks in large part to his books for children *Chantefables* and *Chantefleurs*.

Jewish and a *résistant*, he was picked up by the Gestapo on February 22, 1944, and
deported. He died of typhus at the Terezin concentration camp on June 8, 1945, a few
weeks after its liberation by the Red Army. He was forty-three years old.

Desnos is buried in Montparnasse Cemetery.

Saint-André-des-Arts

PLACE SAINT-ANDRÉ-DES-ARTS

This lively square tucked behind the Saint-Michel fountain is named for an early-thirteenth-
century church, demolished in 1808. François-Marie Arouet, the future Voltaire, was baptized in the church in 1694. The son of a lawyer, he grew up in a solid middle class milieu
and attended the prestigious Jesuit Collège d'Harcourt (now Lycée Louis-le-Grand). He
would spend the rest of his life railing against the idiocies he associated with his social
class.

Like a scene right out of *La Bohème*, in the nineteenth century the square was ringed
with young, impoverished artists' ateliers. In the 1850s, London-born art student George
du Maurier lived in one of them. Years later, when he was a famous caricaturist for *Punch*,
he used to regale his friend Henry James with tales of his Parisian youth. James loved the
stories and urged him to write them down. The result was Du Maurier's 1894 novel *Trilby*.
It opens on what he calls "Place Saint-Antoine-des-Arts," where three young artists from
the British Isles are charmed by the lovely milkmaid Trilby and by her sweet voice crying,

"Milk below, milk below." She may be forgotten, but no one has forgotten the mesmerizing mastermind of her fabulous singing career: Svengali.

Trilby was an enormous success, with 200,000 copies sold in the United States alone the year it was published. Henry James was so jealous it ruined their friendship.

YOUNG BAUDELAIRE

Charles Baudelaire was born on April 9, 1821, in a house on Rue Hautefeuille later demolished to make way for the Boulevard Saint-Germain. His father, Joseph-François, was a charismatic ex-priest, art connoisseur, painter, and the retired head of the administrative office of the Senate. He was sixty-one, his wife Caroline twenty-seven when their only child was born. Charles was just short of six years old when his father died, devastating the hypersensitive boy, but he and his mother drew close in their mutual grief.

The following year they moved to a cheaper apartment in the seventeenth-century Hôtel de Monthlou at No. 30 rue Saint-André-des-Arts, where a plaster medallion and a couple of floral clusters survive over the entrance. It was the happiest time of the boy's life, as he basked in the love of his adoring mother and the doting housemaid. He later wrote:

> Men who have been raised by women and among women are not at all like
> other men . . . The precocious taste of the feminine world, *mundi mullebris*,
> with all that undulating, scintillating, and perfumed apparatus, makes supe-
> rior geniuses.

His attachment to his mother became a romantic passion. Less than two years after his father's death, he was stunned when she abruptly remarried. He never learned the reason for the haste, but less than a month later she delivered a stillborn child.

Baudelaire's feelings of rejection and betrayal erupted violently in adolescence and continued for the rest of his life, a pattern of ardent love alternating with rage. In the more than ten thousand letters he wrote to his mother, mostly begging for money, this pattern is constantly at work.

His stepfather, Jacques Aupick, was a military man devoted to *"la règle"* of duty, discipline, and hard work. He tried to convert his stepson to these sturdy values, but Charles would have none of it. "To be a useful man has always seemed something hideous to me," he later said. Baudelaire was a brilliant but rebellious student, fascinated with bohemians and prostitutes, including the cross-eyed Sarah, from whom he caught gonorrhea when he was eighteen. He spurned the diplomatic career General Aupick planned for him: His heart was set on becoming a poet.

In later years Baudelaire would come back to the Saint-André-des-Arts quarter with Jeanne Duval, his "Vénus noire." Together they frequented the Caveau de la Bolée, an atmospheric cabaret in a thirteenth-century cellar, still in business at No. 25 rue de l'Hirondelle.

YOUNG HUYSMANS

The pot-bellied seventeenth-century house at No. 9 rue Suger was the birthplace of Joris-Karl Huysmans, on February 5, 1848, as a plaque on it notes. He was baptized at the church of Saint-Séverin with the given name of Charles-Marie-Georges, but adopted the *nom de plume* of Joris-Karl in honor of his father, a lithographer and descendent of Dutch painters. When Huysmans was only a child, his beloved father died and, as with Baudelaire, his mother soon married a stepfather he hated: no doubt one cause of the strain of misogyny that runs through his novels.

Rue Gît-le-Coeur

CHESTER HIMES AT THE BEAT HOTEL

In the late 1950s the elegant four-star Hôtel du Vieux Paris at No. 9 was a fleabag known—thanks to its guests Allen Ginsberg, Peter Orlovsky, Gregory Corso, and William Burroughs—as the Beat Hotel. Photos of them are in the lobby. But the first important writer to stay here was Chester Himes, who checked in with his German girlfriend in the spring of 1956.

Like many other African Americans, Himes was driven to France by his rage about racism in America. But complete escape was impossible: He was turned away by several hotels because, as the receptionists told him, white American guests didn't want blacks staying there.

Chester Himes

Himes had started writing in the 1930s while serving eight years for armed robbery in Ohio State Prison. By the time he arrived in Paris in 1953, he was forty-four years old and had four powerful novels to his credit, including *If He Hollers Let Him Go* and *The Lonely Crusade*, but they had not brought him the fame or financial stability he needed. In 1957 Marcel Duhamel, the director of Gallimard's *Série noire*, signed Himes to a contract to write detective novels. In *La Reine des pommes* (*A Rage in Harlem*), he introduced two minor characters who would eventually dominate his eight-novel Harlem cycle: detectives Coffin Ed Johnson and Grave

Digger Jones. The best known of these novels is *Cotton Comes to Harlem*, thanks to the hit movie.

La Reine des pommes won the prestigious Grand Prix du Roman Policier in 1958. In his autobiography, *My Life of Absurdity*, Himes says, "Now I was a French writer and the United States of America could kiss my ass."

He and Marlene left the hotel for Majorca in September 1957, missing the Beats by a few weeks.

THE BEATS AT THE BEAT HOTEL

Ginsberg, Orlovsky, and Corso checked into a room with a double bed on October 15, 1957. Corso, who was straight, slept on the floor. Then thirty-one, but looking and acting ten years younger, Ginsberg had been traveling with his "wife," as he called Orlovsky, for six months in various spots in Europe and in Tangiers, where they stayed with Burroughs. In the meantime, a censorship case in San Francisco was making Ginsberg famous.

On March 5, 1957, his poem "Howl" was seized on the grounds of obscenity, and its publisher, City Lights Bookstore owner Lawrence Ferlinghetti, was arrested. Between the "Howl" case and the publication of Jack Kerouac's *On the Road* that summer, the Beat Generation was big news. *Life* magazine sent a writer and photographer to the Beat Hotel the month Ginsberg and company arrived. The article made them look ridiculous, but they loved it, because

Peter Orlovsky (in cap) and Allen Ginsberg in Paris, December 1957

their new celebrity status got them what they wanted: drugs, and access to other celebrities. And that status got them a meeting with Jean Genet, their living saint. But their relationship with Genet ended abruptly when Corso painted pictures on the walls of an apartment where one of Genet's friends had graciously let him stay.

In Paris, Ginsberg wrote the lovely poems "At Apollinaire's Grave," "The Lion for Real" and "To Aunt Rose," and he composed fifty-six lines of his most moving work, "Kaddish," about his mother's madness, weeping as he wrote them in café Sélect.

Corso, a Greenwich Village street kid who spent most of his youth behind bars, discovered poetry at seventeen while serving time for robbery. He reached his peak as a poet in Paris, writing "Bomb," "Marriage," and "The Happy Birthday of Death."

Burroughs arrived at the Beat Hotel in January 1958, armed with his messy manuscript of the Sade-tinged, hallucinatory extravaganza he then called *Interzone*. Ginsberg, who had previously tried to pitch it to Olympia Press owner Maurice Girodias, returned home in July, but Burroughs's new best friend Brion Gysin took over the task. When Girodias finally decided to publish the book a year later, Gysin and other Beat Hotel cronies—fortified by copious lashings of cocaine and speed—typed the chaotic mess into a legible manuscript to make Girodias's two-week deadline. *Naked Lunch* came out a month later.

Life magazine paid another visit to the Beat Hotel.

Rue Séguier

EDGAR ALLAN POE

Rue Séguier was named Rue Pavée-Saint-André when Poe made it the setting of "The Mystery of Marie Rogêt." Marie, the unfortunate *grisette* who lives in her mother's *pension bourgeoise*, suddenly disappears. Four days later, "her corpse was found floating in the Seine, near the shore which is opposite the Quartier of the Rue Saint-André." Published in 1842, this was the second of Poe's *Tales of the Grotesque and Arabesque* to feature C. Auguste Dupin, the prototype of the brilliant, aristocratic amateur sleuth who steps in and solves murders that bewilder the police. Dupin—Sherlock Holmes's forebear—also appears in the first detective story ever written, Poe's "The Murders in the Rue Morgue," and in "The Purloined Letter."

Baudelaire, Poe's great champion in France, shared his taste for the strange and the morbid. He translated the first of many Poe stories in 1848, a year before Poe died. Four years later, he published the first serious study of Poe's life and work.

Albert Camus in the late 1940s

ALBERT CAMUS

From 1946 to 1950 Albert Camus lived with his beautiful wife, Francine, and their young twins in a cramped duplex apartment at the rear of the courtyard of No. 18 rue Séguier. This self-described "mixture of Fernandel, Humphrey Bogart, and a samurai," was the brightest light in the intellectual firmament of post–World War II France, along with the binary star Sartre-Beauvoir. He had come into his own as a writer during the Occupation with *The Stranger* and *The Myth of Sisyphus*, both published in 1942, and as the editor-in-chief of the leading clandestine newspaper *Combat*. Sartre, eight years Camus' senior, became a sort of older brother. But the two began drifting apart politically after the Liberation: Sartre supported the Stalinist line, and Camus spoke out about Soviet political repression. "It is better to be wrong by killing no one rather than be right with mass graves," he said.

Camus completed *La Peste* (*The Plague*) in 1947. Considered by many his finest novel, it was also an enormous success, selling 52,000 copies in its first few months. But this was a trying time for him, torn as he was between philosophy and politics, literature and journalism. He fought hard to keep *Combat* alive, but it collapsed the same year.

Like Henri Perron, the character based on him in Beauvoir's *The Mandarins*, Camus found it almost impossible to resist attractive women. He had countless liaisons and several affairs, the most serious by far with the Spanish-born actress Maria Casarès. They had a passionate affair when they first met early in 1944, but he broke it off that fall when his wife, who was stranded in Algeria during the war, finally made it to Paris. When he ran into Maria again on the Boulevard Saint-Germain in 1948, their passion reignited. He remained married, but Maria was the love of his life.

Rue des Grands-Augustins

HEINRICH HEINE

In 1841, ten years into his exile from Germany, Heinrich Heine, then living in the townhouse at No. 25 rue des Grands-Augustins where Jean de La Bruyère, the author of *Les Caractères*, had lived in the late seventeenth century, fell in love with a *grisette* named Mathilde in a glove shop in the Palais-Royal. George Sand and his other literary friends put up strenuous objections to his wish to marry her: At twenty-one, she was less than half Heine's age; her brains were no match for her undeniable beauty; Heine had paid off her aunt to allow the marriage; and he was already ill in the secondary stage of syphilis. Surprising his friends, Mathilde became a loyal and affectionate wife, who cared for him as he degenerated into helplessness. She never learned German and could not understand his poetry. But this endeared her all the more to him: As he told his friends, she loved him for himself rather than for what he produced.

Rue Christine

GERTRUDE STEIN AND ALICE B. TOKLAS

In 1938 Gertrude Stein and Alice B. Toklas had to leave their legendary atelier in Montparnasse when the owner reclaimed it for his son. Stein took it in stride, saying, "Now we need the picturesque the splendid we need the air and space you only get in old quarters." So they packed up their Picassos and Cézannes and moved to a large second-floor apartment in the courtyard of the seventeenth-century house at No. 5 rue Christine. It was just around the corner from Picasso's studio at No. 7 rue de Grands-Augustins.

But with the Fall of France in 1940, Stein and Toklas, both Jewish, went into hiding in Savoy, where Stein had a country home. Meanwhile, the Gestapo searched the Rue Christine apartment. Their opinion of Stein's Picassos: "Jewish trash, good for burning."

When Stein and Toklas returned after the Liberation, some blankets, linen, and china were missing:

> But the treasures, they left them all there, all the youth of me and Picasso,
> everything was there. Picasso and I kissed and we almost wept together. All
> of his things were there, nothing was broken, not even a plaster bust that
> Picasso himself sculpted in our youth, no everything was there.

The ladies delighted in the company of GIs and turned the apartment into an unofficial enlisted men's club. In 1945 Stein published *Wars I Have Seen*, essays on the two wars she had lived through in France. The following year, when the U.S. government refused to issue a passport to Richard Wright because of his leftist past, she convinced the French to send an official invitation, which the U.S. could not refuse.

Wright said his ears had been opened to "the magic of the spoken word" in literature by Melanctha, the black servant in Stein's *Three Lives*, saying it was "as if I were listening to my grandmother for the first time, so fresh was the feeling it gave me." On her part, Stein was impressed by Wright's *Native Son* and *Black Boy*. He arrived in May 1946 and called on her at Rue Christine. Two months later she was diagnosed with cancer. She died in the American Hospital on July 27, 1946, at seventy-two. According to Alice, her last words were, "What is the answer?" And when Alice failed to reply, she asked, "In that case, what is the question?"

Quai des Grands-Augustins

BECOMING GEORGE SAND: STEP TWO

After a month at her brother's apartment on Rue de Seine at the start of 1831, Baroness Dudevant, *née* Aurore Dupin, moved in with her twenty-year-old lover Jules Sandeau at his boarding house at No. 21 quai des Grands-Augustins. While here, the baroness began wearing men's clothes to go about the city, a complete outfit that included top hat, frock coat, trousers, and hobnail boots.

> I was no longer a woman, nor was I a man . . . No one knew me, no one
> looked at me, nobody stopped me. I was an atom lost in that immense crowd.

In men's clothing, she could do many things ladies could not: smoke cigars, clomp along the streets in her boots, and buy standing-room tickets to plays.

After achieving success as George Sand, she became one of many writers who frequented Lapérouse, the glamorous restaurant at No. 51 quai des Grande-Augustins, in business since 1766. She and Musset were regulars, as were their contemporaries Hugo and Dumas. Colette, Proust, Simenon, and countless other writers have dined at the Lapérouse, and, if on an expense account, many still do.

Quai de Conti

HOURS PRESS

In the late 1920s and early 1930s, the storefront at No. 15 rue Guénégaud, by the Quai de Conti, was home to the Hours Press, launched by British-born poetess and shipping line heiress Nancy Cunard. It published works by such distinguished writers and poets as George Moore, Arthur Symons, Richard Aldington, and Robert Graves. But Cunard's most remarkable literary discovery was a poem by an unknown writer submitted for a contest she and Aldington had launched. They were discouraged by the mundane verses they were receiving, but on the morning after the midnight deadline had expired, June 16, 1930, Cunard arrived at the office to find an envelope stuffed through the mail slot. In it was a ninety-eight line poem whose brilliant language, subtle versification, and erudite references floored her and Aldington. They were all the more astounded to learn that the poet was a twenty-four-year-old man who had heard about the contest on the day of the deadline and, inspired by the ten-pound award, had written the poem in a few hours. His name was Samuel Beckett. He was teaching English at the École Normale Supérieure, and "Whoroscope" was to be his first published work.

Manning the bulky seventeenth-century Mathieu printing press, which Cunard bought from Bill Bird's defunct Three Mountains Press, was her lover Henry Crowder, an African American pianist who quit his jazz orchestra in 1928 and became a skillful typesetter and printer. Her American-born mother cut her off because of the relationship. But Cunard was fascinated with African art and African American jazz, and Crowder's dramatic stories of racial injustice in America inspired her to compile and edit a massive anthology of the history and arts of Africa and the African Diaspora entitled *Negro*. It was Hours Press's last publication, in 1934.

On and Off Rue Dauphine

BORIS VIAN AT THE TABOU

In April 1947, Le Tabou, the first jazz club in the district, opened in the cellar of the Hôtel d'Aubusson at No. 33 rue Dauphine. An immediate hit, the "*rats de cave*" danced to the wee hours of the morning to the music of trumpeter and bandleader Boris Vian, the twenty-seven-year old Pied Piper of Saint Germain-des-Prés. Also a talented novelist, songwriter, journalist, translator, avant-garde playwright, jazz critic, and leading proselytizer of bebop, he was astonishingly prolific despite a rheumatic heart condition that had endangered his

Boris Vian at the 1949
Paris Jazz Festival

life since childhood. Sartre and Beauvoir were among the literary regulars he attracted to the club. Richard Wright joined them, but only once: He couldn't bear the Dixieland the band played.

Vian's most enduringly popular book is his exhilarating absurdist novel *L'Écume des jours* (playfully entitled *Foam of the Daze* in English), but the book that created the greatest stir in its time was *J'irai cracher sur vos tombes* (*I Spit on Your Graves*). Published in 1946 as the work of Vernon Sullivan, the plot involves a black man from the American South who rapes and murders white women as a form of racial revenge. Vian posed as the book's translator, and wrote an introduction claiming that Sullivan—an African American writer—was unable to get published in the United States. A *scandale* erupted over the misogynous sex and violence in the novel. Two years later Vian was forced to admit in court that he was the author of *I Spit on Your Graves*. He was fined 100,000 francs and the book was banned. But by then it had sold 100,000 copies.

On June 23, 1959, Vian attended the screening of a dreadfully inept adaptation of the novel. Ten minutes into the movie, he growled, "These guys are supposed to be American? My ass!" and collapsed, his sickly heart finally giving out. He was thirty-nine. His friend Louis Malle said it was the film that killed him.

LES DÎNERS MAGNY

The Restaurant Magny, in vogue during the 1850s and 1860s, stood at what is now a modern building at No. 9 on tiny Rue Mazet. It was here the great literary figures of Paris—Gustave Flaubert, Ivan Turgenev, Edmond and Jules de Goncourt, Charles Augustin Sainte-Beuve—met twice a month for "les dîners Magny." George Sand, then living in Nohant, was an occasional guest, as was Théophile Gautier. Flaubert and Turgenev first met at the restaurant on December 6, 1862. Already ardent admirers of each other's work, they developed a deep friendship, and the "*bon Moscovite*" became Flaubert's most trusted literary advisor.

The conversations at Magny were lively and wide-ranging, but always came back to the writers' main preoccupations: literature and women. Most of the regulars were bachelors and, except for Turgenev, they were terrible misogynists. In his book *Dinner at Magny's*, Robert Baldick masterfully captures the flavor of these get-togethers, reconstituted from the letters, memoirs, and journals. The dinners were held at Magny's from 1862 to 1872, after which the survivors, Flaubert, Turgenev, and Edmond de Goncourt, moved on to other restaurants.

Odéon

THE THÉÂTRE DE L'ODÉON

The presence of the Théâtre de l'Odéon and many other buildings dating from the late eighteenth century makes this one of Paris's most architecturally harmonious neighborhoods. The great-columned neoclassical theater—the city's largest with 1,900 seats—was built for the Comédie-Française on the site of the Condé estate's garden. In 1784, Beaumarchais's satirical comedy *The Marriage of Figaro* finally had its premiere. It had been blocked by the censors for years, but the delays only piqued the public's appetite. Louis XVI, who once declared, "This play will never go on," finally had to give in.

Carrefour de l'Odéon, Rue Monsieur-le-Prince on the left, Rue de Condé on the right, and Rue de l'Odéon in the center, with the Théâtre de l'Odéon at the top of the street.

In the play the valet Figaro outsmarts his master, Count Almaviva, and holds him (and by inference, his whole class) in contempt:

> Because you are a great nobleman you think you are a great genius . . .
> Nobility, fortune, rank, position! How proud they make a man feel! What
> have *you* done to deserve such advantages? Put yourself to the trouble of
> being born—nothing more!

The play was a smash hit. Even the aristocrats, only five years before the Revolution, had to laugh at the mirror Beaumarchais held to their faces.

The Théâtre de l'Odéon's other extraordinary success came during the directorship of Jean-Louis Barrault and Madeleine Renaud, from 1959 to 1968. They staged many memorable productions: Ionesco's *Rhinoceros*, a world premiere with Barrault as Bérenger; Beckett's *En attendant Godot* (*Waiting for Godot*) and *Oh les beaux jours* (*Happy Days*) with Renaud as Winnie; and Genet's *Les Paravents* (*The Screens*) with Maria Casarès, Camus's great love, in a lead role. But after Barrault let rebel students hold meetings in the theater during the "events" of May 1968, Minister of Culture André Malraux declined to renew the company's lease.

LA MAISON DES AMIS DES LIVRES

Thanks to an insurance settlement from a railway accident, a working man named Clovis Monnier was able to help his twenty-three-year-old daughter fulfill her dream of owning

James Joyce and Sylvia
Beach at Shakespeare
and Company

a bookshop. On November 7, 1915, Adrienne Monnier opened the Maison des Amis des Livres at No. 7 rue de l'Odéon. Auspiciously, the first writer to come through the door was the reigning Prince of Poets, Paul Fort. She endeared herself immediately by buying all the back issues of his magazine *Vers et Prose*, which had gone out of business a year earlier. André Gide, Paul Valéry, Léon-Paul Fargue, and Valery Larbaud were soon giving readings, and unknown writers were offered the chance to present their work. "I'm not interested only in famous personalities," said Monnier. "The great joy is to discover. And then, you know, famous people weren't born so."

In March 1917 an American woman came to the shop looking for a back issue of *Vers et Prose*. At thirty, she was five years older than Monnier, but the slim, nervous *américaine* seemed younger than the plump, serene owner. They took to each other immediately. When Sylvia Beach returned from war relief work in Serbia two years later, Monnier encouraged her to open an English-language bookshop.

SHAKESPEARE AND COMPANY

"My loves were Adrienne Monnier, James Joyce, and Shakespeare and Company," said Sylvia Beach in her memoirs.

In November 17, 1919, she opened Shakespeare and Company in a narrow storefront at No. 8 rue Dupuytren. The first American writer to come in was Gertrude Stein, accompanied by Alice B. Toklas. Stein became a "bunny," as Beach called the members of her lending library, after the French word for subscriber, *abonné*. But, as Beach noted, "Gertrude's subscription was merely a friendly gesture. She took little interest, of course, in any but her own books."

In July 1920 Beach met the writer she most admired. James Joyce and his family had been living in Zürich, but Ezra Pound convinced him that Paris would be a better place to arouse publishers' interest in his unfinished novel *Ulysses*. Joyce and his supporters suffered a crushing setback the following February when a judge in New York found *The Little Review* guilty of obscenity for publishing an excerpt from *Ulysses*. Now, no publisher in England or America would dare touch it. Though Beach had never considered publishing a book before—and she knew this one would place her struggling business in jeopardy—her belief in Joyce was so strong that she made the offer. With nowhere else to turn, he gladly accepted.

Stein was furious at Beach for choosing Joyce's work over her own, and wrote a curt note canceling her *abonnement*. "A thorn is a thorn is a thorn," Beach responded.

On July 27, 1921, Shakespeare and Company moved to a larger shop at No. 12 rue de l'Odéon, across from the Maison des Amis des Livres. The timing could not have been better. Robert McAlmon arrived that fall, and Hemingway a few months later. Djuna Barnes and Ford Madox Ford came the following year. The bookshop became the center of a literary earthquake, especially after the publication of *Ulysses* in February 1922. As Janet Flanner recalled, Joyce's book "burst over the Left Bank like an explosion in print whose words and phrases fell on us like a gift of tongues, like a less than holy Pentecostal experience."

The bookshop also became the main outlet for magazines like *The Little Review*, *Broom*, Ford Madox Ford's *Transatlantic Review*, Eugene and Maria Jolas's *transition*. In order to remain unsullied by philistine influences, the magazines accepted no advertising, and few lasted more than a year or two. As Stein put it, "They died to make verse free."

With the onset of the Great Depression, the departure of most Americans left Beach in desperate financial straits. Compounding her problems, Joyce sold the American rights to *Ulysses* to Random House in 1932, and there was no sharing of the revenue with her. Though she remained cordial, this singular act of ingratitude tainted her love for him. For the rest of the decade, contributions from loyal patrons and benefit readings by friends such as André Gide, T. S. Eliot, and Paul Valéry kept the business from going under.

In December 1941 Beach made a sudden decision to close when a German officer, angry because she refused to sell him her personal copy of *Finnegans Wake*, threatened to return with a squad and confiscate her books. Adrienne and other friends helped Syliva pack up—five thousand books, correspondence files, photographs, and furniture—and they lugged everything upstairs to a vacant fourth-floor apartment. She then hired a carpenter to rip out the bookshelves, and a painter to paint out the sign. Twenty-two years of "steering a little bookshop between two wars" were over in a matter of hours.

Rue Monsieur-le-Prince

LE POLIDOR
On this narrow street, where the moat of Philippe Auguste's medieval ramparts once ran, the Crémerie Polidor at No. 41 opened in 1845. Verlaine and Rimbaud, Valéry, Joyce, and the ever-hungry young Hemingway were among the army of writers who dined on its belly-filling staples at long communal tables, elbow to elbow with teachers and students from the nearby schools. After its founding in 1948, the Collège de 'Pataphysique, inspired by the off-the-wall teachings of Jarry's Dr. Faustroll, held meetings at the Polidor. Boris Vian was elevated to the lofty rank of Transcendent Satrap at a ceremony in 1953.

YOUNG ZOLA
Seventeen-year-old Émile Zola arrived from Aix-en-Provence in February 1858 to enroll

in the Lycée Saint-Louis, around the corner from the garret he shared with his widowed mother at No. 63. Since the death of his father, an engineer, when Zola was seven, he and his mother had been living in poverty. They moved from garret to garret on the Left Bank during their first five years in the city. After failing the *baccalauréat* exam twice, Zola took a job as a clerk at the Hachette book shop on Boulevard Saint-Michel, where his fresh ideas about promotion caught the manager's attention. By twenty-three he was the director of publicity for the publishing and book-selling empire. He and his mother could live in comfort at last. Zola now began writing.

RICHARD WRIGHT

Unlike most American writers who came to Paris, Richard Wright could afford to live well, thanks to the proceeds from his best sellers *Native Son* and *Black Boy*. After a visit

in 1946, he returned the following year with his wife, Ellen, and their young daughter Julia, this time to stay. In 1948 he leased an eight-room apartment in the building at No. 14. As the plaque in his honor indicates, he stayed until 1959.

Wright came to France for three reasons: racial prejudice in America (particularly malicious for him because his wife was white); political harassment (he had once been a Communist Party member); and greater opportunities to expand his intellectual horizons. With Sartre, he explored existentialist philosophy, and he supported Sartre and Camus's attempt to create a movement of Leftist intellectuals critical of both the United States and the Soviet Union. With his African and African Diaspora friends Léopold Senghor, Alioune Diop, Aimé Césaire, and others in the *Présence Africaine* group, he worked on issues of colonialism and pan-African culture, which led to the nonfiction studies *The Color Curtain*, *Black Power*, and *White Man, Listen!*

Richard Wright

Wright was the central figure in the formidable African American literary presence in post–World War II Paris, which also included James Baldwin, Chester Himes, and William Gardner Smith. His circle gathered at the Monaco (now the Comptoir du Relais) on the Carrefour de l'Odéon, and later the Café de Tournon.

Wright also became close friends with his neighbor Sylvia Beach, who wrote her sister:

> Of all the writers I have known, he is the most unselfish and thoughtful.
> In fact, none of the others—the so-called white ones—were interested in
> anyone but themselves. Fellas like Hemingway appear uncouth beside Dick
> Wright.

When Richard Wright died suddenly at fifty-two in 1960, his death was ruled a heart attack. But conspiracy theories abounded—about the CIA, the weird Russian doctor who was treating him, a mysterious woman who showed up at the clinic the night he died. No proof of a crime was ever established, because he was cremated without an autopsy. His ashes rest in a funerary box at the Père-Lachaise Cemetery.

Rue de Condé

THE MARQUIS DE SADE

On this gently curving fifteenth-century street which cut through the abbey of Saint Germain-des-Prés's medieval vineyards, Donatien-Alphonse-François de Sade was born at the Hôtel de Condé, which stood at No. 9–15 rue de Condé. Born on June 2, 1750, he was baptized the following day at the Church of Saint-Sulpice. A cousin of the princely Condé family, Sade spent most of his youth at his family's chateau in Provence or at military school. He served as a boy officer in the Seven Years War, promoted to captain at eighteen.

The Marquis de Sade at twenty, his only known portrait from life, by Charles-Amédée-Philippe Van Loo

Five years later, back in Paris, he was pressured by his financially strapped father into marrying the daughter of a rich family of recent nobility. His father also hoped that marriage would temper his son's evident libertine tastes. Five months after his high society wedding at the church of Saint Roch, he was arrested in Paris for subjecting a prostitute to the sort of treatment that would make his name an "ism." (Krafft-Ebbing, who invented the term sadism, defined it as the inflicting of pain on others for one's sexual pleasure). In this case, the instrument of Sade's pleasure was a whip. He spent two weeks in prison at the Château de Vincennes.

In 1778, at his château in La Coste, Sade staged the marathon orgy of buggery, flagellation, and revoltingly unhygienic sexual practices upon which he would enlarge in *The 120 Days of Sodom*. At the instigation of his mother-in-law, he was imprisoned the same year. All but ten of his remaining thirty-six years were spent in prison cells, either at Vincennes, the Bastille, or the insane asylum at Charenton outside Paris.

BEAUMARCHAIS, THE PARNASSIANS, AND RACHILDE

The first writer to live in the seventeenth-century house at No. 26 rue de Condé was Beaumarchais, who took up residence in 1763. Five years later, this *parvenu* son of a clock-maker took a wealthy aristocrat as his second wife. She died two years later—as his first wife, another wealthy aristocrat, had also done two years after they were married. Rumors flew that he had poisoned them both for their fortunes. The rumors were wrong: Both wives died of natural causes, and he had surrendered all rights to their property in pre-nuptial agreements.

Beaumarchais wrote *The Barber of Seville* here in this house, but when it premiered at the Comédie-Française on February 23, 1775, it laid an egg. He immediately plunged into round-the-clock rewrites, slashing the comedy from five acts to four. At its next performance three days later, it was a resounding success.

The following year, 1776, Beaumarchais, an early champion of American independence, secured Louis XVI's backing to set up a clandestine trading company to ship arms and equipment to the rebels, and he moved to the Marais to run it.

The next writer to live at No. 26 was poet Théodore de Banville, whose Parnassian cohorts gathered at his Thursday evening salon throughout the 1860s. Young Paul Verlaine and Stéphane Mallarmé also attended, though they were not members of the "art for art" school. One of Verlaine's first published poems was in the group's 1866 anthology *Parnasse contemporain.*

In 1889 Alfred Vallette and his wife, Rachilde, acquired this remarkably literary house as their residence and the office of their magazine and publishing company the *Mercure de France.* They published Mallarmé, Heredia, and other Symbolists, counterbalancing their subtle *oeuvre* with works by the most uninhibited prose writers of the period, Rachilde among them. This *"homme de lettres,"* as she called herself, wrote the gender-bending novels *La Marquise de Sade* and *Monsieur Vénus,* in which the dominatrix heroine makes her passive male lover dress in drag. When a Belgian court sentenced her in absentia to two years in prison, Verlaine wrote her, "Ah, my dear child, if you have invented a new vice you are the benefactor of humanity."

But Rachilde's and Vallette's aim was not simply to shock: it was to escape from all bourgeois literary constraints, in form and in content. The *Mercure* publishing house brought out the first books by Gide, Claudel, and Apollinaire. Vallette and Rachilde published many offbeat luminaries: Huysmans, whose *décadent* novels shocked the nation; Rémy de Gourmont, the author of *Lettres à l'Amazone,* about Natalie Barney; poetess Renée Vivien, one of Barney's lovers; and Barney herself, who wrote reams of poetry in French.

Works by Alfred Jarry, the wildly eccentric creator of *Ubu Roi,* appeared in the literary magazine. He became a sort of adoptive son to Vallette and Rachilde, who tried, in vain, to save him from self-destruction.

Purchased by Gallimard in 1958, the *Mercure de France* is still headquartered in the Vallettes' house, and continues their tradition of publishing innovative contemporary French fiction, along with earlier literary works, letters and memoirs, and foreign fiction.

A plaque at No. 26 honors Rachilde, who died at ninety-three in 1953.

The Luxembourg Gardens

The lovely Jardin du Luxembourg is the most literary park in Paris. Statues and busts of writers abound. Stendhal, Sand, and her friend Flaubert can be found on the woodsy plateau on the Boulevard Saint Michel side, and Baudelaire and his nemesis Sainte-Beuve by the orchard. *Scènes de la vie de bohème*'s Henri Mürger and Parnassian poet Théodore de Banville are to the east of the Palais du Luxembourg. Banville is bare-chested; Verlaine called his bust "the one with the tits." To the west of the palace are Symbolist poet José Maria de Heredia and Paul Verlaine, whose jumbo, grey granite bust looks more like Lenin than like the poet who wrote of "*les sanglots longs des violons de l'automne...*"

PARIS. — Le Palais du Luxembourg

In *The Three Musketeers*, Athos, Porthos, Aramis, and d'Artagnan played tennis at a *jeu de paume* court in the garden. In *Les Misérables*, Marius and Cosette stole their first amorous glance on a secluded pathway by the tree nursery. The lovers George Sand and Alfred de Musset strolled these same paths, and Balzac circled the garden at night in his monk's cowl, candelabra in hand.

HENRY JAMES

In James's *The Ambassadors*, Lambert Strether, the proper middle-aged gentlemen from Wollett, Massachusetts, is on a diplomatic mission for Mrs. Newsome: to extricate her son Chad from the seductions of Paris and bring him home. With Chad out of town for a few days, Strether takes the time to put himself "in relation" to the city. In a penny chair by the water basin of the garden, memories of his first trip to Paris with his young wife, now long dead, start to flood his mind, and with them, thoughts of "his elaborate, innocent plan of reading, digesting, coming back, even, every few years." But the deep feelings Paris stirs up in Strether frighten him:

> His greatest uneasiness seemed to peep at him out of the possible impression that almost any acceptance of Paris might give one's authority away. It hung before him this morning, the vast bright Babylon, like some huge iridescent object, a jewel brilliant and hard, in which parts were not to be discriminated nor differences comfortably marked. It twinkled and trembled and melted together; at what seemed all surface one moment seemed all depth the next.

OTHER AMERICANS IN THE LUXEMBOURG

Gertrude Stein, a devotee of the garden, settled in her atelier down the street on the Rue de Fleurus the year *The Ambassadors* was published, in 1903. Henry James was the American

writer she most admired. In the 1920s, as high priestess of expatriate Montparnasse, she
would tick off the four greats of American literature: "Poe, Whitman, Henry James, and
myself." And since James had died a few years earlier . . .

Young Ernest Hemingway often crossed the garden to visit Stein, and, as he recounts
in *A Moveable Feast*, it was also the best place to avoid the tantalizing odors of food when
he was "belly-empty, hollow-hungry." He later told friends that, while living at Rue Notre-
Dame-des-Champs, he used to trap and strangle pigeons in the garden, hide them in his
son Bumby's pram, and smuggle the birds home to eat.

ANDRÉ GIDE

The writer who dominates the Luxembourg Gardens is Gide. He was born in 1869 in a
house overlooking the park at No. 19 rue de Medicis (now No. 2 place Edmond-Rostand)
and, aside from stays in Languedoc with the family of his father, a Sorbonne professor,
and with his mother's family in Normandy, he spent his childhood and adolescence in the
vicinity. His formal education was at the upper-class Protestant École alsacienne on Rue
Notre-Dame-des-Champs, and he received his *baccalauréat* at the age of eighteen in 1888
at the Lycée Henri IV on Place du Panthéon.

Gide's *Les Faux-monnayeurs* (*The Counterfeiters*) was published in 1926, but is set at the
turn of the century. The novel's action starts in "Le Luco," and it involves students who
live and go to school around the garden.

The street where Bernard Profitendieu had lived until then was quite close
to the Luxembourg Gardens. There in the path that overlooks the Medici

fountains, some of his school-fellows were in the habit of meeting every Wednesday afternoon between four and six. The talk was of art, philosophy, sport, politics and literature.

The *lycéen* Bernard has just discovered that he is illegitimate. He decides to leave home and comes to the meeting place to ask his best friend, Olivier, to put him up for the night. Olivier's rascally younger brother, Georges, and his schoolmates pass counterfeit coins at shops along Boulevard Saint-Michel. At the Taverne du Panthéon, Alfred Jarry disrupts the *Argonaut* literary magazine's launch party by blasting away with his revolver. Bernard sees an angel in the garden and follows it around the *quartier*. And the shocking event that ends the novel takes place at the Vedel-Azais school on Rue Vavin.

The first important writer to deal openly with homosexuality, Gide explored the theme in most of his literary works, beginning in the 1890s and including *The Counterfieters*. At twenty-two he fell under the moral and aesthetic sway of Oscar Wilde, in Paris that winter to write *Salomé*. Physical intimacy between them seems unlikely, and Gide always denied it, but three excised pages for December 1891—from his otherwise scrupulously-kept journal—have raised suspicion.

Gide was a bundle of contradictions, which only seems to have nourished his work: a *grand bourgeois* who became a militant Communist; his era's grand heir to the French classical literary tradition, delivering explosive content in the most limpid of styles; married platonically for decades while leading an extraordinarily active gay sex life and fathering an illegitimate daughter by another woman. In his autobiography, *Si le grain ne meurt* (*If It Die*), published the same year as the *Counterfeiters*, Gide expressed regret "not for having sinned, but for not having sinned more, for having let some opportunity for sinning slip by unused."

Saint-Sulpice

THREE MUSKETEERS COUNTRY

In this quaint corner of the Left Bank, between the heart of Saint Germain-des-Prés and the Luxembourg Gardens, every step you take follows in the floppy-booted footprints of Alexandre Dumas's deathless cape-and-sword heroes. When the eighteen-year-old D'Artagnan arrives in Paris, the first thing he does—after selling the ridiculous yellow nag that transported him from Gascony—is rush to the headquarters of the King's musketeers on Rue du Vieux-Colombier, with hopes of joining the illustrious company. One by one, he meets Athos, Porthos, and Aramais, and manages to get challenged to duels by all three.

The first duel, with Athos, is set for noon in a field by the church of Saint Joseph-des-Carmes at No. 70 rue de Vaugirard. (It dates from 1620, five years before the fictional duel takes place). D'Artagnan is amazed when Porthos and Aramis show up as Athos's seconds;

new to the city, he doesn't know about their "all for one, and one for all" motto. Barely have he and Athos clicked swords when a squad of Richelieu's guards arrives to arrest them for dueling, which has been outlawed by the Cardinal. Athos refuses to surrender. Naturally, Porthos and Aramais back him up. Without hesitation, D'Artagnan throws in his lot with the musketeers. In the rousing combat that follows, the young Gascon's dazzling swordsmanship saves the day. After defeating Richelieu's men (one dead, four badly wounded), D'Artagnan and his new comrades return to headquarters

> . . . arm in arm, taking up the whole width of the street and calling out to
> every musketeer they met, until finally they had formed a triumphal march.
> D'Artagnan was between Athos and Porthos. He felt drunk with happiness.

All of them live in Saint-Sulpice: Aramis on Rue de Vaugirard; Porthos on Rue du Vieux-Colombier; Athos on Rue Férou; and D'Artagnan on Rue Servandoni, then called Rue des Fossoyeurs, where his sniveling landlord's young wife falls under his charm.

The real D'Artagnan was a musketeer captain under Louis XIV. Dumas set his tale a little earlier to give his heroes a worthy nemesis, Louis XIII's Prime Minister Richelieu. Dumas came across the names of Athos, Porthos, and Aramis in D'Artagnan's memoirs, and though he learned nothing about the men, the odd-sounding names sparked the novel. Published in 1844, it was a phenomenal success. Dumas followed it the next year with the sequel, *Vingt ans après* (*Twenty Years After*), and in 1848 he published the last of the musketeer novels, *Le vicomte de Bragelonne* (*The Man in the Iron Mask*).

Mme de La Fayette

MME DE LA FAYETTE

In a century that produced the likes of Molière, Corneille, Racine, and La Fontaine, Mme de La Fayette ranks among its greatest writers. *La Princesse de Clèves* is the first modern French novel, and the only one from the seventeenth century still widely read. She lived practically all her life at the Hôtel de la Vergne, the mansion behind the tall blue *porte cochère* at No. 50 rue de Vaugirard. She was born in the hotel, as Marie-Madeleine Pioche de la Vergne, in 1634, and remained there after marrying Jean-François Motier, comte de La Fayette, when she was twenty-one. But they had little in common: He loved farming, hunting, and the great outdoors; she loved Parisian society, the life of the mind, and the great indoors. In 1661, after six years of marriage and two sons, they agreed to live separately, he on his estates in Auvergne, she in Paris. No rancor. They simply acknowledged that they were not made for each other.

Mme de La Fayette attended the great ladies' salons, where she met Racine, Corneille, Boileau and other leading men of letters. After avoiding him for years, she formed the most important relationship of her life with the duc de la Rochefoucauld. She had been certain that anyone who could write the godless and relentlessly cynical epigrams in his *Maxims* had to be depraved. "Ah! What corruption there must be in the mind and heart to imagine all that!" she told a friend. But in 1664, when she was thirty and he fifty-one, they began a strong and ever-deepening friendship. La Rochefoucauld helped her sharpen her analytical abilities, and she brought out his hidden tender side. "I believe no passion could surpass the force of that liaison," wrote her close friend Mme de Sévigné. But if they were lovers, nobody knew.

La Princesse de Clèves was published in 1678, but the action takes place in the sixteenth century, at the court of Henri II. In a splendid ballroom scene at the Louvre, the heroine, a beautiful, married noblewoman, falls passionately in love with the dazzling duc de Nemours. But far from surrendering to passion, she keeps her love secret, even after the death of her husband. This work of psychological analysis was a striking departure from the wildly overblown novels of the period. It was a stylistic revelation as well, using the clean, deceptively simple style of quintessential French prose for the first time in a work of fiction. Her heirs are Stendhal, Flaubert, Maupassant, Gide, and all the other masters of clear, logical, sinewy French.

Place Saint-Sulpice

With slim trees fringing it and the busy Fontaine des Quatre Points Cardinaux at its center, this wide granite square was one of Henry Miller's favorites during the bumming-around period he describes in *Tropic of Cancer*, when he sometimes slept on a park bench:

> . . . in the morning I'd be sitting there myself, taking a quiet snooze in the sunshine, cursing the goddamned pigeons gathering up the crumbs everywhere. St. Sulpice! The fat belfries, the garish posters over the door, the candles flaming inside. The Square so beloved of Anatole France, with that drone and buzz from the altar, the splash of the fountain, the pigeons cooing, the crumbs disappearing like magic and only a dull rumbling in the hollow of the guts.

THE CHURCH OF SAINT-SULPICE

The Marquis de Sade and Baudelaire were baptized in the church of Saint-Sulpice. It is where Victor Hugo married Adèle, with Alfred de Musset and Alfred de Vigny as witnesses. Mme de La Fayette is entombed here, as is Molière's wife, Armande Béjart. However, it was rarely visited by tourists until Dan Brown's *The Da Vinci Code* brought them in droves.

The Left Bank's largest church was built over a very long period, from 1646 to 1780, and

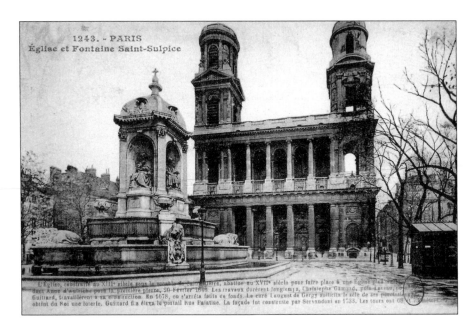

1243. - PARIS
Église et Fontaine Saint-Sulpice

L'Église, construite au XIII° siècle sous le vocable de Saint-Sulpice, abattue au XVII° siècle pour faire place à une église plus grande, dont Anne d'Autriche posa la première pierre, 20 Février 1646. Les travaux durèrent longtemps, Christophe Gamard, puis Laveau, puis Guittard, travaillèrent à sa construction. En 1678, on s'arrêta faute de fonds. Le curé Languet de Gergy sollicita le zèle de ses paroissiens et obtint du Roi une loterie. Guittard fils éleva le portail Rue Palatine. La façade fut construite par Servandoni en 1733. Les tours ont 68 mètres.

The church of Saint-Sulpice and its Place

it looks it. "What a mess," Huysmans's hero Durtal observes in *Là-bas*. "And it's taken five or six architects to raise this pitiful pile of stones!" Durtal meets regularly with his friend Des Hermies in the bell-ringer Carhaix's rooms to explore their fascination with the Black Mass and the sadistic and sexual perversion of Catholic rituals.

Huysmans lived practically all his life in the vicinity of the church, almost half of it in a former convent at No. 11 rue de Sèvres. His final decade, after the mystical vision which brought him back to religion, was marked by long retreats at monasteries. He died in 1907, at fifty-nine, at No. 31 rue Saint-Placide, and is buried at Montparnasse Cemetery.

THE CAFÉ DE LA MAIRIE

In the 1920s this unpretentious-looking café fronting on the square was a favorite of the Surrealists, and of Hemingway, Fitzgerald, and Faulkner when they lived nearby. But the American writer most deeply linked to it is Djuna Barnes. She lived nearby from 1920 until 1933, and made this café the local of "Dr. Matthew-Mighty-grain-of-salt-Dante-O'Connor" in her haunting 1936 novel *Nightwood*:

> Close to the church of St. Sulpice, around the corner in rue Servandoni, lived
> the doctor. His small slouching figure was a feature of the Place. To the pro-
> prietor of the Café de la Mairie du VIème he was almost a son.

The tortured, egocentric Dr. O'Connor is the most mesmerizing figure in this dense poetical novel about the night world of lesbian, homosexual, and transvestite Paris. He watches,

comments pyrotechnically, and plays a role in the fates of the love-ravaged characters. The semi-autobiographical novel parallels Barnes's own affair with the artist Thelma Wood. They met in 1921, when Wood—"a girl who resembles a boy," like Robin Vote in the novel—was twenty, Barnes twenty-nine. Wood moved in with Barnes the following year, at No. 173 boulevard Saint-Germain, and five years later, they moved to No. 9 rue Saint-Romain. But Wood had numerous adventures with other women over those years, including Edna St. Vincent Millay, and Barnes eventually found her infidelities unbearable. When Wood became the lover of Henrietta McCrea Metcalf ("the squatter" Jenny Petherbridge in the novel) in 1928, Barnes broke with her. She later claimed, "I'm not a lesbian. I just loved Thelma."

Rue de Tournon

CASANOVA

In the late 1750s Jacques Casanova lived in the *hôtel particulier* at No. 27 rue de Tournon, "the most Italian of Paris streets," as Alberto Moravia called it. Then in his early thirties, Casanova was already earning the reputation that made his name a common noun ("a man known for his amorous adventures; a rake; a Don Juan"). Besides being a virtuoso of *la galanterie*, Casanova was a man of wit, taste, and learning, who traveled widely, even to Catherine the Great's Russia, making his living as a soldier, violinist, gambler, spy, alchemist, secretary to well-connected gentlemen, and writer. Born to a Venetian theatrical family—his mother an actress in Goldoni's troupe—he used his adventures, much embellished in the retelling, to charm the rich and the famous. During Casanova's first stay in Paris, the elderly playwright and *homme de lettres* Crébillon *père* (who has a street near the Théâtre de l'Odéon named for him) took the bright young Venetian under his wing and taught Casanova to write the elegant French we find in his memoirs.

During the same stay, he encountered the gorgeous artists' model Marie-Louise O'Morphy, then thirteen years old. According to his account, the girl happily allowed him to give her a bath, but it went no further because she was saving herself for a man who could afford her; after seeing a nude of "la petite O'Morphy" by Boucher the following year, Louis XV became that man. The king took her as a mistress and fathered a child, but when she tried to supplant Mme de Pompadour as the official royal mistress, she was promptly married off and sent into provincial exile.

Following his amazing escape from the seemingly escape-proof Leads Prison in Venice in 1757, Casanova stayed on Rue de Tournon for two years, creating a successful lottery and an unsuccessful silk factory and, as ever, having plenty of affairs.

At sixty he retired from his life of adventure and became the librarian for the Count of Waldenstein at his castle in Bohemia. But far from slipping into oblivion, he lived his life over again by writing the memoirs that would secure his fame.

BALZAC

From 1827 to 1829, Honoré Balzac (still no "de") lived in a second-floor flat in the Hôtel de Châtillon at No. 2. A year after his move, his printing business on Rue Visconti collapsed, and he plunged into writing a novel about a failed 1793 counter-revolutionary revolt in Brittany. Published in 1829, *Les Chouans* became his first successful novel.

On the romantic front, while continuing his affair with Mme de Berny, twenty-two years his senior, he formed a liaison with the duchesse d'Abrantès, the witty and glamorous widow of Napoléon's Marshall Junot, only fifteen years his senior. Balzac helped her write her lively memoirs, and she appears thinly disguised in two of his novels.

ALPHONSE DAUDET

Across the street at No. 7 was the Hôtel du Sénat, a cheap lodging house popular with southerners in the mid-nineteenth century, where Alphonse Daudet, born in Nîmes, shared a room with his older brother, a journalist, when he arrived at seventeen in 1857. Daudet spent his first years scratching for a living, but went on to become one of France's most successful writers of fiction. Though he lived in Paris, he remained deeply attached to his roots in the South. Most of his novels have gone out of vogue, but his delightful Provençal stories in *Lettres de mon moulin* (*Letters from my Mill*) remain among the most popular in French literature. Everyone in France knows M. Seguin's goat—"*Ah! Grignoire, qu'elle était jolie la petite chèvre de M. Seguin*"—and the curate of Cucugnan, "*bon comme le pain, franc comme l'or.*"

AT THE FOYOT

The little Square Francis-Poulenc at the corner of Rue de Vaugirard occupies the site of the former Hôtel-Restaurant Foyot. Founded in 1848 by the chef of the deposed king Louis-Philippe, it remained in vogue with the literary elite for almost a century.

In the 1890s Count Robert de Montesquiou shocked the diners one day when he arrived for lunch, not because of the red pearls and blue hydrangea he was wearing (they were used to that), but because of the guest he had with him: the semi-clochard Paul Verlaine. Despite Montesquiou's notorious snobbery, he befriended the destitute poet in his final years, helping him financially and promoting his work. Montesquiou claimed to be the one who gave Gabriel Fauré Verlaine's poem "Clair de lune" to set to music.

Rainer Maria Rilke, T. S. Eliot, Dorothy Parker, Robert McAlmon, and his wife Bryher and her lover Hilda Doolittle (H. D.) were among the writers who stayed in the rooms upstairs at the Foyot.

Another guest, Raymond Radiguet, fell fatally ill here in 1923. His novel *Le Diable au corps* (*The Devil in the Flesh*) had been published to critical huzzahs and excellent sales that March, thanks in part to the vigorous publicity campaign by his lover Jean Cocteau, fourteen years his senior. Their affair turned sour, however, when Radiguet fell in love with the enchanting sixteen-year-old artists' model Bronia Perlmutter, and let it be known that he planned to marry her. To escape Cocteau's fits of jealousy, Radiguet moved from hotel to hotel, ending up at the Foyot. In early December, he came down with typhoid, which normally could have been cured, but his excessive drinking, opium smoking, and generally dissolute life had broken his resistance. By the time Cocteau's doctor had him hospitalized, it was too late. He died at twenty years old on December 12, 1923, leaving a quasi-widow and a quasi-widower behind. Bronia recovered and married film director René Clair, but Cocteau fell into a long depression, aggravated by periods of heavy opium use. He didn't fully recover from Radiguet's death until he met Jean Marais fourteen years later.

At the Café de Tournon

JOSEPH ROTH

When German and Austrian Jewish writers were forced into exile by the Nazis in the 1930s, many holed up in little hotels on Rue de Tournon, and cafés became their places of refuge. Berliner Hermann Kesten wrote in *Ma Vie au café*:

> In exile the café becomes everything: home, or even country, church and parliament, desert and battlefield, cradle of illusions and cemetery. Exile provokes solitude and isolation, but also enlivens and regenerates: Here the café is the only place where one feels a sense of continuity in things.

LEFT Café de Tournon, a refuge for many expatriates

RIGHT Joseph Roth

A simple plaque on the wall of the Café de Tournon's building, at No. 18, honors Joseph Roth, who spent his final two years in its hotel and made the café his headquarters. He was born in 1894 in the Galicia region of Ukraine, then part of the Austro-Hungarian Empire. A brilliant storyteller in the tradition of Stendhal, Roth made his name as the poetic chronicler of the lost worlds of Eastern European Jewry and the sprawling multi-cultural Hapsburg Empire, the subject of his 1932 novel *The Radetzky March,* his masterpiece. At the peak of his career his works were outlawed and burned by the Nazis, and he left Berlin in 1933 for six alcohol-clouded years of exile. On May 23, 1939, he collapsed in the Café de Tournon upon hearing that his friend Ernst Toller, the dramatist, had committed suicide. Roth was rushed to the Hôpital Necker, where, after four days of delirium tremens, he died at age forty-four.

Roth's works fell into oblivion, but in 1956 his friend Kesten published a three-volume edition which began the literary resurrection of a writer now recognized as one of the finest German-language novelists of the twentieth century.

THE "MERLIN JUVENILES"

The Café de Tournon again became a gathering place for expatriate writers after World War II, but this time for English-speaking groups.

Merlin was an ambitious but pitifully underfunded avant-garde magazine, initiated by the brilliant, charismatic young Scotsman Alexander Trocchi, who had fled Glasgow to make a name for himself in Paris. The magazine's funding came from the modest allowance of his nineteen-year-old American girlfriend, Jane Lougee, whom he named publisher. Though they managed to put the magazine out only sporadically between 1952 and 1955, they were among the first to publish Beckett, Ionesco, Italo Svevo, and Pablo Neruda in English.

Richard Seaver, an American graduate student and *Merlin* editor, was the member who discovered Beckett. Riding his bike to the Sorbonne in 1952, he passed Editions de Minuit on tiny Rue Bernard-Palissy and noticed two recently published novels in the window, written in French, by an unknown Irish expatriate. Enthralled by *Molloy* and *Malone meurt*, he searched for the reclusive author, finally found him, and learned that he had an unpublished novel in English in a drawer. Since Seaver and his associates needed a French partner to publish books, "the Merlin juveniles," as Beckett called them, entered into a loose partnership with Maurice Girodias's Olympia Press. Together they created Editions Merlin. Beckett's *Watt* was their first novel, published in 1953.

PARIS REVIEW

The other young editors to settle into the Tournon created the *Paris Review* in 1953. They were affluent, resolutely non-political Americans, and recent Ivy League graduates for the most part. The French publisher La Table Ronde gave them an office in its splendid *hôtel* around the corner on Rue Garancière, but this was Paris and, naturally, they preferred to work in a café.

Yale graduate Peter Matthiessen launched the magazine and made his friend George Plimpton, from Harvard, the editor-in-chief. When four fat, beautifully printed issues per year appeared like clockwork, most expatriates assumed CIA backing. But people stopped speculating when Prince Sadruddin Aga Khan, another Harvard graduate, became the publisher.

The impetus of the review was frankly nostalgic, harkening back to the days of the Lost Generation. Its success was due in large part to its "The Art of Fiction" interviews, starting with E. M. Forster, Plimpton's don at Cambridge. Plimpton spotted Hemingway buying the *Paris Review* one day at the Ritz, and talked him into an interview. Other early subjects were François Mauriac, Graham Greene, Alberto Moravia, Georges Simenon, and James Thurber.

After the first few years, the bloom of the American-in-Paris experience faded, and the top editors drifted home. Plimpton was among the last to leave, in 1956. Since then the *Review*, still in operation, has been *Paris* in name only.

THE AFRICAN AMERICANS

Richard Wright, the dean of post-World War II American literary expatriation, frequented the Tournon in the early 1950s after the Monaco, his customary haunt near his home on Rue Monsieur-le-Prince, became too popular for his taste. Other African American writers and artists followed. The camaraderie of black men enjoying freedom from the daily pressures of racism in America made their get-togethers especially exhilarating. In Chester Himes's autobiography, *My Life of Absurdity*, he describes his early days at the café, where cartoonist Ollie Harrington ("the best raconteur I'd ever met") was the life of the party:

We were fantastically absurd, all us blacks. But Ollie was funny. I could always follow Ollie's lead. The absurdity of the other blacks was ofttimes hurting. But ours never was, it was only entertaining. During that spring the Café de Tournon became the most celebrated café in all of Europe, and from here one could select entertainments of all types.

The main entertainment was scoring with white women, at which Himes and Harrington excelled. The availability of white women was the most striking difference between their lives in Paris and their lives in the States, where interracial sex was taboo, even dangerous. In 1955, in a case that shocked the world, white men in Mississippi murdered fourteen-year-old Emmett Till because they believed he had flirted with a white woman. The laissez-faire attitude about interracial relationships in Paris (at least among foreigners) worked out well for Himes: A happy marriage to a fine and devoted English wife complemented the success he achieved as a writer.

The African American contingent was tight-knit in the beginning, but the FBI and CIA began planting spies and agents provocateurs among them, and their cohesion unraveled. Himes became convinced that the novelist and journalist William Gardner Smith was a CIA fink. Smith suspected Wright. Some saw Ollie Harrington's vociferous support for the Left as a cover for CIA ties (he was a dedicated Communist who soon moved to East Germany). Wright suspected everyone *but* Harrington. By 1958, none of them were going to the café. The magnitude of U.S. intelligence operations against African Americans in Paris came to light in the 1970s when thousands of classified pages were released through the Freedom of Information Act. There were 250 pages of FBI reports on Richard Wright alone.

Faulkner, Hemingway, and Fitzgerald

FAULKNER ON RUE DE VAUGIRARD, 1925

In August 1925, just short of his twenty-eighth birthday, William Faulkner moved into a garret overlooking the Luxembourg Gardens in the Grand Hôtel des Principautés-Unies at No. 42. Then a cheap rooming house, it is now a swanky hotel with a plaque on the Rue Servandoni side commemorating the stay of the 1949 Nobel laureate.

Faulkner had published his poetry collection *The Marble Faun* the year before and was working on his first novel, *Soldier's Pay*. He planned to spend two or three years in Paris, but other than the Luxembourg Gardens, which he loved, he found little to inspire him. After five months he cut short his stay and went back to what the Paris experience helped clarify as his true creative milieu, Yoknapatawpha County.

His only literary use of his months in Paris is the final scene in *Sanctuary*, in which Temple Drake's father has taken her to Europe, hoping she will her forget her ordeal with Popeye. We find them at concert in the Luxembourg Gardens:

. . . she seemed to follow with her eyes the waves of music, to dissolve into the dying brasses, across the pool and the opposite semicircle of trees where at somber intervals the dead tranquil queens in stained marble mused, and on into the sky lying prone and vanquished in the embrace of the season of rain and death.

HEMINGWAY'S LAST PARIS RESIDENCE

At the top of narrow, cobblestone Rue Férou is the Luxembourg Museum on Rue de Vaugirard, where Hemingway learned much from Cézanne's paintings. Just down from the museum, with twin sphinxes guarding its gate, is the eighteenth-century Hôtel de Luzy at No. 6, where Hemingway lived with Pauline Pfeiffer, his new wife, from late 1927 to the start of 1930. To assuage his guilt over leaving his first wife, Hadley, he had signed over to her the revenues from *The Sun Also Rises*. And having given up journalism, he was practically broke. Even so, he and Pauline lived well on Rue Férou, where their apartment included a salon, dining room, superb kitchen, big master bedroom, two baths, a study, and a spare room. Pauline's Uncle Gus picked up the tab.

Hemingway began writing *A Farewell to Arms* and finished it at Rue Férou, but over the two years during which this was his principal address, he and Pauline traveled most of the time. They spent the better part of 1928 in America, where their son Patrick was born, and where Hemingway's father committed suicide that December, a crushing blow Hemingway would never get over.

In the spring of 1929, when Hemingway and Scott Fitzgerald were both in town, Hemingway's notorious boxing match with Canadian writer Morley Callaghan took place at the American Club in Montparnasse, with a well-oiled Fitzgerald acting as referee. In a round in which Hemingway was getting trounced, the ref let it continue well past the one-minute limit, calling time only when Hem finally thudded to the mat. Scott swore that it was unintentional, that he got carried away by the action and lost track of the time. Though Hemingway was furious, but it might have blown over if the story hadn't ended up in American newspapers. It galled him to be laughed at for taking a licking from a much smaller man.

Hemingway was at Rue Férou when *A Farewell to Arms* came out in September 1929 to sensational reviews and sales. It made him America's most famous young writer, displacing Fitzgerald, whose career was in a tailspin.

In January 1930, Ernest, Pauline, and Patrick sailed for America, settling in Key West.

THE FITZGERALDS ON RUE DE VAUGIRARD

In April 1928, Scott and Zelda and six-year-old Scottie moved to a fourth-floor apartment overlooking the Luxembourg Gardens at No. 58. There were flashes of happiness during their five-month stay, but for the most part it was sheer hell.

The idea for this trip was Zelda's. She had become obsessed with becoming a ballet dancer, and at the age of twenty-eight began taking lessons with the director of the Diaghilev school. Fitzgerald would later see this fixation as the first clear sign of her mental illness.

Scott's drinking was worse than ever. There were frequent shouting matches with Zelda, nasty episodes with friends, brawls with strangers, and two trips to jail. But he continued to churn out stories and sell them for top dollar. He was working on *Tender is the Night*, but by the time it was published in 1934, the Depression was on, Marx-tinged realism was selling, and tales of the Jazz Age in expatriate France were passé. The novel sold less than 13,000 copies in two years.

In *Tender is the Night*, Dick and Nicolle Diver and the starlet Rosemary Hoyt lunch in Abe and Mary North's apartment (based on Gerald and Sara Murphy's apartment at No. 14 rue Guynemer) "high above the green mass of leaves" of the Luxembourg Gardens. At this lunch, Rosemary, who has fallen in love with Dick, realizes that he is falling in love with her too. Though Fitzgerald modeled Dick Diver's stylish bearing on Gerald Murphy, at its core the character is a self-portrait of Fitzgerald on the path to emotional bankruptcy.

THE FITZGERALDS ON RUE PALATINE, 1929

Scott, Zelda, and Scottie returned to Paris in March 1929 and spent two months on Rue Palatine. In Fitzgerald's story "Babylon Revisited," the reformed alcoholic Charlie Wales goes to the apartment of his late wife's sister on this street to try to regain custody of his daughter Honoria. The fictional address and the Fitzgeralds' own was almost certainly one of the twin Haussmann-style buildings at Nos. 3 and 5 rue Palantine.

Though they were only steps from Hemingway's house on Rue Férou, Fitzgerald was unaware of it when he arrived, because Hem had asked their mutual editor Maxwell Perkins not to tell him. A football weekend at Princeton the previous fall featuring an outrageously drunk Fitzgerald seems to have been the last straw. Though he was pained by the snub, Scott sent a message when he learned Hem's whereabouts, inviting him and Pauline to dinner.

Compounding the tension was Zelda's and Ernest's mutual contempt. To her, he was "a phony," "a professional he-man," and "a pansy with hair on his chest," and *The Sun Also Rises* was "bullfighting, bullslinging, and bullshit." To him, she was "crazy" and a wrecker of Scott's talent. But that night at dinner they were all on their best behavior.

While living at this apartment, Zelda accused Scott of having a homosexual relationship with Hemingway. Scott later wrote to her, "The nearest I ever came to leaving you was when you told me you [thought] that I was a fairy in the rue Palatine."

In 1929 Scott predicted that Hemingway would have a new wife for every big book he wrote. There had been Hadley for *The Sun Also Rises*, and he now had Pauline for *A Farewell to Arms*; and there would be Martha Gellhorn for *For Whom the Bell Tolls*, and Mary Welsh for *Across the River and into the Trees*.

Fitzgerald stayed with Zelda despite her love affair with a French flyer in 1924, her frivolity (a match for his own), and her madness. He supported her in sanatoriums in Europe and America, visited her, and corresponded with her regularly until his death in 1940.

Rue Madame

ALBERT CAMUS

In 1950 Camus, his wife Francine, and their five-year-old twins Catherine and Jean moved to the pleasant early-nineteenth-century house at No. 29 rue Madame, where he bought a five-room apartment. Every morning he would have his coffee and read the papers at the Café de la Mairie before heading to his office at Gallimard. Although *The Stranger* and *The Plague* were generating enough income to live on, he chose to keep working as a member of Gallimard's prestigious selection committee. Born in rural Algeria, the son of a farm worker killed in World War I and an illiterate Spanish-born mother who raised him, Camus was ill at ease in Parisian intellectual circles, and found the emotional support he needed in the Gallimard family. His working-class origins could have been an advantage in leftist Saint Germain-des-Prés, but since he did not trust the Communist Party, of which he had once been a member, his man-of-the-people background did him no good. At the time he moved to Rue Madame, he was the only famous French writer on the Left to have publicly attacked the abuses of Stalinist Russia.

In October 1951 Camus published *L'Homme révolté* (*The Rebel*), his "intellectual gene-alogy of totalitarianisms," which immediately became a best seller. The following May, Sartre's fiery associate Francis Jeanson wrote a scathing critique in *Les Temps Modernes*, heaping scorn on Camus for his "thirst for moderation." This was the spark that set off the intellectual cause célèbre of the decade. Far more than the content of the article, Camus was hurt that Sartre had not critiqued the book himself, and he wrote him an emotional open letter. Sartre replied with nineteen vitriolic pages attacking him for his "somber self-importance," "vulnerability," and "mournful moderation." The press played it up as a personal feud between famous writers, but it was essentially a political dispute over the nature of Communism in the Soviet Union.

The bitterness stirred up by the affair unnerved Camus so much that he stopped going to places frequented by Sartre and his crowd. Sartre, on the other hand, forgot about Camus immediately. In *The Force of Circumstance*, Beauvoir wrote, "Camus, who had been dear to me . . . no longer existed." But he did exist for her, at least in a fictionalized version in *The Mandarins*, published in 1954. He appears as Henri Perron, the editor-in-chief of a Left-leaning but non-Communist newspaper. Henri is a fine writer, well-meaning but fragile, torn by his moral qualms and shaky political convictions, who keeps his emotion-ally disintegrating mistress Paula in constant anxiety because of his other women. Camus kept his reactions to *The Mandarins* to himself, but his wife Francine fell into a depression and had to be hospitalized.

Camus returned to the literary fray in 1956 with his novel *La Chute* (*The Fall*), 126,000 copies sold in its first six months, and he received the Nobel Prize in Literature the fol-lowing year. At forty-three, he was its second-youngest recipient, after Rudyard Kipling, who was forty-two when he received the prize in 1907. A little more than two years later, on January 4, 1960, Camus died in a car crash.

Le Premier homme (*The First Man*), the novel he was working on before his death, was published in its unfinished state in 1994 to enormous success, confirming the timeless appeal of the writer whom François Mauriac dubbed "the conscience of his generation."

Rue Cassette

ALFRED JARRY

From 1897 until his death ten years later, the brilliant and outlandish Alfred Jarry lived on "the second and a half floor" of the building at the rear of the courtyard at No. 7. "Notre Grande Chasublerie," as he called his home (there was an ecclesiastical garment-maker on the floor below), was an *entresol* room with a ceiling so low it barely cleared the pint-sized Jarry's head. Plaster flaked off and made Jarry look like he had the world's worst case of dandruff. Apollinaire joked that the ceiling was so low the only thing one could eat in the room was flounder.

Jarry moved to his Grande Chasublerie shortly after the riotous premiere of his play *Ubu Roi* in December 1896. The play made Jarry and his ludicrous, obscene, cowardly, amoral, murderously power-hungry, pear-shaped hero Père Ubu instantly famous. By then Jarry was already employing the royal *nous* and rattling off Ubuish dialogue ("that which chirps" was a bird, "that which blows" was the wind) in a high-pitched machine-gun-like delivery. He would charge off into the Paris night on "that which rolls" with two pistols in his belt, which he became notorious for firing in public places.

By thirty, Jarry had burned himself out creatively. He isolated himself in his Ubu identity, and was using absinthe and ether to induce hallucinations. His sex life was apparently nonexistent. The disease that killed him, in 1907, was acute meningitic tuberculosis, aggravated by heavy drinking, ether, poor nutrition, and the cold and humidity in his unheated apartment. "Suicide by hallucination" is what Roger Shattuck calls Jarry's unraveling in *The Banquet Years*, his marvelous study of avant-garde artists at the dawn of the twentieth century.

Alfred Jarry, 1897 drawing by F. A. Cazals

Under the alias of Dr. Faustroll, Jarry was also the founding father of 'Pataphysics, defined as the science of all sciences: " 'Pataphysics is to metaphysics what metaphysics is to physics." The Collège de 'Pataphysique, founded after World War II, conducts 'Pataphysical research to this day. Raymond Queneau, Jacques Prévert, Boris Vian, and Georges Perec were dedicated *'pataphysiciens*.

THE FAUBOURG SAINT-GERMAIN AND THE EIFFEL TOWER

Up to the late seventeenth century this district was a vast stretch of farmland owned by the Abbey of Saint Germain-des-Prés. But finding itself short of funds due to corruption and mismanagement, the abbey began selling off land. Some went to other religious orders to build convents, and a big piece went to Louis XIV for the Hôtel des Invalides, but the main buyers were rich nobles planning to build mansions with huge private gardens. After the Pont-Royal was completed in 1689, making it easy to "cross the waters" to this hitherto remote stretch of the Left Bank, many aristocrats abandoned the Marais for the wide open spaces of the *faubourg*. Until the end of the *belle époque*, in literature as in life, the name Faubourg Saint-Germain was synonymous with wealth, elegance, and social exclusiveness.

Voltaire, Chateaubriand, Fenimore Cooper, Edith Wharton, Rainer Maria Rilke, and

André Gide lived in the *faubourg*, as did an army of fictional characters. And a certain James Joyce lived and worked in the shadow of the Eiffel Tower.

The Quais

VOLTAIRE ON THE QUAI VOLTAIRE

After twenty-eight years in exile, Voltaire returned from his estate in Ferney, arriving in Paris on February 10, 1778. He chose the premiere of his play *Irène* as the excuse for his return, but in truth, he was eighty-three years old, he was ill, and he wanted to see his native city before he died. He moved into the townhouse of his friend the Marquis de Villette at No. 27 quai des Théatins (now Quai Voltaire). The house is still there, decayed and semi-deserted.

Voltaire was the archetype of the politically *engagé* intellectual. *Ecrasez l'infâme*—"crush the infamous one"—was his motto. His principal target was the Church, which he had been flailing for much of his life. But the end was approaching, and wishing to be buried in consecrated ground, the old atheist wrote a recantation witnessed by a priest—after which Voltaire's health suddenly improved. On March 30, he attended a performance of *Irène* by the Comédie-Française at the Tuileries Palace, where his bust was crowned with laurels. He received a standing ovation. A torchlight procession escorted his carriage back to Villette's residence, where the marquis had changed the street signs to read "Quai Voltaire." The government changed them back to Quai des Théatins the next day.

Two months to the day later, Voltaire died at the marquis's home. But the Church refused him a burial in Paris. The marquis hid the body overnight in his garden, and the next day Voltaire's nephew, the Abbé Mignot, spirited it to a Cistercian monastery in Champagne for interment. Thirteen years later, the Revolution had Voltaire's remains transferred to the Panthéon, and renamed the quay in his honor.

BAUDELAIRE AT THE HÔTEL DU QUAI VOLTAIRE

A plaque on this atmospheric hotel at No. 19 notes the names of former guests Charles Baudelaire, Richard Wagner, Oscar Wilde, and Jean Sibelius, and quotes from, "Le Crepuscule du matin," a poem by Baudelaire written during his stay:

L'aurore grelottante en robe rose et verte
S'avance sur la Seine déserte
Et le sombre Paris, en se frottant les yeux,
Empoignait ses outils, vieillard laborieux.

The Quai Voltaire, Pont Royal, and Gare d'Orsay, early 20th century

(Shivering dawn robed in pink and green
moves up the deserted Seine
and gloomy Paris, old drudge rubbing its eyes
grabs it tools.)

Then in his mid-thirties, Baudelaire moved to the hotel on June 9, 1856, to write and revise poems to be published as *Les Fleurs du mal*. His garret room, No. 47, can be rented or, if not occupied, viewed.

In July 1857, shortly after *Les Fleurs du mal* went on sale, the Minister of the Interior seized it as an offense against public morals. Flaubert, whose *Madame Bovary* had been in court on the same charge earlier that year, sent Baudelaire a letter of support (a framed copy can be seen in the hotel room). The court ordered six of Baudelaire's poems suppressed, and slapped fines on him and his publisher.

The impact of *Les Fleurs du mal* on French poetry—on Mallarmé, Verlaine, Rimbaud, and the Symbolists—cannot be exaggerated. Verlaine pinpointed Baudelaire's "expert vagueness" as an essential condition for poetry from this point on. Baudelaire also introduced a shocking range of subject matter—filth, carrion, sexual deviation—never before treated as material by poets. Leconte de Lisle called *Les Fleurs du mal* a "Dantesque nightmare pierced here and there with luminous outlets through which the spirit flies to ideal peace and joy."

In November 1858 Baudelaire left the hotel to care for Jeanne Duval, his longtime mistress. He had broken with her two years earlier, but now she was desperately ill. He broke with her for good when he learned, four years later, that the brother she was living with was not her brother.

OSCAR WILDE AT THE HÔTEL DU QUAI VOLTAIRE

Oscar Wilde lived in a second-floor suite overlooking the river during his stay in Paris from January to May 1883. Then twenty-eight, with none of his famous works yet written, he was living on his youthful poetry, his wit ("I have nothing to declare but my genius," he told the customs agents in New York), and his flamboyant dress and foppish manners, already satirized by Gilbert and Sullivan in *Patience*. He visited many important artists of the time: octogenarian Hugo, who nodded off as Wilde talked; "the divine Sarah," as he dubbed Bernhardt; Degas at his studio, with a letter of introduction from their mutual friend Whistler; and Edmond de Goncourt at his famous *grenier* in Auteuil, who described Wilde in his *Journal* as "*au sexe douteux.*" Wilde carried an ivory cane with a turquoise head as a token of his extravagant admiration of Balzac:

> A steady course of Balzac reduces our living friends to shadows and our acquaintances to shadows of shadows. Who would care to go out to an evening party to meet Tomkins, the friend of one's boyhood, when one can sit at home with Lucien de Rubempré?

Balzac's description of Lucien's astonishing beauty in *Lost Illusions* inspired Wilde's vision of Dorian in *The Picture of Dorian Gray*, and the magical device employed by Balzac in *La Peau de chagrin* (*The Wild Ass's Skin*)—the wish-granting parchment shrinks, and Valentin's life shortens, as each of his wishes comes true—is echoed in what happens to Dorian's portrait as he sinks into his life of debauchery and crime.

GERTRUDE STEIN AND VIRGIL THOMSON

In November 1927 Gertrude Stein's young composer friend Virgil Thomson moved into an attic apartment she found for him in the townhouse at No. 17. They had met the previous year while he was studying with Nadia Boulanger. According to him, he and Stein "hit it off like two Harvard men." They went right to work on their opera *Four Saints in Three Acts*, based loosely on the lives of four sixteenth-century Spanish saints, and completed it the following year. It premiered in 1934 to critical raves in Hartford, Connecticut—a provocative production with an all-African American cast—and went on to a two-month run in a Broadway theater. It made Thomson's name as a composer. His 1947 opera *The Mother of Us All*, about Susan B. Anthony, also had a libretto by Stein.

The Musée d'Orsay

BAUDELAIRE AND FRIENDS

This vast structure with its ornate, vaulted ceiling opened as the Gare d'Orsay railway station in 1900, closed in 1939, and came back to life half a century later as the Musée d'Orsay,

which shows artworks from approximately 1848 to 1914, a period when artists and writers were particularly close. Baudelaire was the most perceptive art critic of his time and was close friends with Delacroix, Manet, and Apollonie Sabatier, the woman who inspired the sexiest sculpture in the museum. The model for Auguste Clésinger's 1847 *Femme piquée par un serpent* (*Woman Stung by a Snake*), a nubile young nude writhing in an agony that could easily be mistaken for ecstasy, was also the muse of some of Baudelaire's finest poems and, very briefly, his lover. They appear together in Courbet's vast canvas *L'Atelier du peintre*, painted in 1855. Her lightly-draped body, considerably fleshier by then, occupies the center of the canvas, and Baudelaire is on the far right, reading a book.

In Fantin-Latour's *Hommage à Delacroix*, Baudelaire stares out with his dark and ironical eyes from a group portrait which includes his friends Whistler, Manet, and Fantin-Latour himself.

VERLAINE AND RIMBAUD

In *Un Coin de table*, Fantin-Latour's group portrait of Symbolist poets, was shown at the 1872 Salon. In it we see Verlaine, then twenty-eight, seated next to the mischievous-looking adolescent Rimbaud. Fantin-Latour had planned to call it *Hommage à Baudelaire*, but had to change the title because the most eminent *Baudelairiens* refused to pose with Rimbaud. At one reading, the youngster had grunted loudly while poets were reciting their works. At another he punctuated the end of each line of a long, boring poem with the word *merde*. When one of the poets scolded Rimbaud, he slashed his hand with Verlaine's sword stick. Rimbaud's *bêtises* in the artist's studio were so offensive to one of the sitters that he dropped out; Fantin-Latour replaced him with a pot of flowers.

ZOLA AND FRIENDS

Émile Zola, one of the boldest champions of Manet and the Impressionists, appears in three paintings by artist friends: Manet's 1867 portrait *Émile Zola*; Fantin-Latour's 1870 group portrait *Un atelier aux Batignolles*; and Frédéric Bazille's *Atelier de Bazille rue de la Condamine*, which shows Zola on the staircase of Bazille's studio conversing with Renoir. Zola was Cézanne's best friend at *lycée* in Aix-en-Provence. They remained close in their early years in Paris, but later drifted apart. The tormented painter Claude Lantier in Zola's *L'Oeuvre* (*The Masterpiece*) is partially based on Cezanne, who has many paintings in the Musée d'Orsay.

PROUST AND FRIENDS

In Jacques-Émile Blanche's 1892 portrait *Marcel Proust*, the would-be writer is depicted as a twenty-one-year-old dandy, ghostly pale in his black evening clothes. Two of Proust's most important friends are also to be found in the Orsay. Mme Straus, his favorite salon hostess, appears in Elie Delaunay's somber portrait *Madame Georges Bizet*, painted in 1878, three years after her first husband's tragically early death. In Giovanni Boldini's 1897 portrait *Le comte Robert de Montesquiou*, Proust's principal model for the Baron de Charlus displays all his exquisite dandyism.

MARGUERITE DURAS AT THE GARE D'ORSAY

Between the Gare d'Orsay's demise as a railway station and rebirth as an art museum, the building's most spectacular use was as Joseph K's office in Orson Welles's 1963 movie adaptation of Kafka's *The Trial*, in which a thousand typists clattered away at their desks. Its most heartrending use was as a reception center for French POWs being repatriated from German camps at the end of World War II. In Marguerite Duras's *La Douleur* (*The War: A Memoir*), a personal account of the Occupation and its aftermath, she spends the spring of 1945 at the station seeking news about her husband, Robert Antelme, a Résistant deported by the Gestapo, and gathering information for a newsletter created to provide up-to-date lists for families of returning POWs. Disorder reigns:

> People keep on arriving. Truck after truck. From Le Bourget. The prison-
> ers are dumped at the center in groups of fifty. Whenever a group arrives
> the music strikes up: *"C'est la route qui va, qui va, et qui n'en finit pas . . ."* For

larger groups it's the *Marseillaise.* There are silences between the songs, but very short ones. The "poor boys" look at the hall, they all smile. They're surrounded by repatriation officers. "Come along boys, get in line!" They get in line and go on smiling. The first ones to arrive at the identity window say, "Slow work!" but still smile pleasantly. When they're asked for information they stop smiling and try to remember.

On and Off Rue du Bac

D'ARTAGNAN ON RUE DU BAC

Cut through the farms of the Abbey of Saint Germain-des-Prés in 1564 to transport stones for the construction of Catherine de Medicis's Tuileries Palace, the Rue du Bac became the main north-south street of the *faubourg.*

From 1659 to 1673, the man on whom Alexandre Dumas based his most popular hero lived at No. 1, where there is a commemorative plaque. Charles de Batz de Castelmaure d'Artagnan served Louis XIV. The king held him in such high regard that he acted as godfather to one of his sons, and the dauphin was godfather to another. In 1661 Louis XIV gave d'Artagnan the sensitive assignment of arresting Nicolas Fouquet after his lavish fête at Vaux-le-Vicomte. D'Artagnan was appointed governor of the region of Lille in 1672 and was killed at the siege of Maastricht the following year.

ELIOT, JOYCE, AND POUND

Twenty-two-year-old T. S. Eliot lived "on the old man's money" at a pension at No. 9 rue de l'Université, now the Hôtel Lenox, while attending Henri Bergson's lectures at the Sorbonne and studying French poetry during the 1910–1911 academic year. His tutor was Alain-Fournier, whose haunting novel of adolescence *Le Grand Meaulnes* (*The Wanderer*) came out in 1913, a year before he was killed in World War I. In the summer of 1911, Eliot wrote the first version of "The Love Song of J. Alfred Prufrock," edited by his mentor Ezra Pound and published in the London magazine *Poetry* in 1915. After Pound relocated to Paris in 1920, Eliot would come and work with him on *The Waste Land.*

James Joyce also stayed at the Lenox when he arrived with his family in July 1920. He came to discuss publishing strategy with his "John the Baptist," as Sylvia Beach called Pound, who was then living at a hotel around the corner on Rue de Beaune. Joyce planned to stay in Paris for a week. As it would turn out, he stayed for twenty years.

After completing *Ulysses* at Valery Larbaud's apartment in the summer of 1921, Joyce and his family returned to the Lenox where Sylvia Beach placed the first copy of *Ulysses* in his hands on February 2, 1922, Joyce's fortieth birthday.

LEFT André Malraux in 1933, the manuscript of *Man's Fate* on the desk

RIGHT Guillaume Apollinare after his head wound, photograph by Harlingue

With the publication of *The Waste Land* a few months later, 1922 was a banner year for Pound. Eliot acknowledged Pound's invaluable editorial help by dedicating the poem to him, calling Pound "*il miglior fabbro*," "the better craftsman."

ANDRÉ MALRAUX

As the plaque on the big, run-down seventeenth-century house at No. 44 rue du Bac indicates, André Malraux here wrote his gripping novel of revolutionary China *La Condition humaine* (*Man's Fate*), and it won the Prix Goncourt for 1933. His daughter Florence was born the same year, and he and his wife, Clara, sheltered many Leftists and Jews fleeing Germany after the burning of the Reichstag. Though Malraux never joined the Communist Party (nor did they ever try to recruit him), he sympathized strongly with the ideals of the Left. In 1936 he organized and led a volunteer fighter squadron, the Escuadrilla España, in support of the Republicans during the Spanish Civil War. Out of that experience came his novel *L'Espoir* (*Man's Hope*), one of the outstanding literary works to emerge from the conflict, along with Orwell's *Homage to Catalonia* and Hemingway's *For Whom the Bell Tolls*.

GUILLAUME APOLLINAIRE

Tiny Rue de Gribeauval, directly across Rue de Bac from Malraux's house, leads to the Baroque church of Saint Thomas d'Aquin, an important landmark in the life of Apollinaire. He lived around the corner in his "pigeon coop," six tiny rooms piled high with books on the top floor of the old house at No. 202 boulevard Saint-Germain. The year Apollinaire moved in, 1913, he published *Alcools*, one of the most popular books of French poetry of all time, and *Les Peintres cubistes*, his pioneering essays on the controversial new style, which included illustrations of works by his comrades Picasso, Braque, Gris, Léger, Duchamp, and others.

As an Italian national, Apollinaire could have sat out World War I in France. Instead, he applied for French citizenship, joined the Army, and went to the front. In March 1916 a piece of shrapnel ripped through his helmet and hit him above the temple. After a seemingly successful trepanation, his personality changed. He could still think and work, but beyond occasional flashes, his remarkable freshness of perception, analysis, and poetic inspiration had vanished.

On May 2, 1918, at the church of Saint Thomas d'Aquin, with Picasso and Vollard as his witnesses, Apollinaire married Jacqueline Kolb, the lovely redhead he called "Ruby," his mistress since his release from the hospital in 1916. Six months after the wedding, he fell victim to the worldwide influenza epidemic. His funeral was held at the church on November 13, 1918, little more than a day after the Armistice. As the funeral cortege wound its way up to Père Lachasise, it passed through a city still exploding with joy. People were shouting "A bas, Guillaume!" But not for Apollinaire. The Guillaume in question was the kaiser of Germany. It was just the sort of thing the man who invented the word "surreal" would have enjoyed.

René de Chateaubriand

CHATEAUBRIAND AND MME RÉCAMIER

From 1838 until his death ten years later, René de Chateaubriand lived in the handsome early-eighteenth-century *hôtel* at No. 120 rue du Bac which belongs, as in Chateaubriand's time, to the Missions Étrangères missionary society. His apartment was on the ground floor at the rear of the courtyard. It is here he wrote the final sections of *Mémoires d'outre-tombe* (*Memoirs from Beyond the Grave*), his autobiography:

> As I write these last words, on 16 November 1841, my window, which looks
> west over the gardens of the Foreign Missions, is open; I can see the pale and
> swollen moon; it is sinking over the spire of the Invalides . . . behold the light
> of a dawn whose sunrise I shall never see.

He was seventy-three when he wrote those lines, ill and depressed, feeling that his end was very near. But he was wrong: He had another seven years to go.

Chateaubriand was an aristocrat who, as a young army officer, welcomed the Revolution. But when it turned vindictive, he sailed for America in 1791. He saw Niagara Falls, the Great Lakes, and the frontier settlement of Pittsburgh, but came back after five months to join the *émigré* army. Wounded in 1792, he took refuge in England, and he returned in 1800 to France, where he became famous with his wildly successful novels *Attala* and *René*, about a young French aristocrat's encounters with American Indians, nature's noblemen. A classical stylist with a romantic sensibility, he was the most admired French writer of the dawn of the nineteenth century. While still a young boy, Victor Hugo vowed to be "Chateaubriand or nothing."

Chateaubriand's life was a heady mix of literature, politics, and love affairs. His most celebrated affair involved the exquisite Juliette Récamier, whom he met in 1801 when she was twenty-four. In his memoir he says:

> As I draw near my end, it seems to me that everything I love I have loved in
> Mme Récamier, and that she was the hidden source of my affections.

He would leave his place on Rue du Bac daily at three o'clock on the dot—passing the neighbors' houses at so precisely the same time that they could set their clocks by him—on his way to Mme Récamier's apartment at the convent of the Abbaye-aux-Bois at No. 7 rue de la Chaise, where she held her long-running literary salon. Lamartine, Benjamin Constant, Stendhal, Sainte-Beuve, Hugo ("enfant sublime," she called him), Balzac, and Musset were some of the other writers who attended. The Square Chaise Récamier, a secluded *jardin à l'anglaise* on the former grounds of the abbey, commemorates the great lady.

Chateaubriand died on July 4, 1848. The funeral was held in the Baroque chapel of the Missions Étrangères at No. 128 rue du Bac, with Balzac, Hugo, Sainte-Beuve, and all France's literary world in attendance. There is a commemorative plaque at No.120 and a weathered bust of Chateaubriand across the street in the little Square des Missions Étrangères.

BECKETT'S FIRST PLAY

In what is now a nondescript multi-purpose room in a language school, one of the most earthshaking events of twentieth-century theatrical history took place on January 3, 1953: the premiere of Samuel Beckett's *En Attendant Godot* (*Waiting for Godot*). The play was performed at the Théâtre de Babylone, a 230-seat playhouse in the cobblestone alleyway entered at No. 38 boulevard Raspail.

Though Jean Anouilh, Jacques Audiberti, and Alain Robbe-Grillet recognized the play's worth right away, most of the audience did not know what to make of it. *Godot* played to sparse audiences for the first couple of weeks, but after a claque of well-dressed spectators created a *scandale* one night when they stood up, whistled, and booed during Lucky's dazzling monologue, the play became a must-see event for Parisians in the know. Journalists found themselves fascinated with the reclusive Irishman who wrote in

French. They discovered he already had two novels in print, *Molloy* and *Malone meurt*, and another, *L'Innommable*, coming out in July. Beckett's *annum mirabilis* ended with the publication of *Watt*, a novel he had written in English during the war. By then, his name was everywhere.

The Noble Houses of the Faubourg Saint-Germain

The most written-about part of the *faubourg* is the area that stretches from Rue du Bac to the Esplanade des Invalides, where the biggest, most glamorous eighteenth-century mansions were built on its long, semi-deserted streets such as Rue de Varenne, Rue de Grenelle, and Rue Saint-Dominique. Ministries and embassies occupy the mansions now. Few can be seen from the street, much less entered. But it was the same when the aristocrats lived here, as Christopher Newman discovers when he first calls on Mme de Cintré in James's *The American*:

> He walked across the Seine, late in the summer afternoon, and made his way
> through those gray and silent streets of the Faubourg St.-Germain, whose
> houses present to the outer world a face as impassive and as suggestive of
> the concentration of privacy within as the blank walls of Eastern seraglios.
> Newman thought it a queer way for rich people to live: his ideal of gran-
> deur was a splendid façade, diffusing its brilliancy outward too, irradiating
> hospitality.

Novelists have been mining the literary riches of the district at least since the days of Lawrence Sterne, when Parson Yorick, from *A Sentimental Journey*, goes calling on Madame de V*** to test the proposition that flattery, the more outrageous the better, can get you anywhere with French ladies.

In Stendhal's *Le Rouge et le noir*, Julien Sorel works at the Hôtel de la Mole (based on the Hôtel de Castries at No. 72 rue de Varenne), where he enters into a dangerous love affair with Mathilde, the marquis's willful daughter.

In Balzac's *Père Goriot*, young Rastignac ingratiates himself with his cousin Clara, vicomtesse de Beauséant, at her palatial home on Rue de Grenelle.

C. Auguste Dupin, Poe's aristocratic amateur detective, lives in "a time-eaten and grotesque mansion in a retired and desolate portion of the Faubourg Saint-Germain."

In Dickens's *Tale of Two Cities* the office of Tellson's Bank is in the mansion of "a great nobleman who had lived in it until he made a flight from his troubles, in his own cook's dress, and got across the borders." Tellson's Bank is where Mme Defarge has her fatal confrontation with the indomitable ("I am a Briton") Miss Pross.

THE GUERMANTES IN THE FAUBOURG

In *The Guermantes Way*, Proust takes readers into the twilight of the *faubourg*'s aristocratic era. At the the the novel begins, the star-struck young narrator and his bourgeois family are living in a rented apartment on the property of "the leading house in the Faubourg Saint-Germain," that of the ultra-aristocratic Guermantes family. The young man worships the exquisite duchesse de Guermantes from afar and despairs of ever catching her notice, much less receiving an invitation to her home. Only people from the loftiest level of society cross her threshold:

> Even for small and intimate gatherings it was only from among them that
> Mme de Guermantes could choose her guests, and in the dinners of twelve
> assembled around the dazzling napery and plate, they were like the golden
> statues of the apostles in the Saint-Chapelle, symbolic, dedicative pillars
> before the Lord's Table.

When she eventually invites him to dinner, he gets to know these "golden statues" in person, and he sees what a shallow, utterly self-centered lot they are. The duchess, so admirable for her wit and learning, can't resist pointing out that every old-line aristocrat whose name comes up is a cousin. As for the duke, he is a boor and a philanderer:

> Thus I beheld the pair of them, divorced from the name Guermantes in
> which long ago I had imagined them leading an unimaginable life, now just
> like other men and other women.

In the final scene, set in the courtyard of the *hôtel*, Swann reluctantly reveals to the duchess that he has only a few months to live. Faced with the choice of staying to console her old friend or leaving with her husband for a routine society dinner, she hesitates only briefly, and then tells Swann, "I expect they've frightened you quite unnecessarily. Come to luncheon, any day you like." She rides away in the carriage with the duke.

For a sense of the palatial size and décor of the sort of house Proust had in mind, the Hôtel de Galliffet at No. 50 rue de Varenne, one of the *faubourg*'s finest mansions and currently home to the Italian Cultural Center, is open to the public on weekdays.

EDITH WHARTON

In 1906 Edith Wharton and her husband Teddy sublet George Vanderbilt's spacious apartment at No. 58 rue de Varenne, now an annex of the Prime Minister's office. She was forty-four years old, a famous novelist since the publication of *The House of Mirth*, but she was suffocating intellectually in the New York and Newport high society. Fluent in French thanks to a childhood spent in Europe, she wanted to challenge her mind in Paris's vibrant cultural climate, which she adored. "*Je l'ai dans mon sang*," she wrote in her diary. Planning to stay through the winter, the Whartons arrived with six servants, a cook, their automobile and chauffeur, and two dogs.

In 1908 they moved to a larger apartment across the street at No. 53, where she is quoted on a plaque:

> "My years of Paris life were spent entirely in Rue de Varenne—rich years, crowded and happy years."

Edith Wharton,
Christmas 1905

But they were blighted by her relationship with Teddy, a mentally unstable man twelve years her elder, with whom she had never had an emotionally, intellectually, or sexually fulfilling marriage. He was also a philanderer, and embezzled money from her. His financial losses would force her to sell The Mount, the splendid house she built in Lenox, Massachusetts.

In the spring of 1907 she met a dark, handsome, mustachioed American named Morton Fullerton. He was a Paris correspondent for the *Times of London* and a friend of Henry James, her mentor (Fullerton was the inspiration for the journalist Merton Densher in James's *The Wings of the Dove*). He was cultivated, seductive, and "very intelligent, but slightly mysterious, I think," she told a friend. They became regular theater and travel companions and, early in 1908, they became lovers. As her letters and poems to him make clear, she experienced, at long last, her erotic awakening.

The next year, however, Fullerton alternated between brief periods of passion and long unexplained silences, and the affair ended in 1910. Though she never learned the full range of his erotic involvements, they included numerous lovers of both sexes, a short-lived marriage to a French opera singer, and an affair with his young cousin Katherine. He was also being blackmailed by a woman with proof of his homosexual past. But Wharton's fiction took on a new emotional depth as her ability to describe love, in its full range of emotions, expanded in such novels as *Ethan Frome*, *The Reef* (with Fullerton the model for George Darrow), and in her masterpiece *The Age of Innocence*, in which the Countess Olenska lives on Rue de Varenne.

After twenty-eight increasingly difficult years of marriage, she finally divorced Teddy in 1913. With the outbreak of war the next year, she threw herself into relief work, creating orphanages, hostels, clinics, and workshops for displaced persons in Flanders and northeastern France. Her friends André Gide and Jean Cocteau worked for "Mrs. Wharton's Charities," as they were called. In 1916 she was made a chevalier of the Légion d'honneur.

Wharton's final decades were rife with rewards, including the Pulitzer Prize in 1921 for *The Age of Innocence*, and an honorary doctorate from Yale two years later, the first woman

Rodin Museum

to be so honored by the university. In 1937 she died at her home in Saint-Brice-sous-Fôret, north of Paris. She is buried at the American Cemetery at Versailles.

ANDRÉ GIDE

In 1926 André Gide, then fifty-six, moved to a spacious sixth-floor apartment in the building with Art Deco *rondeurs* and marvelous iron grillwork at No. 1 *bis* rue Vaneau, where there is a plaque in his honor. That same year, his novel *The Counterfeiters* and the final edition of *If It Die*, his early autobiography, were published. Many of his great works were well behind him, including *The Fruit of the Earth*, *The Immoralist*, *Strait is the Gate*, *Lafcadio's Adventures*, *Croyden*, and *The Pastoral Symphony*, but Gide remained extremely active during the quarter-century he lived on Rue Vaneau. He traveled and wrote for political purposes, arguing against colonialism in Africa, for Communism, then against it after a visit to the Soviet Union in 1936. His essay *Return from the USSR* infuriated the French Left and resulted in the banning of all his works in Russia. He rejected the Vichy government after the Fall of France, embraced Gaullism, made his way to Tunisia, and worked for the liberation of France until the end of the war. He received the Nobel Prize in Literature in 1947 and died on February 9, 1951. Following in the footsteps of the Kremlin, the Vatican put all Gide's writings on its Index of Prohibited Books the following year.

RILKE AND RODIN AT THE HÔTEL BIRON

Built in 1730 for a wealthy wig manufacturer from Languedoc, the magnificent Hôtel Biron, now the Musée Rodin, is named for the tulip-loving Duc de Biron, who owned it from 1753 to 1788. It became a convent in the nineteenth century, but the government acquired it when the religious orders were disenfranchised in 1904, and allowed artists to divide the building into studios.

In August 1908, when Rainer Maria Rilke's sculptress wife, Clara Westhoff, returned to Germany, he moved into her studio. Realizing that the vast, unoccupied main gallery would be ideal for a sculptor who worked on a grand scale, Rilke thought of his former boss Auguste Rodin. They had fallen out two years earlier, but the time for reconciliation had come. He wrote to him:

> You must see this handsome building and the room I have been living in since this morning. Its three picture window open prodigiously onto an abandoned garden, where from time to time we see naïve rabbits jumping through the trellises, as in an ancient tapestry.

Rodin came for lunch, loved the ground floor, and moved in barely a month later.

Rodin and Rilke now renewed their friendship, but on far more equal terms than in the past, because Rilke's two volumes of *New Poems* had made him famous. Their big disagreement was about women: Rodin could not separate them from their sexuality (his "French temperament," as Rilke saw it), while Rilke defended the model of "Nordic women," whose sensual purity did not get in the way of aesthetics.

In his rooms overlooking the garden, the melancholy poet enjoyed one of his happiest periods, despite his struggle with *The Notebooks of Malte Laurids Brigge*. Rilke had been working on the novel since 1902, but it remained a jumble of fragments. In December 1909 he traveled to Germany, lugging the mess with him. At the suggestion of his publisher in Leipzig, he started dictating his pages to a stenographer. Miraculously, everything fell into order. Two weeks later, on January 27, 1910, it was ready for the printer.

In 1912, to prevent the planned demolition of the Hôtel Biron, Rodin offered to will a large body of his work to the French government if it would convert the property to a museum after his death. His offer was accepted. When he died five years later, the Musée Rodin was born.

Literature inspired Rodin's art. He borrowed imagery from Dante's *Inferno* for his *Gates of Hell*, illustrated a deluxe edition of Baudelaire's *Les Fleurs du Mal*, and sculpted a splendid bust of Victor Hugo from life when the great writer was eighty-three. Each work is displayed at the museum. But the writer who dominates Rodin's art is Balzac. A massive bronze casting of him in his monk's cowl stands to the right of the museum's entrance. This statue was rejected by the Société des Gens de Lettres in 1898. And Rodin's previous trial version resulted in total outrage: A naked Balzac, the barrel-shaped dynamo positively bursting with male vigor. A glistening black bronze of the notorious nude stands in the Balzac room of the museum.

JAMES FENIMORE COOPER

From 1831 until their return to America in 1833, James Fenimore Cooper, his wife, and five children lived in a huge apartment in the Hôtel de Kinsky at No. 59 rue Saint-Dominique. Cooper had arrived in 1826, a year after the publication of *The Last of the Mohicans*, a sensation in Europe, making this child of the American frontier the first American novelist to be acclaimed on the Old Continent. Balzac described Natty Bumppo, Cooper's half-white Christian, half-Indian hero, known by his Indian name of Hawkeye, as "a magnificent moral hermaphrodite, between the savage and civilized states." Balzac acknowledged the influence of *The Last of the Mohicans* on *Les Chouans*, his first successful novel. Cooper wrote *The Prairie* in 1827 while living on Rue de l'Abbé-Grégoire. He had planned to stay for only a year, but he became fascinated by European history and politics, and ended up remaining in Paris for seven. It was a bad career move. The American public rejected his "continental" attitudes, and his books about Europe failed to sell. He had to revert to the Leatherstocking saga to win back his readers, publishing *The Pathfinder* in 1840 and *The Deerslayer* in 1841.

The Eiffel Tower

Established writers hated the tower when it went up in 1889. Verlaine called it a "*squelette de beffroi*" (a skeleton of a belfry), Huysmans a "*chandelier creux*" (a hollow candlestick holder), and Zola "a tower of Babel." Maupassant signed a petition protesting its con-

293 M. PARIS — La tour Eiffel - La foule au Champ de Mars

struction. After it was built, he said that he liked the tower's restaurant because it was the only place in Paris where he did not have to look at the structure. But the writers of the next generation saw it as a symbol of modernity. In his poem "Zone" Apollinaire likened the tower to a shepherdess whose "flock of bridges is bleating this morning. You've had enough of living in Greek and Roman antiquity." The Surrealists also appreciated this great lady "*au sexe feminin entre ses jambes de feré cartées,*" as Louis Aragon called her. And Cocteau celebrated the tower in his play *Les Mariés de la Tour Eiffel*.

JAMES JOYCE IN THE SHADOW OF THE EIFFEL TOWER

After scraping by for sixteen years teaching English in Trieste and Zürich to support his family, followed by two difficult years in Paris, James Joyce finally had the means to lease a place of his own, thanks to his income from Sylvia Beach's edition of *Ulysses* and the generosity of patrons. In the fall of 1922, this paragon of literary Modernism moved with Nora and their children, Giorgio and Lucia, to the bourgeois vicinity of the Eiffel Tower. They lived on Avenue Charles Floquet until June 1925, when they moved to the *belle époque* apartment house at No. 2 square Robiac.

Joyce first met Samuel Beckett at this apartment in November 1928, when Joyce was forty-six and Beckett twenty-two, shortly after the young Irishman's arrival to teach English at the École Normale Supérièure. Contrary to many accounts, Beckett did not become Joyce's "secretary." He was merely a young friend and admirer, who would read to the nearly-blind Joyce, find books for him in libraries, and occasionally take dictation for *Work in Progress*, the future *Finnegans Wake*.

Joyce liked Beckett and considered him the brightest and most talented of the young men around him. He brought him into the family circle, which included Sylvia Beach, Adrienne Monnier, Tom MacGreevy, and Eugene and Maria Jolas. A rift developed in 1930, however, when Lucia convinced her parents that Beckett was trifling with her affections. When Joyce told him he was no longer welcome in their home, Beckett was devastated. But two years later, after Joyce came to see that Lucia was mentally unstable, and Beckett was not to blame, he renewed their friendship.

In the mid-1930s, the Joyces moved to No. 7 rue Edmond-Valentin, almost literally in shadow of the Eiffel Tower. They were living here when Beckett was stabbed in the chest, and they rushed to the hospital to lend their support.

The Joyces spent their last year in Paris across the river in the Sixteenth Arrondissement, on Rue des Vignes, near the Balzac Museum, where they had just moved when *Finnegans Wake* finally came out in May 1939.

The German invasion chased them from the city in June 1940. Seven months later, on January 13, 1941, Joyce died in Switzerland of a perforated duodenal ulcer at the age of fifty-eight. He is buried in Fluntern Cemetery in Zürich.

MONTPARNASSE

In the seventeenth century, university students began venturing to a no-name wasteland on the fringe of the Latin Quarter to declaim poetry, using a mound of rubble as their platform. They nicknamed it Mount Parnassus, after the legendary home of Apollo, the god of poetry. The mound was eventually leveled, but the name remained. Other than Balzac and Chateaubriand, forced by their financial woes to live on the outskirts of Paris, no writers of importance settled in Montparnasse until the dawn of the twentieth century. But after World War I, Montparnasse suddenly found itself the new literary hot spot of the city.

The Heart of Montparnasse

LE DÔME
The first of the big cafés to open, in 1898, was the Dôme at No. 108 boulevard du Montparnasse, a haunt from the beginning for bohemian artists and models. But the atmosphere changed after World War I, when the Dôme became the rage for American

The Dôme and the Boulevard
du Montparnasse

writers, artists, journalists, hip tourists, and hangers-on who packed its giant *terrasse*—
triple the size of today's glassed-in version—day and night.

One of its most conspicuous habitués was Robert McAlmon, whose eight years in
Paris overlapped Hemingway's almost exactly, but whose trajectory was Hemingway's in
reverse. McAlmon arrived in the fall of 1921, a published writer at twenty-five, and considered a rising star. Thanks to his *mariage blanc* to the young English writer Winifred
Ellerman (*nom de plume* Bryher), arranged to conceal her lesbianism from her fabulously
rich father, McAlmon had a lavish allowance from Sir John—enough to start his own
publishing company, *Contact Editions*. Sylvia Beach told him that he was "talking his talent away in cafés," but he pooh-poohed her warning. By the time he returned to America
in 1929, he was an embittered man. The only company to have published his books was
his own, and his chief claim to fame was that he had published Hemingway's first book,
Three Stories and Ten Poems, in 1923.

The regulars at the Dôme were terrible snobs. One night when Sinclair Lewis, the
hugely successful author of *Main Street* and *Babbitt,* was overheard boasting about one of
his books on the *terrasse,* someone at a table shouted, "Sit down, you're just a best seller."

In the late 1930s the Dôme was Simone de Beauvoir's favorite café. "I have the feeling of
being part of a family that protects me against depression," she said, and scenes in her first
novel, *L'Invitée* (*She Came to Stay*), take place in the café. It is the story of a mature couple's
attraction to a young woman, and their attempt to draw her into a *ménage à trois,* based on
Beauvoir's romantic attraction to a girl in a *lycée* philosophy class she was teaching and the
burning desire Sartre also felt for the student. Their wishes remained unfulfilled, however,
because Olga (to whom the novel is dedicated) refused to join in the game.

Beauvoir abandoned the Dôme after the fall of France. The sight of German officers at the tables depressed her. She switched to the Café de Flore.

LA ROTONDE

When La Rotonde opened across the boulevard at No. 105 in 1904, it was a tiny workman's bar and no threat to the Dôme. But in 1911, Victor ("Papa") Libion bought it, expanded it, and created a large *terrasse*, nicknamed "*Raspail plage.*" In March 1922, three months after his arrival, twenty-two-year-old correspondent Ernest Hemingway fired off this report to the *Toronto Star*:

> The scum of Greenwich Village, New York, has been skimmed off and deposited
> in large ladles on that section of Paris adjacent to the Café Rotonde . . . They are
> nearly all loafers expending the energy that an artist puts into his creative work
> in talking about what they are going to do and condemning the work of all art-
> ists who have gained any degree of recognition . . . The artists in Paris who are
> turning out creditable work resent and loathe the Rotonde crowd.

On March 2, 1932, two years to the day after arriving in France, Henry Miller made a date for a drink with Anaïs Nin, with whom he had fallen deliriously in love. He declared his love at the Rotonde and tried to coax her to his hotel. He would have to wait almost a week.

Simone de Beauvoir was born upstairs from the café in 1908 and spent her first eleven years in the building, an upbringing described in *Mémoires d'une jeune fille rangée* (*Memoirs of a Dutiful Daughter*). Her prickly father was an aristocrat by birth, but lacked the means to support his entitled behavior. With his submissive wife's dowry exhausted, the family could no longer afford their large apartment. In 1919 the Beauvoirs moved to a cramped, five-flight walk-up on Rue de Rennes.

LE SÉLECT

Le Sélect at No. 99, the least-changed of the old hangouts, opened in 1925, at the height of the expatriate frenzy, and was the first spot in the Quarter to stay open all night. That and its Welsh rarebit made it very popular. Jake Barnes stops in four times in *The Sun Also Rises*.

In Jean Rhys's *Quartet*, the fragile heroine, Marya, has to endure a nasty scene at the café with Heidler, her lover, and his testy wife, Lois. To lighten the tension, Heidler beckons the very drunk Guy Lester to the table, but Guy calls Marya a hussy.

> "Darling Marya," said Lois, laughing on a high note. "You don't know her,
> you don't. She's as harmless at they're made, Guy. A sweet young thing on the
> sentimental side."

The thinly disguised models for Heidler and Lois were Ford Madox Ford and his longtime mistress Stella Bowen. Rhys was her own model for Marya.

In July 1929, Hart Crane got roaring drunk, slugged a waiter and a cop, and tangled with several more lawmen until they knocked him cold and dragged him feet first to jail. Gide, Cocteau, Kay Boyle, e. e. cummings, and other admirers rallied to Crane's support, but failed to get him released. Harry Crosby, who was preparing to publish his major poem *The Bridge*, rushed back to Paris as soon as he got word, went to court, and paid the fine. Combined with a strong letter of support from *La Nouvelle Revue française*, it got Crane sprung from La Santé prison. Crosby put him on the first available liner to New York.

The Black Sun Press published *The Bridge* the following year, but without Harry Crosby, who committed suicide with a mistress in New York on January 10, 1930. Two years later Crane took his own life, dropping into the Gulf of Mexico from a ship.

LA COUPOLE

The last of the big Carrefour Vavin establishments was La Coupole, the vast brasserie-style restaurant and café at No. 102, Art Deco in style, with frescos by Montmartre artists atop its forest of columns. It opened on December 20, 1927.

Georges Simenon was a regular from the beginning, as was Josephine Baker, who paraded down the aisles with her pet cheetah. Simenon had called off their affair the year before La Coupole opened. He later claimed he would have married her, but he did not want to be known as "Monsieur Baker."

In one of Simenon's first Maigret novels, *La Tête d'un homme* (*A Man's Head*), La Coupole is the key setting in a murder case investigated by the down-to-earth inspector, rather out of his element in a den of *artistes* and international sophisticates.

On November 6, 1928, the Russian-born writer Elsa Triolet engineered an introduction to Louis Aragon at the bar *américain*. She wanted to meet him for a host of reasons: She loved his Surrealist classic *Le Paysan de Paris*; they were on the same side politically (he had joined the Party the previous year); he was a very attractive man, thirty-one at the time; and he was free, having been dumped by Nancy Cunard. The evening ended back at her room in the Hôtel Istria, and inaugurated their long life together as the First Couple of the literary Left.

La Coupole was the favorite hangout of Henry Miller and his cronies in the 1930s, especially when Anaïs Nin was there to pick up the tab.

THE DINGO

During the benevolent reign of bartender Jimmie Charters in the mid-1920s, the most popular bar in Montparnasse was the Dingo, around the corner from the Dôme at No. 10 rue Delambre. Hemingway would stop by to chat with the jovial Liverpudlian, a former boxer, and later wrote the introduction to Charters's sprightly memoir, *This Must be the*

Place. Kiki and McAlmon were regulars. It's at Dingo that Djuna Barnes met Dr. Dan Mahoney, the defrocked San Francisco physician who was her model for Dr. Matthew O'Connor in *Nightwood*.

Inside the former Dingo, now an Italian restaurant, sits a relic from those heady times: the bar at which Hemingway was drinking with friends on the day F. Scott Fitzgerald walked in and introduced himself.

Just back from the Côte d'Azur, where he had finished writing *The Great Gatsby*, Fitzgerald made the trek to Montparnasse in late April 1925 in search of the young writer whose stories, published in Paris, he had admired so much that he recommended him to his own editor, the celebrated Maxwell Perkins at Scribner's. At twenty-eight, he was three years older than Hemingway, and the most successful young writer in America. But his consuming need for heroes to worship caused him to fall into a sycophantic mode (a no-no in Hem's macho ethic) and get falling-down drunk. In *A Moveable Feast*, written three decades later, Hemingway characterizes Fitzgerald's face as between handsome and pretty, with "a delicate long-lipped Irish mouth that, on a girl, would have been the mouth of a beauty."

> His chin was well built and he had good ears and a handsome, almost beautiful, unmarked nose. This should not have added up to a pretty face, but that came from the coloring, the very fair hair and the mouth. The mouth worried you until you knew him and then it worried you more.

Hemingway was drinking with two friends when Fitzgerald found him at Dingo: Lady Duff Twysden—a striking British aristocrat who could swear like a cockney and drink any man under the table—and Pat Guthrie, her even harder-drinking Scottish cousin and lover. That summer they joined Hem and others at the bullfights in Pamplona, where Lady Duff's fling with a matador aroused the jealousy of Guthrie and another lover, Harold Loeb, sparking in Hemingway the idea for the climactic incident in *The Sun Also Rises*. Lady Duff became the model for Lady Brett Ashley, Pat Guthrie for Mike Campbell, Harold Loeb for Robert Cohn, and Hemingway became his own model for a much-altered Jake Barnes.

DADAISTS AND A SURREALIST ON RUE DELAMBRE

Man Ray lived at the Hôtel des Écoles (now the Lenox) at No. 15 from December 1921 until the following summer, and made some of his most famous photographs of artists: James Joyce (sent by Sylvia Bench for a publicity shot for *Ulysses*), Gertrude Stein (her first photo to appear in print), Jean Cocteau, Sinclair Lewis, Georges Braque, Fernand Léger, and Henri Matisse. A month later his friend and fellow Dadaist Tristan Tzara, then at the height of its influence, took a room on the same floor.

August Strindberg

André Breton spent the year 1921 at the Hôtel Delambre at No. 35, but the future "Pope of Surrealism" found Montparnasse shallow and false. He moved to Rue Fontaine in gritty Lower Montmartre the following year.

RODIN'S BALZAC

Rodin's famous statue of Balzac in his monk's cowl, with its blur of a face and deep pits for his visionary eyes, overlooks the central crossroads of Montparnasse, the Carrefour Vavin. Called "a colossal fetus," "a snowman," "Balzac in a bag," when Rodin first presented the sculpture in 1898, it was rejected by the Société des Gens de Lettres, which had commissioned it. Four decades later, on July 2, 1939, it was installed on the leafy traffic island facing the Rotonde and the Dôme, a decade too late for Balzac to observe the human comedy of *les années folles*.

Rue de la Grande-Chaumière

STRINDBERG

On August 18, 1894, after leaving his wife, Frida, August Strindberg arrived from Austria and moved into a pension at No. 12, where the famed Swedish playwright plunged into chemical experiments. His aim was to get rich by developing a process for refining pure sulfur. On hot days he would strip naked and work at the stove in the makeshift lab in his room, where the temperature would rise to 120 degrees Fahrenheit. Though he had abandoned the theater, Strindberg became the talk of the town in December when Lugné-Poe's avant-garde Théâtre de l'Oeuvre staged *The Father*, which was roasted by critics for its blatant misogynism. He responded with an article in *La Revue Blanche* entitled "The Inferiority of Woman to Man".

Also in December, Strindberg met and became friends with Paul Gauguin, who had a studio on Rue de la Grande-Chaumière. They saw each other almost daily until Gauguin's return to Tahiti the following summer. Gauguin introduced him to a coterie of bohemian artists who gathered nightly at the Crémerie Charlotte at No. 13, a cozy eatery where Strindberg was attracted to the warm, ample Mme Charlotte. But a deep spiritual crisis set in:

> I was living in a strange country, forgetting the past and forgotten by my
> friends, devoting myself to science after having abandoned creative writing,
> when in the year 1896 I entered that phase of my life called the Inferno, and
> it was under that title that there appeared in 1897 the book which represents
> the turning point of my life.

In *Inferno*, Strindberg provides a harrowing account of the paranoia which gripped him—his so-called friends at the Crémerie conspiring against him, and his neighbors at the pension plotting to kill him . . . In February 1896 he fled the nightmare on Rue de la Grande-Chaumière for the seeming calm of the Pension Orfila.

NATHANAEL WEST

In the 1920s and 1930s, the Hôtel Libéria at No. 9, now the modern Villa des Artistes, was the low-budget hostelry where twenty-three-year-old Nathanael West (*né* Nathan Wallenstein Weinstein), a recent Brown University graduate, spent three months in 1926, beginning his first novel, a Surrealist romp called *The Dream Life of Balso Snell*. In one of the hero's elaborate dreams-within-a-dream, Janey—a beautiful, pregnant, young American hunchback—is described in a letter by the poet who impregnated her. In the note, Janey leaps to her death in her pajamas from a window of the Hôtel Libéria to the street below, where "the usual crowds were hurrying to lunch from the Academies Colorossa and Grande Chaumière." Published in 1931, it was a youthful warm-up for West's sardonic masterpieces *Miss Lonelyhearts* and *The Day of the Locust*.

On December 22, 1940, West was killed in a car crash in California, one day after his friend and fellow screenwriter F. Scott Fitzgerald died of a heart attack in Hollywood.

SAMUEL BECKETT

Samuel Beckett moved into Hôtel Libéria in October 1937. He was at the turning point in his life. He had decided to leave Ireland, where he realized he could not live freely and creatively, and had come back to Paris to make a life for himself. At thirty-one, with no income from his few esoteric works and with no prospects for a job, it was a risky move.

In December, Beckett received great news from London: Routledge and Sons had accepted his novel *Murphy*. But less than a month later, on the night of January 7, 1938, Beckett was stabbed in the chest by a deranged man. Suzanne Deschevaux-Dumesnil, a woman he had known slightly a few years earlier, came to visit him at the hospital. They began seeing each other after his return to the Libéria, and he broke off his liaison with the flamboyant American heiress Peggy Guggenheim. Beckett was a shy man, but his brilliant intellect, sensitivity, and lanky good looks made him irresistible to no small number of women. In her memoir *Out of the Century*, Guggenheim confessed, "I was entirely possessed for over a year by that strange creature, Samuel Beckett."

Rue Campagne-Première

VERLAINE AND RIMBAUD

In January 1872, Verlaine rented an attic room for Rimbaud in a little house which stood at No. 14. Soon afterwards Verlaine moved in with him, having been chased from his in-laws' home in Montmartre for hurling his three-month-old son against the wall. He and Rimbaud went back to their life of debauchery. But when Verlaine learned that his wife, Mathilde, was about to file for a divorce, he broke with Rimbaud and returned home.

Years later, when Rimbaud was off in the Horn of Africa, Verlaine wrote a poem about this attic room called "Le Poète et la Muse," published in his collection *Jadis et naguère*:

> La Chambre, as-tu gardé leurs spectres ridicules,
> Ô pleine de jour sale et de bruits d'araignées?
> La Chambre, as-tu gardé leurs formes désignées
> Par ces crasses au mur et par quelles virgules?

> (Room, have you kept their ridiculous ghosts,
> O room full of dirty daylight and spiders' sounds?
> Room, have you kept the vestige of their forms
> Outlined by stains and marks on the wall?)

HÔTEL ISTRIA

A plaque on the Istria at No. 29 notes the stays of a remarkable contingent of artists and writers: Man Ray and Kiki, Marcel Duchamp, Francis Picabia, Moïse Kisling, Rainer Maria Rilke, Tristan Tzara, Louis Aragon and Elsa Triolet, and Vladimir Mayakovsky.

Kiki moved here in 1922 to be close to Man Ray, who had rented a studio in the magnificent artists' building next door (his was on the ground floor left of No. 31 *bis*).

The following year, trying to escape his jealous lover Jean Cocteau, twenty-year-old Raymond Radiguet hid out with Bronia Perlmutter, his sixteen-year-old girlfriend.

From 1924 to 1929 Russian-born writer Elsa Triolet (*née* Kagan, married briefly to a French officer in Moscow to get out of the country) lived in a miniscule room, with Duchamp and Picabia down the hall. This was where she brought Louis Aragon the night she met him at La Coupole.

On trips to Paris in 1924 and 1925 the poet and dramatist Vladimir Mayakovsky stayed in rooms booked by Triolet, who was an old friend. Passionately idealistic about the Russian Revolution, he would become one of its tragic figures. He committed suicide in Moscow in 1930.

The Closerie des Lilas

The Closerie des Lilas at No. 171 boulevard du Montparnasse is Paris's most self-consciously literary café, with brass name plates of writers on the barroom tables and the magical name of Hemingway bruited about in its promotional material. Named for a lilac grove which no longer exists, the Closerie's literary reputation dates from 1903, when poet Paul Fort inaugurated his Tuesday gatherings. Among the regulars were Max Jacob, André Salmon, Guillaume Apollinaire, American Symbolist poet Stuart Merrill, Maurice Maeterlinck, Paul Claudel, and most spectacularly, Alfred Jarry, who one day fired his revolver into the mirror behind a young lady facing him. It was his way of starting a conversation. "*Maintenant que la glace est rompue, causons*," he told her. "Now that the *glace* is broken" (*glace* meaning both ice and mirror in French), "let's talk."

On February 17, 1922, André Breton was put on "trial" in the café's banquet room upstairs because of an underhanded attack on Tristan Tzara, which had split the Dadaist movement. Before the judge Eric Satie and a jury which included Picasso, Cocteau, and a hundred other avant-gardists, invectives rocketed back and forth between Tzara and his followers and Breton and his proto-Surrealists. Matthew Josephson was astounded by the vituperation:

> Never in my experience were words of such passion and flame hurled at each
> other by men without coming to blows. (If they had been Americans, they
> would have butchered one another).

Breton's "trial" would soon be recognized as the death knell of Dada, clearing the way for the Surrealists to take over.

Though initially contemptuous of expatriates in cafés, Hemingway soon realized that cafés could be fine places to work, and none was better than the Closerie, a few steps from his home on Rue Notre-Dame-des-Champs. It is here that he wrote his classic stories "Big Two-Hearted River" and "Soldier's Home."

After their first introduction at the Dingo, he and Fitzgerald would meet at the Closerie. Fitzgerald was upset about the poor sales of *The Great Gatsby*, published that spring, and asked Hemingway to read it. He was impressed. "If he could write a book as fine as *The Great Gatsby* I was sure that he could write an even better one," he says in *A Moveable Feast*. "But I did not know Zelda yet, and so I did not know the terrible odds that were against him."

Rue Notre-Dame-des-Champs

EZRA POUND

Poet, editor, and all-round cultural gadfly, Ezra Pound lived with his artist wife, Dorothy Shakespear, at No. 70 *bis* from the summer of 1921 until the winter of 1924. There is a small pathway that leads back to the Pounds' pavilion.

A brilliant and omnivorous student and translator of ancient poetry, including Chinese and Japanese verse, this Idaho-born American settled in London in 1908, where he wrote influential poetry ("In a Station of the Metro," and the *Hugh Selwyn Mauberly* cycle), edited the little magazines *Poetry*, the *Egoist*, and *Blast*, and became a guru to younger poets, most notably H. D. (Hilda Doolittle) and T. S. Eliot. But feeling that London had lost its literary edge ("an old bitch, gone in the teeth") and having talked James Joyce into moving to Paris, Pound decided that he should be there too. He arrived in December of 1920.

Sylvia Beach was in for a surprise when he first paid a visit to Shakespeare and Company:

> His costume—the velvet jacket and open-road shirt—was that of the English aesthete of the period. There was a touch of Whistler about him; his language, on the other hand, was Huckleberry Finn's.

The tall, lanky, red-bearded Pound was one of the most influential figures on the expatriate scene as magazine editor, advisor to Bill Bird's Three Mountains Press, and champion of Joyce and Eliot. In Pound's words, this was "a grrrreat littttterary period."

He was also a mentor to Hemingway, giving him lectures on literary style in exchange for boxing lessons. Gertrude Stein was Pound's only known enemy. She called him "the village explainer, excellent if you were in a village, but if you were not, not."

He called her "that tub of guts."

Besides his work for others, Pound started writing his *Cantos*, the vast cycle of poems that would occupy him for the rest of his life.

After four years, he felt that the city had become too crowded with Americans who were "anything but the Passionate Pilgrims of James's day or the enquirers of my own." At the end of 1924, Pound, his wife and his mistress, the concert violinist and musicologist Olga Rudge, moved to Rapallo, where Rudge had a daughter by him the following year. Pound's unbridled support of Mussolini, capped by pro-Fascist, anti-Semitic broadcasts during World War II, irremediably tarnished his reputation and led to his incarceration in a Washington, D.C., mental hospital in 1946 (though he could have faced the death penalty for treason). Twelve years later a group of literary supporters , including his old protégés Hemingway and Eliot, successfully petitioned for his release. He returned to Italy, where he died at eighty-seven in 1972.

FORD MADOX FORD

Pound's friend Ford Madox Ford moved from London to Paris in November 1922, in time to attend Proust's funeral as the self-appointed representative of English letters. He founded the *Transatlantic Review*, joined Pound in promoting Joyce's work—publishing the first excerpt of Joyce's *Work in Progress* in his magazine—and between 1924 and 1928 wrote *The Parade's End*, the greatest fictional treatment of World War I by a British writer. He and his mistress, the Australian painter Stella Bowen, moved to No. 84 in 1925.

Ford, a middle-aged, wheezy fat man with a walrus-like moustache, was quite a ladies' man. Joyce wrote:

> O Father O'Ford you've a masterful way with you,
> Maid, wife and widow are wild to make hay with you.

One of those wives was Mme Jean Lenglet, *née* Ella Gwendolen Rees Williams, born in Dominica, who wrote under the pseudonym Ford created for her: Jean Rhys. She worked for him on the *Transatlantic Review*, and he tutored her in the craft of writing and published her first story. Their affair began early in 1925, after her Dutch husband, Jean Lenglet, went to prison for embezzlement. She was thirty-four (hardly the young thing Marya in *Quartet* seems to be), a beautiful woman, but emotionally shaky and painfully shy.

When Ford and Bowen moved to Rue Notre-Dame-des-Champs, Rhys was in Juan-les-Pins helping a rich American woman write a book (as does Rhys's heroine Sasha Jansen in *Good Morning, Midnight*). But Ford managed to get her fired, forcing her to come back to Paris, where he installed her in a hotel by the Gare Montparnasse. It was just such a place where Heidler installs Marya in *Quartet*:

> It was impossible, when one looked at that bed, not to think of the succession of *petites femmes* who had extended themselves upon it, clad in carefully thought out pink or mauve chemises, full of tact and savoir faire and savoir vivre and all the rest of it.

Ford's final break with Rhys came in the fall of 1926, when he left for an extended book tour in America. Rhys returned to her husband in Holland, where she finished *Quartet*. Its publication two years later sparked alternate versions of the affair by the three other concerned parties: a novel apiece by Ford and Lenglet, and a frontal attack on Rhys by Bowen in her autobiography, *Drawn from Life*.

HEMINGWAY

In February 1924, back from Canada where they had gone for the birth of their baby, Ernest and Hadley Hemingway moved to No. 113. On March 10, Gertrude Stein and Alice B. Toklas served as godmothers: The little boy was christened John Nicanor (after a toreador Hemingway admired) and nicknamed Mister Bumby. The apartment was cramped; even worse, there was a sawmill downstairs. The whine of its buzz saw sent Hemingway to the Closerie des Lilas to write.

In July 1924 he made his second trip to the bullfights in Pamplona, accompanied by John Dos Passos and Donald Ogden Stewart. The next year his group included Hadley, Harold Loeb, Lady Duff Twysden, and Pat Guthrie, the trip that sparked *The Sun Also Rises*. In 1926 he took a break from correcting the proofs of the novel for his fourth trip to Pamplona, with Hadley, Gerald and Sara Murphy, and Pauline Pfeiffer—the attractive young lady whom Hadley had befriended the year before, and who was having an affair with her husband.

A month later, Hadley confronted Hemingway and he moved out.

Nothing remains of the sawmill today, but across the street at No. 110 is the rear entrance of a bakery shop that Hem used as a shortcut "through the good bread smells of the ovens and the shop to the street—to the Boulevard du Montparnasse."

Northern Montparnasse

GERTRUDE STEIN ON RUE DE FLEURUS

For creative Americans coming to Paris in the 1920s, a visit to Gertrude Stein at her art-laden atelier was the cultural equivalent of a private audience with the Pope. A plaque on the Haussmann-style residence at No. 27 rue de Fleurus commemorates the great lady. Her atelier was in the pavilion in the southeast corner of the courtyard.

Newsman William L. Shirer interviewed Stein in 1926 and left with this striking image:

> She was so bulky that, as a note I jotted down reminds me, I thought she looked like a full-blown Irish washwoman. But this first impression soon changed. Above her heavyset body was a face that reminded you of a Roman emperor, masculine and strong and well chiseled, and her eyes were attractive and intelligent. Her hair was closely cropped, like Caesar's. She greeted me in a low, mannish but pleasant voice.

After dropping out of medical school in 1903, Stein left America at the age of twenty-eight and moved in with her adored older brother Leo, an art connoisseur, at his Rue de Fleurus atelier. Following his lead, she developed a passion for modern painting. In 1906, the year Picasso completed his famous portrait of her, she began translating Flaubert's story "Un Coeur simple" to improve her French. But she soon abandoned that task and started writing her own stories, which were published in 1909 as *Three Lives*.

Gertrude Stein and Alice B. Toklas in Stein's atelier at No. 27 rue de Fleurus, 1922 photograph by Man Ray

Alice B. (for Babette) Toklas moved in the following year and became Stein's muse, confidante, secretary, cook, and lover, in effect, her wife. Long-simmering antagonism between Gertrude and Leo over dominance in their relationship eventually became unbearable for Leo, and in 1913 he moved out. The brother and sister never spoke again, even when they passed on the street.

Tender Buttons, her collection of word pictures, baffled most readers. Stein thought of the work as verbal Cubism, because the sound of the words and the images they evoke matter more than any literal meaning. Though her sales were small, certain forward-looking writers, most notably Sherwood Anderson, made a cult figure of her. Her own opinion: "Twentieth-century literature *is* Gertrude Stein."

In March 1922, armed with a letter of introduction from Anderson, Ernest Hemingway made his first visit. He would come often over the next few years. He admired Stein's boldness and artistic integrity, and she loved having a talented young disciple to mold.

He was warned to avoid one subject: James Joyce, whose *Ulysses* had been published the month before Hemingway's first visit. As Stein saw it, Joyce was her sole rival as leader of the Modernist movement in literature. If his name should come up, she would inform the visitor that Joyce "smells like a museum."

Early in his visits, as Hemingway recounts in *A Moveable Feast*, Stein told him he was part of "a lost generation"—"*une génération perdue*"—a phrase used by her garage man to describe World War I veterans. When he protested, she said, "Don't argue with me, Hemingway. It does no good at all. You're all a lost generation, exactly as the garage keeper said." Hemingway used the phrase as the epigraph for *The Sun Also Rises*.

Their friendship soured in 1925. In *A Moveable Feast* Hemingway claims that over-hearing a nasty, sexually-charged tiff between Stein and Toklas at Rue de Fleurus was the cause of his alienation. The true cause of the rift was *The Torrents of Spring*, a parody of Anderson's novel *Dark Laughter*, which Hemingway knocked off in ten days that year. Stein was angered by Hemingway's betrayal of Anderson, her friend (and Hemingway's original mentor). By 1933, when she published *The Autobiography of Alice B. Toklas*, she had relegated her former protégé to the same invidious place as Joyce: "He looks like a modern and he smells of the museums."

STRINDBERG ON RUE D'ASSAS

In the late nineteenth century, the austere house at No. 60 was the Hôtel Orfila, where on February 21, 1896, August Strindberg took refuge from an imagined plot to murder him. A plaque quotes from *Inferno*, about the spiritual hell he was going through:

> Orfila and Swedenborg, my friends, protect me, encourage me and punish me. I don't see them, they don't show themselves to me, neither by visions nor by hallucinations, but little daily events that I take in manifest the vicissitudes of my existence.

But soon the nightmare Strindberg had experienced on Rue de la Grande-Chaumière resumes: people whispering behind his back, deadly ray guns being moved about in the room upstairs . . . After five months, he checks out, calls a cab, and shouts to the coachman to take him to the Gare du Nord. Out of view of the Orfila, he orders the driver to take him to a hotel by the Jardin des Plantes, far from his would-be assassins.

After emerging from his crisis, Strindberg returned to the theater and entered his majestic late period, writing *To Damascus*, *There are Crimes and Crimes*, *A Dream Play*, and *The Ghost Sonata*.

His is a classic story of an artist reborn in Paris. Not surprisingly, Strindberg was an inspiration to Henry Miller, a forty-year-old failure when he arrived. In *Tropic of Cancer* "Henry" visits Strindberg's room at the Orfila and reflects on "the meaning of that inferno which Strindberg had so mercilessly depicted."

> It was no mystery to me any longer why he and others (Dante, Rabelais, Van Gogh, etc., etc.) had made their pilgrimage to Paris. I understood why it is that Paris attracts the tortured, the hallucinated, the great maniacs of love.

Southern Montparnasse: Henry Miller and Anaïs Nin

NIN ON RUE SCHOELCHER

From 1925 to 1928, Anaïs Nin lived in the complex of artists' studios at No. 11 *bis*, along the eastern wall of the cemetery. Then in her mid-twenties, she was in Paris because her

American husband had been posted to France by his New York bank. The young couple occupied one studio, her Danish mother another. Nin was born in Neuilly, but her mother took her to New York at eleven and raised her there after her father, the Cuban-born musician Joachim Nin, abandoned the family. The sensuality of Paris repelled Nin at first, but in December 1926, she wrote in her diary, "I shall try to turn my hate of Paris into writing and make it harmless." She started with close observation of the crowd at the Dôme. A year later she was able to write, "I faced and accepted Paris as a test of my courage."

MILLER ON RUE DE LA GAÎTÉ AND BOULEVARD EDGAR-QUINET

Henry Miller, drawn to the erotic as a bear to honey, loved Rue de la Gaîté, a short tawdry street lined with sex shops and venerable theaters, where Colette once performed in *tableaux vivants* at the Gaîté-Montparnasse, seemingly nude, but wearing flesh-colored tights.

Around the corner at No. 31 boulevard Edgar-Quinet, the glamorous brothel Le Sphinx opened in 1931. On the ground floor were a big Art Deco barroom, a splendid reception hall with frescos by van Dongen, and an orchestra for dancing. Ladies were welcome, but only in the public rooms. Among the visitors were Kiki de Montparnasee, her painter friends Foujita, Kisling, and Pascin; writers Blaise Cendrars, Georges Simenon, Francis Carco; Joseph Kessel, the author of *Belle de Jour*; and Alexandre Breffort, the playwright of *Irma la Douce*. Miller adored the Sphinx but could not afford it. So, as he says in *Tropic of Cancer*, "I got a little rake-off for writing the pamphlets. That is to say, a bottle of champagne and a free fuck in one of the Egyptian rooms."

MILLER AND NIN AT THE HÔTEL CENTRAL

Thanks to freelance work as a copy editor at the *Chicago Tribune*, lined up by his friend Alfred Perlès (Carl in *Tropic of Cancer*), Miller was able to stay at the Hôtel Central at No. 1 *bis* rue du Maine several times during the crucial year of 1931–1932. He began writing *Tropic of Cancer* in August 1931.

That fall his friend Richard Osborn (Fillmore in the book) introduced him to Anaïs Nin at her home in Louveciennes. Miller's intellectual exuberance electrified her, and a passionate literary friendship began, with both of them channeling their erotic attraction into delight in each other's ideas and work. For five months they avoided any mention of sex, afraid it could undermine their connection. To

LEFT Henry Miller, 1931 photograph by Brassaï

RIGHT Anaïs Nin, 1932 photograph by Brassaï

complicate matters further, Nin was attracted to Miller's bisexual wife, June, who made a brief appearance in Paris that winter. But desire eventually got the better of them. On March 6, 1932, Nin joined Miller in Room 401. She did not regret having her "tight secrecy . . . broken for a moment by a man who calls himself 'the last man on earth.'" In *The Diary of Anaïs Nin, 1931–1934*, she wrote:

> After our first encounter I breathed some notes, accents of recognition, human admissions. Henry was stunned, and I was breathing off the unbearable, willing joy. But the second time, there were no words. My joy was impalpable and terrifying. It swelled within me as I walked the streets.

The sexual excitement brought into her life by Henry and June engendered a new fire in the writing of her diary. For Miller, who wanted to marry her, Nin was the only woman he ever loved completely.

On March 20, Miller and Perlès moved to the suburb of Clichy, where Miller and Nin continued their literary-erotic encounters, and Miller finished *Tropic of Cancer*.

Simone de Beauvoir and Jean-Paul Sartre

HÔTEL MISTRAL

Two quotes are engraved on a plaque on the Hôtel Mistral at No. 24 rue Cels. One quote is from Beauvoir's *The Prime of Life*:

> I was cheating when I used to say that we were only one person. Between two individuals, harmony is never a given; it must be conquered again and again.

The other quote is from a letter to her from Sartre:

> But there is one thing that hasn't changed and cannot change: that is that no matter what happens and what I become, I will become it with you.

Beauvoir was living at the Mistral when Sartre was released from a POW camp in Eastern France in March 1941. He joined her, but, as was his custom, in a room of his own.

Sartre tried to organize a Résistance group called Socialism and Liberty, but other than a few former students and an old friend or two, he failed to attract recruits. The Communists were afraid he might have been turned by the Germans in the POW camp. Others did not trust him because he was a compulsive talker who could not be relied upon to keep a secret.

Then thirty-seven, Sartre had already published *Nausea* and *The Wall*, but Beauvoir, thirty-four, had yet to publish. They made their living teaching in *lycées*. Former students gathered around them, and "the family" took shape, with Sartre and Beauvoir acting *in loco parentis*, though incestuously in some cases. Both had sexual relations with at least two of Beauvoir's young women students, though she always denied she had lesbian affairs.

In the fall of 1942 they moved to Saint Germain-des-Près.

BEAUVOIR AT NO. 11 *BIS* RUE SCHOELCHER

In 1956 Beauvoir moved to "the place Goncourt bought," a duplex studio financed by her prize-winning novel *The Mandarins*, located in the artists' complex where Anaïs Nin had lived three decades earlier. Facing the building, the ground floor and mezzanine studio on the left was Beauvoir's. It is here that she wrote her four autobiographies, chronologically and in diminishing order of interest: *Memoirs of a Dutiful Daughter* in 1958, *The Prime of Life* in 1960, *The Force of Circumstance* in 1963, and *All Said and Done* in 1972. Thanks to *The Second Sex*, published in 1949, Beauvoir was hailed as a pioneer in the emerging feminist movement, and she became a revered figure in her later years. But the 1970s were marred by Sartre's disastrous health and a falling-out with his adopted daughter. A month after his death in 1980, Beauvoir was rushed to the Hôpital Cochin with a life-threatening case of pneumonia and complications caused by cirrhosis of the liver. When she recovered she adopted her young friend Sylvie Le Bon and made her the executor of her estate.

Simone de Beauvoir died on April 14, 1986, and she was buried next to Jean-Paul Sartre at the Cimetière de Montparnasse. At the graveside ceremony, feminist writer Elisabeth Badinter proclaimed, "Women, you owe her everything!"

Jean-Paul Sartre and Simone de Beauvoir besieged by journalists after a brief stay in jail for distributing a banned Maoist newspaper, June 26, 1970

SARTRE AT NO. 222 BOULEVARD RASPAIL

After his apartment in Saint Germain-des-Prés was bombed twice by the OAS, Sartre sold it in 1962 and moved to a large, airy studio on Boulevard Raspail. One wall was loaded with books, he had a big leather armchair for reading, and there was a massive work table where editorial meetings of *Les Temps Modernes* were held. He installed his mother a few doors away at the Hôtel l'Aiglon, where she lived until her death seven years later.

During the following decade Sartre's routine was to breakfast at the Café des Arts or Café de La Liberté on Boulevard Edgar-Quinet, work in his studio, and lunch with

Beauvoir or his young mistress Arlette Elkaïm, whom he adopted in 1965, and in the afternoon, he would visit one of the several other mistresses and ex-mistresses he continued to support. While living in the Boulevard Raspail studio he refused the Nobel Prize in Literature, published *Les Mots* (*The Words*), campaigned against the American war in Vietnam, demonstrated for the students in May 1968 and against Soviet occupation of Prague in 1969, became a figurehead for Maoist publications in the early 1970s, published his massive three-volume critique of Flaubert entitled *The Family Idiot*, and helped launch the daily newspaper *Libération* in 1973.

In the fall of that year, at sixty-eight, he suddenly went blind. Without his eyesight he could no longer write, and without writing he could no longer formulate his ideas. Even Sartre's enemies cringed at the sight of the modern heir to the *engagé* tradition of Voltaire being led about in the streets and put on display at public demonstrations.

SARTRE AT NO. 29 BOULEVARD EDGAR-QUINET

Sartre spent his final years in this nondescript, modern building in the shadow of the Tour Montparnasse. "The family" moved him to a two-bedroom apartment here in 1974 so Beauvoir and Arlette Elkaïm could alternately stay overnight. These years were blighted by more than Sartre's blindness: A bitter rift developed between Beauvoir and Elkaïm, whose chief ally was Sartre's new secretary Benny Lévy (pen name Pierre Victor). Beauvoir was angered to see Sartre's name appear on texts of dubious intellectual quality "co-written" with Pierre Victor. For the last two years of Sartre's life, Beauvoir was barred from seeing him. But on the night of March 19, 1980, when he was rushed to the Hôpital Broussais in critical condition, she was allowed to spend the night. She visited him daily during his final month.

On April 15, 1980, more than fifty thousand people marched through the streets of Montparnasse in Jean-Paul Sartre's funeral procession. Waiters came out of cafés to pay their respects. Simone de Beauvoir attended the ceremony at his grave at Montparnasse Cemetery, devastated, clutching a rose in her hand.

Montparnasse Cemetery

Opened in 1824, Paris's classiest cemetery is the final resting place of an extraordinarily distinguished lineup of writers. The main entrance is at No. 3 boulevard Edgar-Quinet, where maps are available at the gatehouse. To the right of the entrance, along the outer wall, Jean-Paul Sartre and Simone de Beauvoir are buried under the same headstone.

The first great writer to be buried here was Baudelaire, who died in 1867 at the age of forty-six. He was interred in the elaborate grave site of his hated stepfather, General Jacques Aupick, deceased a decade earlier. In 1902 Baudelaire's admirers erected a marble cenotaph across the cemetery from the tomb. It is a tall, gloomy affair: A bust of the poet rests on a tall pedestal, dolefully contemplating a sculpture of his own body, which is wrapped like a mummy and stretched out on the slab below.

In the nineteenth century Sainte-Beuve and Guy de Maupassant joined Baudelaire in the cemetery. And in the twentieth century arrived a veritable literary who's who. Besides Sartre and Beauvoir, this is the final resting place for many other leading French writers: Joris-Karl Huysmans; the Parnassian poets Théodore de Banville, François Coppée, and Catulle Mendès; *Arsène Lupin* creator Maurice Le Blanc; poet Robert Desnos, who died in a concentration camp; novelist Emmanuel Bove; poet Léon-Paul Fargue, the author of *Le Piéton de Paris*; Raymond Aron, Sartre's worthy intellectual rival; Pierre Bruller (pen name Vercors), author of *Le Silence de la Mer* and cofounder of Editions de Minuit; poet and songwriter Serge Gainsbourg ("our Baudelaire, our Apollinaire," President Mitterrand called him); Claude Mauriac; and Marguerite Duras.

The foreign contingent buried at Montparnasse Cemetery is impressive as well: Peruvian poet César Vallejo, one of Latin America's greatest; Joseph Kessel, born in Argentina of Lithuanian parents; Julio Cortázar, an Argentinean who lived in Paris for decades; Rumanians Tristan Tzara and Eugène Ionesco; and the Irishman Samuel Beckett.

The Fringes of Montparnasse

CHATEAUBRIAND

The majestic old cedar in the giant ceramic pot in front of the Fondation Cartier at No. 261 boulevard Raspail is the last remaining tree planted by René de Chateaubriand on the property of a hospice created and run by Mme de Chateaubriand.

After quitting his ambassadorship in Rome in 1829, Chateaubriand's career in government was over. Then sixty-one, he was deeply in debt, with no prospect of income. So he moved in with his wife. Victor Hugo, who knew the couple since his teens, wrote that contrary to the image her charitable work might evoke, Mme de Chateaubriand was a shrew—"harsh towards her husband, her relatives, her friends, and her servants, and was sour-tempered, stern, prudish, and a backbiter." The only way to earn money, Chateaubriand reckoned, was to finish the autobiography he had started twenty years earlier. It was the story of his life as a celebrated writer and statesman (once Foreign Minister), in which Chateaubriand details his extraordinarily dramatic history, saying, "[I] met nearly all the men who in my time have played a great or small part in my own or other countries, from Washington to Napoleon."

He was adamant, however, that the work not be published until after his death. To help him find a buyer for the posthumous rights, his muse Juliette Récamier began holding readings of *Mémoires d'outre-tombe* (*Memoirs from Beyond the Tomb*) at her salon at the Abbaye-aux-Bois. After two years of readings, she advised him in 1836 to form a stock company and sell shares in the rights. The scheme worked, guaranteeing him a decent income

Honoré de Balzac in his
famous writing costume

for the rest of his life. Mme de Chateaubriand gave up the hospice, and they moved to Rue du Bac so that her husband could be close to the "arch-madam," as she called Chateaubriand's guardian angel.

Chateaubriand's last cedar marked the rear boundary of the hospice's property. By the front entrance, at No. 92 avenue Denfert-Rochereau, a plaque honors Mme de Chateaubriand, whose tomb rests in the chapel. Her husband's tomb is in his native Saint-Malo.

BALZAC

In 1829 Balzac moved to a country house at No. 1 rue Cassini, renting it under his brother-in-law's name to keep his creditors off his trail. He was thirty years old and had just published his first successful novel, *Les Chouans*. On a filing cabinet in his study he placed a statuette of Napoléon and fixed to it a note: "What he did not complete by the sword, I shall accomplish by the pen." He signed it "Honoré *de* Balzac." Though he had no legal or hereditary right to the aristocratic particle, as an artist and a royalist, he liked the ring. The first novel he signed with the particle was *La Peau de chagrin* (*The Wild Ass's Skin*) in 1831.

While on Rue Cassini, Balzac adopted his famous monk's cowl as his writing costume, and kept his equally famous coffeepot ever at hand, drinking up to twenty cups a day to maintain his furious pace. His schedule: to bed at six in the evening, rise at midnight, on with the monk's cowl, write for twelve to fifteen hours, go out in the afternoon, go to bed at six, and on and on without a day off. He hired Jules Sandeau as his secretary after Sandeau's breakup with George Sand, but being awakened by his boss at all hours of the night—so that Balzac could read aloud what he had just written—brought the young man to nervous collapse.

Balzac wrote more than two dozen books in his five years in this house, including the novels *La Peau de chagrin, Louis Lambert, Eugénie Grandet, Ferragus, La duchesse de Langeais, La fille aux yeux d'or,* and *Le Père Goriot.*

He also made the earthshaking discovery that characters could reappear in different novels. Rastignac, Vautrin, Nucingen, and Lucien de Rubempré are a few of the more prominent figures who recur in *La Comédie humaine,* the main title of his vast "novelistic history of the Restoration and the July Monarchy." There are 593 recurring characters in all. Balzac took care, however, that each novel could be read without reference to others.

In 1832 he received his first letter from "*une étrangère,*" who eventually revealed herself to be the Countess Eveline Hanska, a Polish aristocrat married to a Russian count. Their correspondence would lead to his most important love affair, and eighteen years later, to marriage.

Balzac believed that each man had a finite store of vital fluids, and every gratification of sexual desire depleted it. He told Alexandre Dumas *fils* that "a night of love cost half a volume," and "no woman alive is worth two volumes a year." Nevertheless, for Mme de Berny, the duchesse d'Abrantès, Mme Hanska, and others, he willingly sacrificed a shelf or two.

Samuel Beckett

THE STABBING

At about 1:00 AM on January 7, 1938, Beckett was walking his friends Alan and Belinda Duncan home after a Twelfth Night dinner when a man approached them on Avenue d'Orléans (now Avenue du Géneral-Leclerc), pulled a knife, and stabbed Beckett in the chest. He fell to the sidewalk bleeding profusely. The Duncans called the police, and Beckett was rushed to the Hôpital Broussais. James Joyce was notified of the attack, and he and his wife Nora came immediately. "When I came to," Beckett told his biographer James Knowlson, "the first thing I saw was Joyce at the end of the ward and coming to see me. And it was thanks to Joyce and his crazy woman doctor, Fontaine, that he got me a private room."

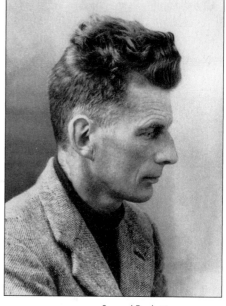

Samuel Beckett, around 1960

The knife had missed Beckett's lungs by less than an inch. Luckily, no complications set in. Joyce showed great concern throughout the ordeal, visiting regularly over the month Beckett was in hospital.

Another visitor was a woman who used to play tennis in a group that included Beckett and his close friend Alfred Péron, and who happened to read about the stabbing in a newspaper. The romance between Beckett and Suzanne Deschevaux-Daumesnil began at his bedside.

The man who stabbed him turned out to be a pimp, apparently deranged. After the trial Beckett asked him why he did it. He said, "Je ne sais pas, Monsieur. Je m'excuse."

THE RÉSISTANCE

The leafy esplanade of Avenue René Coty, a section of which is now named the Allée Samuel Beckett, is in a neighborhood crucial to Beckett's work with Alfred Péron's Résistance network during World War II. His work involved translating documents into English and delivering them to a photographer on this avenue to be microfilmed for transmission to London.

On August 16, 1942, the Gestapo arrested Péron, but his wife managed to call Beckett and warn him. He and Suzanne holed up for a few nights at Mary Reynolds's apartment at No. 24 rue Hallé, near today's Allée Samuel Beckett. The couple moved from place to place in Paris for a month before escaping to the Lubéron, where they hid out for the rest of the war.

THE LAST THIRTY YEARS

By the late 1950s, with money pouring in from productions of *Waiting for Godot, Endgame,* and *Krapp's Last Tape* and from sales of his novels, Beckett could afford a larger, more centrally located home than his little apartment way out in the Fifteenth Arrondissement. In the fall of 1959, he and Suzanne moved to a spacious seventh-floor apartment in the blocky 1950s structure at No. 38 boulevard Saint-Jacques. While Suzanne became increasingly withdrawn, he became more outgoing over the years, drinking with friends, staying out to all hours, and—though he was the soul of discretion—attending to his romances with other women.

While on Boulevard Saint-Jacques, Beckett wrote the play *Happy Days* (*Oh les beaux jours*), *That Time*, and other monologues and short plays, and supervised productions in Paris, London, Germany and elsewhere. He received the Nobel Prize in Literature in 1969 and, as with all the other prizes he received, he gave most of the money away.

He spent his final months in a medical retirement home, Le Tiers Temps at No. 26 rue Rémy Dumoncel, near the house where he and Suzanne had hidden from the Gestapo. She died in July 1989, and he followed that December, at eighty-three. Beckett was buried beside her at Montparnasse Cemetery.

Henry Miller and Friends at the Villa Seurat

The Villa Seurat is a tranquil mews, entered at No. 101 rue de la Tombe-Issoire and built in the 1920s for artists. Dali and Derain lived here. In the spring of 1931, a Lithuanian-born American writer named Michael Fraenkel who owned the house at No. 18, offered his spare room to an amazing talker who had been kicking around Montparnasse for a year, swapping his conversational brilliance for drinks and meals. Henry Miller was enchanted with the Villa Seurat. "The whole street is given up to quiet, joyous work," he wrote to his friend Emil Schnellock. "Every house contains a writer, painter, musician, sculptor, dancer, or actor. Is it such a quiet street and yet there is such activity going on, silently, becomingly, shall I not say reverently too?"

Miller's stay at the Villa Seurat gave him time to think about "the Paris book" he was burning to write. And after years of failed efforts at writing fiction in America, he found his true voice—explosive, uninhibited, erotic, nihilistic, and anarchistic. In the opening paragraphs of *Tropic of Cancer* he writes:

> I have no money, no resources, no hopes. I am the happiest man alive. A year
> ago, six months ago, I thought I was an artist. I no longer think about it, I *am*.
> Everything that was literature has fallen from me. There are no more books
> to be written, thank God. This then? This is not a book. This is libel, slan-
> der, defamation of character. This is not a book, in the ordinary sense of the

word No, this is a prolonged insult, a gob of spit in the face of Art, a kick in the pants to God, Man, Destiny, Time, Love, Beauty . . . what you will. I am going to sing for you, a little off key perhaps, but I will sing. I will sing while you croak, I will dance over your dirty corpse . . .

Henry Miller's beloved Villa Seurat, where he spent much of the 1930s

Three years later, on September 1, 1934, Miller returned to live at No. 18 villa Seurat on the very day *Tropic of Cancer* was published. Eric Kahane had accepted the book for his Obelisk Press almost two years earlier, but only when Anaïs Nin stepped in and paid the printing costs did he publish it. Nin also paid the rent for Miller's top-floor studio.

Praise for *Tropic of Cancer* poured in from Blaise Cendrars, Miller's favorite French writer, who wrote the first review. More praise followed from Marcel Duchamp, Louis-Ferdinand Céline, Raymond Queneau, Aldous Huxley, and George Orwell.

If his first stay had kickstarted his miraculous birth as a writer, Miller's second stay resulted in five of his most joyous and productive years, surrounded by a colorful band of literary adventurers, including Nin, Fraenkel, Alfred Pèrles, Walter Lowenfels, and Lawrence Durrell.

After the publication of *Tropic of Capricorn* in 1939, Miller left Paris to join Durrell and his family in Corfu. Out of that trip came *The Colossus of Maroussi*, considered by many to be Miller's finest book, written in the exuberant Millerian voice that had emerged in Paris, but without the *fucks*, *cunts*, and *cocks* that made his *Tropics* illegal in the United States. He would have to wait another quarter of a century for his controversial books to be sold legally in America. On June 22, 1964, in a landmark case establishing a new, more liberal code of censorship, the United States Supreme Court ruled that *Tropic of Cancer* was not obscene.

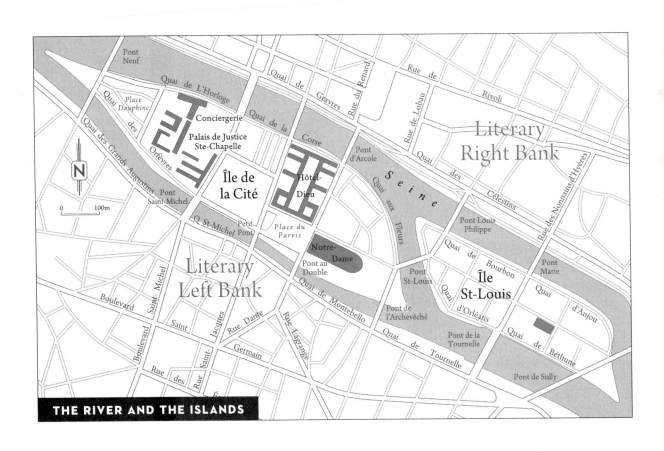

THE RIVER AND THE ISLANDS

The River and the Islands

2147. PARIS – *Panorama de la Seine vers la Cité*   C. M.

THE SEINE

So key is the Seine to the beauty of Paris that we may take for granted that it has always been so. It has not. Paris's stretch of the river became aesthetically appealing only in the late nineteenth century, after Haussmann and his successors rid it of its malodorous mud flats, cleaned up its sewage-tainted water, sent the tripe-cleaners packing, demolished the rows of houses blocking the view, lined the banks with stone quays (a few already existed, but not many), and created the tree-shaded walkways so beloved to literary browsers. The famous green boxes of the *bouquinistes*, standardized in 1895, run more than a mile on each bank, creating the world's longest open-air bookshop.

DEATH ON THE SEINE

Before gentrification, writers took little interest in the river except as a setting for death or its contemplation in their fiction.

In Poe's "Mystery of Marie Rogêt," the mutilated corpse of the *grisette* is found "floating in the Seine, near the shore which is opposite the Quartier of the Rue Saint-André." And in Zola's *Thérèse Raquin*, Thérèse's lover Laurent engineers the drowning of her husband, Camille.

Characters often consider suicide, but rarely carry through. In Balzac's *The Wild Ass's Skin*, the despairing young Raphaël de Valentin prepares to take the fatal plunge from the Pont-Royal one morning, but, noticing a rescue boat on duty, decides to wait until nightfall. Once he discovers the magical wish-granting parchment in the strange antique shop on the Quai Voltaire, Valentin quickly forgets the urge to end his life. More recently, in Jean Rhys's *Quartet*, as Marya stares into the river from the Quai des Orfèvres, a passerby shouts, "Hé, little one. Is it for tonight the suicide?" And in Sartre's *The Age of Reason*, Mathieu is about to plunge from the Pont-Neuf, but at the last moment changes his mind: "That will be for the next time."

Of all the suicides that do take place in fiction, none matches Inspector Javert's in Hugo's *Les Misérables*. Unhinged by the extraordinary magnanimity shown him by Jean Valjean in sparing his life during the 1832 uprising, the inspector realizes that his entire *raison d'être*, his obsessive pursuit of this man, has been a sham, and he goes to his neatly calculated demise. He walks to a spot between the Pont Notre-Dame and the Pont-au-Change noted by boatmen for its swift current, where "a man falling into the river at this point, even a strong swimmer, does not emerge." On a night as dark as the tomb, he stands on the parapet and looks down:

> There was a sound of running water, but the river itself was not to be seen. What lay below him was a void, so that he might be standing at the edge of infinity. He stayed motionless for some minutes, staring into nothingness. Abruptly he took off his hat and laid it on the parapet. A moment later a tall, dark figure, which a passer-by might have taken for a ghost, stood upright on the parapet. It leaned forward and dropped into the darkness.
> There was a splash, and that was all.

ZOLA'S *L'OEUVRE*

The first writer to put the beauty of the Seine to elaborate use was Émile Zola in his 1886 novel *L'Oeuvre* (*The Masterpiece*). Early on, Claude and Christine's enchantment with the riverscape reflects their budding love, while "the soul of the great city, rising from the waters, wrapped them in all the tenderness that had ever pulsed through its age-old stones."

Years later the half-mad painter drags Christine over the same terrain in the desperate hope of recapturing his inspiration, searching for a perspective for a vast painting he has in mind, to "put all of nature on one canvas." He finally pauses at the Pont du Carrousel, facing the Île de la Cité:

> There he stopped again, his gaze fixed upon the island riding forever at anchor in the Seine, cradling the heart of Paris through which its blood has pulsed for centuries as its suburbs have gone on spreading themselves over the surrounding plain. His face lit up, as with an inward flame, and his eyes were aglow as, with a broad sweeping gesture, he said, "Look! Look at that!"

Much later, distraught after years of obsessive work on what he conceived as his master-piece, he slashes the vast canvas to pieces in his studio, and hangs himself in front of it from a beam.

APOLLINAIRE

"Adorable river," Apollinaire called it. In "Véndemiaire" the great poet of the Seine speaks of "voices limpid and distant" which rose from it:

> And long did I hear all those songs and cries
> That called forth in the night the song of Paris.

After the breakup of his affair with Marie Laurencin, the Seine became a source of con-solation, which he expressed in his poem "Le Pont Mirabeau" about the bridge where he and Marie used to rendezvous:

> Sous le pont Mirabeau coule la Seine
> Et nos amours
> Faut-il qu'il m'en souvienne
> La joie venait toujours après la peine
>
> Vienne la nuit sonne l'heure
> Les jours s'en vont je demeure
>
> (Under the Pont Mirabeau flows the Seine
> and our loves
> I must recall
> joy always comes after pain.
>
> Come the night, sound the hour
> the days go by, I remain.)

ÎLE DE LA CITÉ

The original settlement of Paris, the Île de la Cité is often compared to a boat, much like the city's emblem of a medieval ship buffeted by waves: *Fluctuat nec mergitur*—"It is bat-tered but does not sink."

Practically no writers have lived on this little isle, but through kingdom, revolution, empire, and republic, it has provided much grist for their literary mills. The Palais de

Justice, France's vast, sprawling center for law and order, and the glorious Gothic cathedral of Notre-Dame have been their main sources of inspiration.

Notre-Dame de Paris

FRANÇOIS RABELAIS

In 1534 the none-too-reverential lay priest and former Benedictine monk Rabelais published *La vie très horrifique du grand Gargantua* (*The Very Horrifying Life of the Great Gargantua*), which chronicled the adventures of the famed giant. During Gargantua's first days as a student at the University of Paris, he is constantly pestered by Parisians in awe of his size. To get away, he takes refuge on the towers of the cathedral, where he decides to play a joke—*un ris*—on the mob gathered below:

Gargantua on the towers of Notre-Dame Cathedral, illustration by Gustave Doré

> Then, with a smile, he undid his magnificent codpiece and, bringing out his john-thomas, pissed on them so fiercely that he drowned two hundred and sixty thousand, four hundred and eighteen persons, not counting the women and small children.
>
> A number of them, however, were quick enough on their feet to escape this piss-flood; and when they reached the top of the hill above the university, sweating, coughing, spitting, and out of breath, they began to swear and curse, some in a fury and others in sport (*par ris*), "Carymary, Carymary! My holy tart, we've been drenched in sport! We've been drenched *par ris*."
>
> Hence it was that the city was ever afterwards called Paris.

VICTOR HUGO

Hugo's *Notre-Dame de Paris* (*The Hunchback of Notre-Dame*) is a tale of a beauty, the enchanting gypsy girl La Esméralda, and two beasts madly in love with her: Frollo, the perverted archdeacon of the cathedral, and Quasimodo, the deformed bell ringer with a heart of gold. This grand melodramatic romp was a work of youthful exuberance, written when Hugo was twenty-nine, but it is also a meticulously researched and passionately committed portrait of medieval Paris.

"Victor Hugo invented Paris," said Louis Aragon. Published in 1831, *The Hunchback of Notre-Dame* was the first work of fiction to bring the city alive as a full-fledged character. But the most important character of all was "the immense church of Notre-Dame, which seemed, with her two towers, her flanks of stone and her monstrous haunches darkly silhouetted against the sky, an enormous two-headed sphinx seated in the midst of the city."

At the time Hugo wrote his novel, the cathedral had fallen into severe neglect, and there was talk of tearing it down. But, as Hugo had hoped, the success of the book reawakened the public's interest and eventually sparked a campaign to save it. Gothic architecture, sneered at since the Renaissance, made a comeback. All over France cathedrals were restored.

Le Quartier des Cloîtres

ABÉLARD AND HÉLOÏSE

In the early years of the Middle Ages, a prestigious center for theological studies developed in the Cloister District, in the vicinity of the Romanesque predecessor of today's cathedral, where the most brilliant teacher and writer in the early twelfth century was the monk Pierre Abélard. Cast iron medallions on the doors of Nos. 9–11 quai aux Fleurs, depict Abélard and Héloïse, the niece of the canon of Notre-Dame, who lived in her uncle Fulbert's home on this spot. In his *Historica Calamitatum* (*The Story of My Misfortunes*), published in 1132, Abélard confesses that "utterly aflame with my passion for the maiden, I sought to discover means whereby I might have daily and familiar speech with her, thereby the more easily to win her consent." He had little trouble convincing Fulbert to let him move into the house and tutor his teenage ward:

> We were united first in the dwelling that sheltered our love, and then in the hearts that burned with it. Under the pretext of study we spent our hours in the happiness of love, and learning held out to us the secret opportunities that our passion craved. Our speech was more of love than of the books which lay open before us; our kisses far outnumbered our reasoned words.

When Héloïse became pregnant, the couple fled to Brittany, where a son named Astrolabe was born. They married in secret, and Abélard later returned to Paris in hopes of placating Fulbert by formalizing the hasty marriage, but the canon would have none of it. Fulbert sent his kinfolk to Abélard's cell in the cloister of Notre-Dame:

> There they had vengeance on me with a most cruel and most shameful punishment, such as astounded the whole world; for they cut off those parts of my body with which I had done that which was the cause of their sorrow.

Abélard and Héloïse were kept apart for the rest of their lives, he in a monastery, she in a convent, but they were allowed to correspond by letter. Published the following century, their tender exchanges made them the great romantic figures of the Middle Ages.

In the early nineteenth century, their remains, buried separately after their deaths, were brought together at the Père-Lachaise Cemetery.

The Conciergerie

Built as a royal palace at the start of the fourteenth century, the Conciergerie changed its function a half-century later when Charles V moved off the Île de la Cité, leaving it to the Concierge, the royal superintendent, to run. As one of the duties of the Concierge was to maintain order, he converted part of the former palace into a prison. Many celebrated unfortunates were incarcerated in its dank cellars. Gabriel de Montgomery, the Scottish knight who accidentally killed Henri II, and Ravaillac, the deranged assassin of

The Conciergerie

Henri IV, spent their last days here before paying the penalty for regicide: drawing and quartering. Marie Antoinette spent two months in her bare cell before going to the guillotine.

The public entrance is on the Boulevard du Palais, near the fourteenth-century clock tower La Tour de l'Horloge.

SIDNEY CARTON

In Dickens's *A Tale of Two Cities*, Sidney Carton cajoles a spy to sneak him into the prison at night and lead him to the cell of Charles Darnay, who had been condemned as a descendant of the noble Evrémonde family, and was scheduled to go to the guillotine in the morning. Out of love for Darnay's wife, Lucie, and his own need to finally do something useful with his life, Carton has determined to take the condemned man's place. He chloroforms Darnay, for whom he is a dead ringer, switches clothes, and has the spy carry the unconscious man to a waiting carriage. Then he calmly awaits his fate:

> Sounds that he was not afraid of, for he divined their meaning, then began to
> be audible. Several doors were opened in succession. A gaoler, with a list in
> his hand, looked in, merely saying, "Follow me, Evrémonde!"

ANDRÉ CHÉNIER

The only poet of the Revolutionary period to go to the guillotine was André Chénier. Condemned for writing anti-Jacobin pamphlets, he spent the night before his execution in the Conciergerie, and he went to his death on July 27, 1794, the day before Robespierre met the same fate and the Terror came abruptly to an end. Chénier, thirty-four when he died, had been writing poetry for his own pleasure since he was sixteen, never dreaming of having it published. He wrote his last three *lambes*, or fragments, in prison on tiny slips of paper 1½ to 2¼ inches wide, in handwriting so minute that a magnifying glass is needed to read it. He had them smuggled out of prison in baskets of dirty laundry only few days before his execution. (The amazing mini-manuscripts are in the collection of the Bibliothèque Nationale de France.)

In Balzac's *Lost Illusions*, set in 1819, the aspiring young poet Lucien de Rubempré and his friend David Séchard read aloud the poems of André Chénier, whose work had been recently discovered:

> So that is what André Chénier is like!" Lucien exclaimed again and again. "It drives one to despair," he repeated for the third time when David, too moved to go on reading, handed the volume over to him, "A poet discovered by another poet!" he cried, when he saw by whom the preface was signed. "After writing all those poems," David continued, "Chénier still thought he had produced nothing worthy of publication."

Eleven years after first marveling over André Chénier's poetry, Lucien finds himself in a cell in the Conciergerie in *Lost Illusions*'s sequel *Splendeurs et misères des courtisanes*. Though he is innocent of the murder of which he is accused, he is so deeply remorseful about failing to protect the two people who loved him most, the courtesan Esther and his benefactor the abbé Carlos Herrera, that he hangs himself from a bar in the cell window.

"One of the greatest tragedies of my life is the death of Lucien de Rubempré," said Oscar Wilde. "It is a grief from which I have never been able to completely rid myself. I remember it when I laugh."

The Palais de Justice

QUASIMODO IN LA GRANDE HALLE

Upstairs from the Conciergerie is the vast reception hall for the Palais de Justice known as the Salle des Pas Perdus, "the room of wasted steps," which is reached via the main entrance to the sprawling Palais de Justice complex on the Boulevard du Palais. Originally, the Salle de Pas Perdus was the magnificent Grande Halle of the medieval Conciergerie, where the opening scene of *The Hunchback of Notre-Dame* takes place. It is the sixth of January, 1482, the day of the Feast of Fools, and the Pope of Fools is to be elected.

Here Hugo gives us our first view of Quasimodo:

> We shall not try to describe for the reader that tetrahedron nose, that horseshoe mouth, that small red eye obscured by red, bushy eyebrows; the right

eye which disappeared completely under an enormous wart; those jagged teeth, with gaps here and there, like the battlements of a fortress; that horny lip, over which one of those teeth protruded like the tusk of an elephant; that forked chin, and above all, the expression on the whole face, a mixture of malice, astonishment, and sadness.

On top of all that, there are the stumpy, bowed legs, the simian arms, and the hump. The bell-ringer is elected by a landslide.

THE SECOND EMPIRE VS. FLAUBERT AND BAUDELAIRE

There was standing room only in the courtroom the day *Madame Bovary* went on trial for "outrage to public morality, religion, and good moral standards." Press coverage of the case had been fervent, with outraged defenders of literary freedom on one side, outraged right-thinkers on the other. Installments of the novel had run in November and December of 1856 in the *Revue de Paris*, where, over Flaubert's howls of protest, the editor, his old friend Maxime Du Camp, had expurgated potentially offensive sections, including the scene where the heroine receives the last rites of the Church while a drunk passes by her window singing an off-color song. But for Napoléon III and his moralistic (and profoundly immoral) administration, that was not censorship enough.

So, on January 29, 1857, in the 6ème Chambre Correctionnelle, where pimps, whores, con men, and small-time thieves were normally found in the defendant's box, there sat the bourgeois son of the respected chief surgeon of Rouen's Hôtel-Dieu. Luckily for Flaubert, the prosecutor Ernest Pinard was an ass, whose pronouncements such as "Art without rules is not art any more! It is like a woman who takes off all her clothes" had the spectators in stitches. Representing Flaubert was Maître Sénard, Rouen's finest, who mesmerized the courtroom with his eloquence.

On February 7, the court cleared *Madame Bovary* in its entirety. The first edition sold out immediately. But Flaubert was far from happy: He knew that his first novel's reputation would dog him for the rest of his career.

Five months after Flaubert's acquittal, the Minister of the Interior ordered that all copies of Baudelaire's collection of poems *Les Fleurs du mal* be seized on the same grounds. Flaubert sent Baudelaire a strong letter of support where he was living at the Hotel du Quai Voltaire. But unlike *Madame Bovary*, *Les Fleurs du Mal* did not leave the 6ème Chambre Correctionnelle unscathed. The judge ordered six poems suppressed—"Les Bijoux," "Le Léthé," "A celle qui est trop gaie," "Les Femmes damnées," "Lesbos," and "Les Métamorphoses du vampire"—shockers in their day and still capable of making our heads spin. And he slapped fines on Baudelaire and his publisher. The ban on the six outlawed poems, though long ignored, remained in force until 1949.

The courtroom where Flaubert and Baudelaire went on trial no longer exits. It was demolished at the start of the twentieth century when the *chambres correctionnelles* were moved to a new wing at the corner of the Boulevard du Palais and the Quai des Orfèvres. In this new location, Jean Genet was convicted on March 10, 1942, in the 16th Chambre Correctionnelle of stealing a bolt of cloth from a fabric shop, one of several botched thefts that kept him in prison during most of the early 1940s.

INSPECTOR MAIGRET ON THE QUAI DES ORFÈVRES

The PJ, Police Judiciare headquarters—"*la maison*" as Maigret and his colleagues call it—is housed in the early-twentieth-century wing of the Palais de Justice at No. 36 quai des Orfèvres, where a plaque on the Rue de Harlay corner acknowledges the fame Georges Simenon's inspector has brought it. So real is Maigret to readers that they send him letters at this address.

Maigret may dominate the building, but this is not where he wants to be, as we sense in *Maigret et la jeune morte* (*Maigret and the Young Girl*):

Two or perhaps three times that afternoon Maigret looked up from his papers and gazed at the sky. It was limpid blue, in it floated white clouds fringed with gold. Sunlight was pouring over the roofs. Then he stopped his work, sighed and opened his window. Hardly had he sat down again, inhaling a breath that gave a special fragrance to his pipe, when the papers on his desk started to tremble, to take flight and to land all over his room.

Georges Simenon's most famous character on a stamp commemorating Belgium's most famous author

The character first entered Simenon's mind while the Belgian-born writer was cruising the waterways of Holland in October 1929. Simenon saw his detective as "a big man who ate a lot, drank a lot, followed suspects patiently and eventually uncovered the truth." He put him right to work, investigating a murder on a Dutch canal.

Simenon never studied the procedures of the Police Judiciare while writing his *Maigrets*—103 of them—which were published from 1931 to 1972. His approach to the *roman policier* was purely literary. Maigret investigates a crime by absorbing the atmosphere of a place, picking up odd little behavioral details, and slowly, relentlessly getting inside the minds of the suspects. Psychological identification with the murderer is the key to his method of solving the crime.

With seventy-seven of the *Maigrets* set in Paris, along with numerous "psychological" novels, Simenon is one of the great literary explorers of the city. From the tawdry streets of Montmartre to the most ordinary bourgeois and working class districts, there are few corners his inspector does not visit.

Place Dauphine

At the middle of the Pont Neuf, where the bridge touches down on the leafy western tip of the island, stands the jaunty equestrian statue of Henri IV. From atop his bronze mount, the Vert Galant looks into the narrow entrance of the lovely triangular square that he ordered built in 1609 and named in honor of his *dauphin*, the future Louis XIII.

ANDRÉ BRETON

In 1927 André Breton kept running into a young woman at places in Paris where he almost never set foot. According to the Surrealists, coincidences (or what passed as such) offered important keys to the meanings hidden below even the most banal surfaces of everyday life. Women, particularly the authentic *femme-enfant*, non-analytical and open to spontaneous impressions—such as the one he kept running into—offered another. The year after meeting her, Breton published his Surrealist classic *Nadja*, a more or less factual narrative about the strange relationship that developed between him and the mysterious young woman.

At one point in the narrative, Nadja intends to take Breton to one place, but for some mysterious reason they end up at another—at Place Dauphine, which he considers "one of the most profoundly secluded places I know of." The light is fading when they arrive. They dine on the terrace of the wine cellar at No. 19, where Nadja calls his attention to strange things. Though the square is practically empty, she seems to see a crowd. "And the dead, the dead!"

She points out a house:

"Do you see that see that window up there? It's black, like all the rest. In a minute it will light up. It will be red." The minute passes. The window lights up. There are, as a matter of fact, red curtains.

And there is yet another connection with the Surrealists: Nadja identifies with the water nymph Melusina, their favorite divinity, intimately linked to that inexhaustible source of supernatural meanings, the city of Paris. According to Surrealist mythology, the Île de la Cité is the trunk of the goddess's body, the rose windows of Notre-Dame are her eyes, the two branches of the Seine are her legs, and as Breton pinpointed it, the delta-shaped Place Dauphine is "le sexe féminin de Paris."

ÎLE SAINT-LOUIS

If the Île de la Cité is the medieval flagship of Paris, the Île Saint-Louis is its neoclassical yacht. It dates from the early seventeenth century, when Henry IV had two tiny

Île Saint-Louis

unpopulated islands, the Île Notre-Dame and the Île aux Vaches, joined together to create a residential development for aristocrats. Many of the houses still exist on this neatly preserved slice of the *grand siècle*.

MONSIEUR NICOLAS

In the eighteenth century the secluded quays of the island became popular places for trysts. But the lovers were not as alone as they thought, thanks to Nicolas-Edmé Restif de la Bretonne. Every night the self-described "perverted peasant" would cross from his lodgings in the Latin Quarter, spy on couples, scratch coded notes on the walls, and continue his rounds. The next day he would come back and copy his notes for use in his chronicles *Le Paysan perverti* and *Les Nuits de Paris*. Hugely popular in their time, with twelve volumes coming out in the 1780s and 1790s, they still make for piquant reading. But the scratches are gone, erased over the centuries by prudes and the elements.

THE BYRON OF POLAND

In 1838 the poet Adam Mickiewicz, one of the most charismatic Europeans of his day, established a Polish library at No. 6 quai d'Orléans. It is now home to the Musée Adam Mickiewicz, devoted to the life and times of Poland's greatest poet. He was a leader in his nation's struggle for independence, for which he was imprisoned in Russia as a young man. In 1832, when he was thirty-four, the "Byron of Poland" exiled himself to Paris, where he was befriended by George Sand and the Romantics, and wrote the Polish national epic *Pan Tadeusz*, published in 1834.

The attractive little museum has manuscripts by Mickiewicz, busts of him by David d'Angers and Bourdelle, drawings by Delacroix, and letters from Goethe, Pushkin, and other writers. In the Chopin Room hangs a portrait of his friend George Sand.

BAUDELAIRE ON THE ISLAND

In the summer of 1841 Baudelaire's mother and his hated stepfather, General Aupick, sent him on a voyage to India. They hoped that a long absence from France would make the young man forget about becoming a poet. But after three months, he jumped ship in Mauritius and made his way back to France. With his twenty-first birthday approaching, he was eager to get his hands on his inheritance from his father's estate.

In March 1842, a month before reaching his majority, he moved to the Île Saint-Louis, to the house at No. 22 quai de Béthune, where a plaque marks his stay. He received his legacy the following month and immediately plunged into a dandified Bohemian style of life, spending freely at the finest tailor shops, and buying paintings and *objets d'art*. His friend Nadar described his look at this time:

Charles Baudelaire, photograph by Nadar

> Dark black pants tight about shiny boots, blue, highly starched roll-collar blouse with sharp pleats, his long black naturally curly hair his only hair-style, linen of dazzling material, unstarched, and pink gloves. Dressed and un-coiffed like that, Baudelaire walked around his area and the city with a jerky step, nervous and soft like a cat's, and choosing each paving stone as if he had to be careful not to crush an egg.

As befit a young man of means, he also took a mistress. She was Jeanne Duval, "La Venus Noire," the illegitimate daughter of a mulatto prostitute from the West Indies, and a bit-part player in a vaudeville house when he met her. He installed her in a flat at No. 6 rue le Regrattier. She was a drinker, a drug user, and an unfaithful woman, without heart or mind by most accounts, who held him in the trap of his sexual attraction to her during their tempestuous twenty-year-long affair. "The strange thing about Woman, her preordained fate," Baudelaire would later write, "is that she is simultaneously the sin and the Hell that punishes it." But Jeanne Duval also inspired some of his finest poems, including "Les Bijoux," "La Chevelure," and "Parfum exotique":

> Quand, les deux yeux fermées, et un soir chaud d'automme,
> Je respire l'odeur de ton sein chaleureux
> Je vois se dérouler des rivages heureux,
> Qu'éblouissent les feux d'un soleil monotone . . .

> (Warm autumn nights when, eyes closed, I breathe
> the scent of your welcoming breasts
> I see spreading out before me happy shores
> drunk on the fire of a monotonous sun.)

In May 1843 Baudelaire moved to the house at No. 15 quai d'Anjou for a month, and then to the magnificent seventeenth-century Hôtel Lauzun next door at No. 17. Impeccably restored, this gem of a *grand siécle* mansion is one of the most beautiful in Paris, and is now used for prestigious government receptions. But in Baudelaire's day, writers and artists lived in it. His three-room flat was on the top floor, rear.

He continued to play the dandy, supporting his mistress and ripping through his inheritance at a breathtaking pace. Yet, as Théophile Gautier, another writer in residence, observed, "An English coldness seemed to him the height of good taste." Both men were members of the Club des Haschischins, the Hashish Eaters Club, which met in the grand salon. Some dipped heavily into the jar of jellied green substance passed around during the meal, but Baudelaire was not one of them, despite his well-merited reputation as an opium user years later.

Young women came to the soirées, most notably the bright, gorgeous artists' model Apollonie Sabatier. Then in her early twenties, "La Présidente," as Gautier christened her, was at the peak of her physical beauty. Baudelaire's "La Muse et la Madone," "À Celle qui est trop gaie," and "L'Invitation au voyage" ('Luxe, calme, et volupté') were inspired by her.

By the summer of 1844 Baudelaire had run through half of his inheritance. To prevent him from squandering the rest, his mother and stepfather obtained a court order placing his legacy under the control of an administrator. A frugal person could have lived comfortably on his monthly allowance, but not Baudelaire. For the rest of his life he would systematically blow his stipend, borrow money, and beg his mother to cover his debts.

In June 1845 he wrote a suicide note and tried, not very convincingly, to kill himself with a knife. His mother responded by moving him into her and General Aupick's residence on the Place Vendôme. Baudelaire's three glorious years on the Île Saint-Louis were at an end.

CLAUDE LANTIER ON THE QUAI DE BOURBON

Zola's *The Masterpiece* starts with the painter Claude Lantier crossing the Pont Louis-Philippe at two in the morning as a fierce summer thunderstorm breaks out:

> As he turned along the Quai de Bourbon, on the Île Saint-Louis, a flash of lightening lit up the long straight line of big, old houses and the narrow roadway that ran along the bank of the Seine. It was reflected in the panes of their tall, shutterless windows and revealed for a moment their ancient, melancholy-looking façades, bringing out some of their details—a stone balcony, a balustrade, a festoon carved on a pediment with amazing clarity.

Arriving at his building, the Hôtel du Martoy at the corner of Rue Le Regrattier, Claude is surprised to find a young woman huddled on his doorstep. Though he is skeptical of her (perfectly true) story of a lost girl freshly arrived from the provinces, he lets her stay in his attic studio for the night. Except for sketching her half-nude while she's asleep, he behaves like a gentleman. Hesitantly, and platonically, over a period of months, their love develops as Christine visits Claude at his studio and they stroll along the quays of the Seine, a cityscape painted by Zola in marvelously detailed word pictures.

SWANN'S WAY ON THE SEINE

In Proust's *Du côté de chez Swann* (*Swann's Way*), the narrator's great-aunt ("the only person a bit vulgar in our family") hastens to inform guests that their family friend Swann could live on the Boulevard Haussmann, Avenue de l'Opéra, or anywhere else he wanted. Old M. Swann left Swann four or five millions, but living on the Île Saint-Louis, "that was his whim." As the narrator recounts,

> He lived now in an old *hôtel* where he amassed his collection, and which my grandmother dreamed of visiting, but was situated on the Quai d'Orléans, a district that my great-aunt found degrading to live in.

Odette, too, considers this an address unworthy for a man of Swann's means. Nonetheless, she occasionally drops in on him early in their affair, interrupting his work on a study of Vermeer. She begs Swann, an enormously cultivated man, to explain how to appreciate works of art and poetry. He tries, but her attention drifts quickly. She might look as if she stepped out of a Botticelli painting, but he has to admit that she is not very bright.

THREE MOUNTAINS PRESS

The house at No. 29 quai d'Anjou is not much to look at, with its seventeenth-century façade plastered over, and no architectural detail or plaque to hint at an illustrious past. Yet this house was a key spot in the Anglophone literary explosion of the 1920s, thanks to American newsman William Bird and his hobby of traditional hand printing.

In 1922 Bird bought a magnificent seventeenth-century Belgian Mathieu press, installed it in the former wine cellar of this house, and, with no clear notion about what to publish, founded the Three Mountains Press (for Montmartre, Montparnasse, and the Montagne Sainte-Geneviève). At the suggestion of young *Toronto Star* correspondent Ernest Hemingway, whom he met at a conference in Genoa, Bird hired Ezra Pound as his literary guru. The first book to come off the press was Pound's *Indiscretions, ou Une Revue de deux Mondes,* published in 1923. Works by Ford Madox Ford and William Carlos Williams followed that same year, and in March 1924 Hemingway's *in our time,* a collection of stories and sketches, was published. Bird joined forces with the flaky but well-funded Robert McAlmon (whose Contact Editions had published Hemingway's first book, *Three Stories and Ten Poems,* in 1923) in a partnership for joint distribution of their books.

TRANSATLANTIC REVIEW

Early in 1924, Ford Madox Ford installed the editorial office of his new literary magazine the *Transatlantic Review* on the mezzanine at the rear of Bird's printing shop on the Quai d'Anjou, and hired Hemingway, then twenty-five, as his assistant editor. Hemingway talked Ford into publishing Gertrude Stein's *The Making of Americans,* but did not mention how long it was. When Ford returned from a fund-raising trip to America, he was irked to find out that the novel was a thousand-page epic.

Another of Ford's assistants was Dominica-born Jean Rhys, whose first published story was in the *Transatlantic Review*. She would write bitterly about her affair with him in two novels, *Quartet* and *After Leaving Mr. MacKenzie*.

Given the tightness of space in the wine cellar, everyone got along wonderfully, at least in public. Ford threw weekly tea parties, with regulars and guests spilling out on the quay. He later wrote:

> I do not think that there could ever have been an artistic atmosphere younger
> and more pleasurable or more cordial that that which surrounded the *Review*
> offices and the Thursday teas.

HEMINGWAY

Everyone who met Hemingway at this time recognized the power of his writing and wanted to be his friend. Among them was Harold Loeb, eight years his senior, a Princeton graduate, published writer, and editor of the prestigious New York-based literary "little magazine" *Broom*. In his memoir *The Way it Was*, Loeb recalled his first encounter with him at the Quai d'Anjou:

> It was there that I met Ernest Hemingway, who was helping Ford get out
> the review. He had a shy, disarming smile and did not seem interested in the
> other guests; he wore sneakers, my favorite footgear, and a patched jacket. I
> thought never before had I encountered an American so unaffected by living
> in Paris.

Loeb championed Hemingway to his New York publisher Boni and Liveright, which published *in our time* in 1925. But like all other writers who helped him early in his career, Hemingway repaid Loeb with mean-spirited writing. Loeb appears lightly fictionalized as Robert Cohn, Lady Brett Ashley's hapless suitor in *The Sun Also Rises*, which appeared in 1926.

AN ALL-AMERICAN IN PARIS

Rolling in dough from his best-selling novels *From Here to Eternity* and *Some Came Running*, and the movies made from them, James Jones moved to Paris in 1958, when the post–World War II wave of American literary expatriation was already winding down. He and his family lived in the house at No. 10 quai d'Orléans, which had a breathtaking view of the Seine and the Latin Quarter from its fifth-floor penthouse. Over the next seventeen years, he happily shared it with a who's who of literary and show-biz celebrities at his Saturday night open house. Among the guests were Henry Miller, Alexander Calder, Man Ray, Sylvia Beach, Thornton Wilder, Mary McCarthy, William Styron, James

Baldwin, William Burroughs, Gregory Corso, Arthur Miller, Gore Vidal, Gene Kelly, John Frankenheimer, Louis Malle, and Romain Gary, who collaborated with Jones on the screenplay of the 1964 film *The Longest Day*. Here Jones also managed to write *The Thin Red Line* (1962), his best novel, and three other books. *The Merry Month of May*, a cursory look at the events of May 1968, was a failure. It showed him how out of touch he was with life in France, and helped convince him that it was time to return to his roots. He went back to America in 1975, and died two years later.

JULIO CORTÁZAR

The miniscule square at the western tip of the island—"intimate because it was small, not that it was hidden, it offered its whole breast to the river and the sky"—is the key setting of Julio Cortázar's enigmatic story "Blow-up." In it, a French-Chilean translator and dedicated amateur photographer named Roberto Michel comes upon an intriguing scene: An attractive blond woman is behaving seductively with a boy of fourteen

Julio Cortázar

or fifteen. Roberto observes, takes a photo, and notices a mysterious man in a hat watching from a parked car. The woman demands that Roberto destroy the photograph, but he refuses and leaves. He then makes a big blowup of the shot—the size of a poster— tacks it up on his wall, and finds himself drawn into deep speculation about its possible meanings.

First published as "Final del Juego" ("The End of the Game"), the story planted a germ of an idea in Michelangelo Antonioni's mind, which grew into the 1966 movie *Blow-Up*, although the place (go-go London of the 1960s) and the nature of the mystery were altered completely. Cortázar's story is now named after the movie.

Born of Argentine parents in Belgium during the German invasion of August 1914, Cortázar spent four years there before ever seeing Argentina. He grew up in Buenos Aires, but at odds with the Péron regime, he left the country in 1951 on a scholarly grant from the French government and settled in Paris, where he remained for the rest of his life, writing the dazzling stories and novels that made him one of the most respected Latin American writers of the twentieth century. Many other writers from the region were deeply influenced by French literature, particularly Surrealism, and spent important periods in Paris, including Alejo Carpentier from Cuba, Gabriel García Márquez from Colombia, Carlos Fuentes from Mexico, and César Vallejo and Mario Vargas Llosa from Peru.

Cortázar died in Paris in 1984. He is buried in Montparnasse Cemetery.

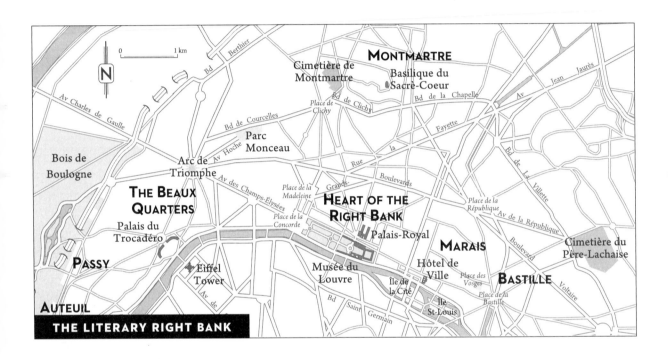

MONTMARTRE

Cimetière de
Montmartre

Basilique du
Sacré-Coeur

Av Charles de Gaulle

Bd de Courcelles

Parc
Monceau

Arc de
Triomphe

THE BEAUX
QUARTERS

Bois de
Boulogne

Palais du
Trocadéro

PASSY

Eiffel
Tower

AUTEUIL

Bd Berthier

Place de
Clichy

Bd de Clichy

Bd de Clichy

Bd de la Chapelle

Fayette

Rue

la

Boulevards

Av Hoche

Av des Champs-Élysées

Place de la
Madeleine

Grands

Place de la
Concorde

HEART OF THE
RIGHT BANK

Musée du
Louvre

Palais-Royal

Av de

Bd

Saint

Germain

Île de
la Cité

Île
St-Louis

Hôtel de
Ville

Place de la
République

Av de la République

MARAIS

Place des
Vosges

BASTILLE

Place de la
Bastille

Av Jean Jaurès

Av

Bd de la Villette

Boulevard

Voltaire

Cimetière du
Père-Lachaise

0   1 km

N

THE LITERARY RIGHT BANK

The Literary Right Bank

A Bird's-Eye View

UNLIKE the Left Bank, with its long, continuously illustrious literary career, the Right Bank began as a commercial district and failed to make its appearance at the great table of literature until considerably later. But when it finally did, it laid out a feast—and a revolutionary one at that—in French language and literature. Surprisingly, the chief instigators were ladies, who, after the rough-and-ready reign of Henri IV, a strong but culturally vulgar king, from 1589 to 1610, decided a bit of elegance was in order. The pioneer was Catherine de Vivonne, the Marquise de Rambouillet, who established the first literary salon in 1620 at her mansion next door to the Louvre. Over the following thirty years, Arthénice (an anagram of her name) received all the leading thinkers, writers, and cultural leaders of the day in her famous *chambre bleue*. She and her fellow salon hostesses and their guests created the sophisticated French language and conversational style which would come to dominate not only France, but all cultivated Europe. Meanwhile, Cardinal Richelieu founded the Académie française, to keep bright men's minds focused on culture rather than politics.

In the mid-1650s, with young Louis XIV securely established on his throne at the Louvre, Paris entered a Golden Age in literature thanks to the theater of Corneille, Molière, and Racine, the fiction of La Fontaine and Mme de La Fayette, the *Maximes* of La Rochefoucauld, the *Pensées* of Pascal, and scores of other outstanding works.

The literary crowd congregated in two neighborhoods: the Marais, home to such lively salon hostesses as Madeleine de Scudéry and Ninon de Lenclos, and the area of the Louvre and the Palais-Royal, where Molière, Mme de Rambouillet's neighbor in her later years, satirized the verbal excesses of the salons in *Les Précieuses ridicules* and staged his most brilliant plays at his theater in the Palais-Royal.

After Louis XIV moved the court to Versailles in 1682, taking the bulk of the nobility with him, the Right Bank went into a long literary decline, but *les enfants du siècle*—Hugo, Balzac, and other writers born at the dawn of the nineteenth century—brought it back to life, launching a literary era far longer than its seventeenth century predecessor, and every bit as rich. From the 1830s through World War I, Paris was, as Walter Benjamin dubbed it, "Capital of the Nineteenth Century." Among the French writers on the Right Bank were Flaubert, Zola, Maupassant, Colette, and Proust, while such foreigners as Turgenev, Dickens, Henry James, and, after the war, Simenon and Fitzgerald also spent important periods there.

The Right Bank of this era covered much more territory than in the seventeenth century, especially after 1860, when Napoléon III and Baron Haussmann incorporated Montmartre, Passy, Auteuil, other villages, and the Bois de Boulogne into the City of Paris.

The northern bank of the Seine was also the stomping ground of Dickens's Sidney Carton, Balzac's Lucien de Rubempré, James's Christopher Newman and Lambert

Strether, Zola's Nana, Maupassant's Georges ("Bel Ami") Duroy, Céline's Bardamu, and most of the characters in *In Search of Lost Time*, and of the *belle époque* personalities on whom Proust modeled them.

The Rive Gauche may have the greater literary cachet, but the Rive Droite offers a lot more surprises.

THE MARAIS AND THE BASTILLE

Le Marais, "the marsh," was a large, soggy stretch of land to the east of the Hôtel de Ville purchased in the twelfth century by the Knights Templar, a rich order of Crusaders who enriched themselves further by draining the swamp and turning it into a profitable market garden. Two centuries later, after Charles V moved to the Hôtel Saint-Pôl, the large estate he built in the Marais, the former swamp suddenly became a fashionable place to live. To protect his property, Charles built a new line of ramparts along a dead branch of the Seine, which became its moat (the line of the Grands-Boulevards today), anchoring it with the sturdy fortress of the Bastille, completed in 1382.

Henri IV enhanced the Marais's aristocratic standing at the start of the seventeenth century by creating the Place Royale (now Place des Vosges, see photo page 143). Work on Paris's loveliest residential square began in 1605, with the king building his Pavillon du Roi on the south side and the Pavillon de la Reine on the north for his little-loved queen Marie de Médicis, and he invited leading nobles to build townhouses with matching red brick facades and arcades. Great lords and newly ennobled bourgeois fell over each other to build elegant *hôtels particuliers* throughout the district, where the social and cultural leaders congregated during one of the most brilliant periods in French history.

THE BIRTHPLACE OF MADAME DE SÉVIGNÉ

Marie de Rabutin-Chantal, the future Marquise de Sévigné, was born in 1626 at her maternal grandfather's house, the Hôtel de Coulanges at No. 1, as a plaque on the building indicates. Known during her lifetime for her wit, taste, learning, and illustrious friendships, Mme de Sévigné is known to posterity thanks to her marvelous letters, which give the best inside view of aristocratic life in the *grand siècle*.

Born to two of France's most influential, aristocratic families, Marie was raised by the Coulanges family after her parents died. They took charge of her upbringing when she was seven, and gave her a superb education, though unfortunately they married her at eighteen to the Marquis Henri de Sévigné, a rakehell who died seven years later in a duel over another woman, leaving her a widow with two young children and little money of her own. Mme de Sévigné received excellent offers of marriage but rejected them all, preferring to concentrate on the upbringing of her daughter Françoise-Marguerite, who she loved obsessively, and her son Charles, a playboy and a bit of joke in the family.

Victor Hugo early in his
Place des Vosges years

Over the years, Mme de Sévigné lived in a number of *hôtels* in the Marais, for the longest time at the Hôtel Carnavalet on the street now named for her. Though she could not afford a salon of her own, she was welcomed wherever she went. In her novel *Célie*, the great Marais salon hostess Madeleine de Scudéry portrays Mme de Sévigné as the Princesse Clarinte:

No one ever understood better the art of having grace
without affectation, raillery without malice, gaiety without folly, propriety without constraint, and virtue without
severity.

VICTOR HUGO

In October 1832, thirty years old and already the titan of French letters, Hugo moved with his wife Adèle and their two sons and two daughters to the large second-floor apartment in the Hôtel Rohan-Guéménée, now the Musée Victor Hugo. It is at No. 6 place des Vosges.

Hugo was riding high on the recent success of *The Hunchback of Notre Dame*, and with several lavishly praised collections of lyrical poetry and the riot-igniting drama Hernani already behind him, he was the acknowledged leader of the Romantic movement. Here he wrote *Ruy Blas*, his most enduringly successful play, as well as three other dramas, several collections of poetry—*Les Chants du crépuscule, Les Voix intérieures, La Tristesse d'Olympio, Les Rayons et les Ombres*—and early drafts of parts of *Les Misérables*. He was elected to the Académie française in 1841, and four years later was made a peer of France with the rank of viscount by Louis-Philippe. During the Revolution of 1848, however, Hugo switched to the democratic side and was elected deputy to the National Constituent Assembly of the Second Republic.

Casting a pall over Hugo's triumphs was the calamitous state of his marriage. Adèle saw her husband as an egotist and a tyrant, and she had an affair with Hugo's friend Sainte-Beuve. Hugo anguished over this double betrayal, and the failure of his marriage depressed him. In January 1833, at the Théâtre de la Porte Saint-Martin, he met a lovely young actress engaged for a bit part in his play *Lucrèce Borgia*. From his first night with Juliette Drouet to her death half a century later, they spent hardly a day apart. "Jugu," as he called her, unleashed in her "Toto" a passion for the erotic, and she thrilled to his poetry, as Adèle never had. Juliette became his copyist, putting his unruly scrawl into legible form until her eyes gave out in old age. Although they saw each other almost daily, they managed to exchange seventeen thousand notes and letters.

Toto set Jugu up in a modest apartment nearby on Rue Sainte-Anastasie. The back door of his house opened onto the Impasse Guéménée, providing convenient cover for his visits to her, and eventually, to many others. In July 1845 Hugo was surprised *in flagrante delicto* by the husband of one of his mistresses, Léonie Biard. Only by invoking his immunity as a peer did he avoid being charged with the crime of adultery. Juliette learned to live with his dalliances, but his serious affairs always hurt her.

Hugo loved the Place des Vosges, but on June 24, 1848, after street fighting broke out during a workers' uprising, he wrote in his journal:

Georges Simenon in his apartment on the Place des Vosges, 1926

> Fourteen bullets hit my coach house door, eleven outside, three inside. A soldier of the line was mortally wounded in my courtyard. We still see the streak of blood on the paving stones.

Hugo quickly moved his family to No. 37 rue de La Tour-d'Auvergne in the then-countrified neighborhood of Saint-Georges in today's Ninth Arrondissement. Three years later, he was forced to flee France after his fiery denunciation of Louis-Napoléon Bonaparte's *coup d'état*. Hugo, his family, and Juliette Drouet all went into exile, first in Brussels, then in the Channel Islands, until the fall of "Napoléon le Petit," as Hugo dubbed him, in 1870.

The rooms of the Musée Victor Hugo are devoted to the three periods of Hugo's life: before exile, exile (principally in Guernsey), and after exile. The reconstituted bedroom from his final home on Avenue Victor-Hugo (named for him during his lifetime, a rare honor) is dominated by the grand Louis XIII bed in which he died on May 22, 1885, at eighty-three. "Je vois la lumière noire"—"I see the black light"—were his last words.

GEORGES SIMENON

In the summer of 1924, Georges Simenon, twenty-one, and his wife Tigy moved into the town house at No. 21, kitty-corner from Ma Bourgogne at No. 19, a favorite café of Inspector Maigret, who would stop in from time to time to knock back a *coup de blanc*. Place des Vosges would be Simenon's home base for the next seven years.

Simenon had come from his Belgian hometown of Liège a year and a half earlier, and by the time he settled on the Place des Vosges was doing fine, thanks in part to Colette, then literary editor of Le Matin, who had called him in to critique stories he had submitted. Her advice: "No literature. Suppress all the literature and it will go fine." He took the tip, and in September 1923, she accepted one of his stories. From then on, all his fiction sold.

With money flowing in, Simenon plunged into the fast life, becoming a regular at Le Boeuf sur le Toit, Le Jockey, and Le Dôme. In 1926 he began a year-long affair with Josephine Baker, the twenty-year-old African American beauty who had set Paris afire the previous year with her nude feather dance in *La Revue Nègre*. While their affair was going on, "La Baker" enhanced her status as an icon of the *années folles* with her comically risqué banana-belt dance at the Folies-Bergère. He called her "the only woman with a bottom that laughs."

Simenon suffered from what he called a "devouring hunger for women," a need that could arise up to four times a day and was easily sated by the army of streetwalkers a few steps away on Boulevard Beaumarchais. Late in his life, Simenon estimated that he had had relations with ten thousand women.

Before he was known for the quality of his writing, Simenon was famous as a speed demon, capable of knocking out eighty pages of fiction a day. Over the years he published 193 novels under his own name, two-hundred-plus novels under pseudonyms, and countless short stories. By his death in 1989 he was reported to have sold more than 550 million books in fifty-five languages (only Shakespeare and Jules Verne had sold more).

It was toward the end of his Paris years that he created the character of Inspector Maigret. He wrote the first Maigret story in 1929, followed by the first three Maigret novels the next year. The twelfth, *L'Ombre chinoise* (*Maigret Mystified*), published in 1932, begins outside Simenon's window:

> It was ten o'clock at night. The iron gates of the garden were shut, the Place des Vosges deserted, with gleaming car tracks on the asphalt and the unbroken murmur of the fountains, the leafless trees and the monotonous outline of the identical roofs silhouetted against the sky.
>
> Under the arcades which form a tremendous girdle around the Square there were few lights. Inspector Maigret saw a family eating in one of them, amidst a clutter of beaded funeral wreaths.
>
> He tried to read the numbers over the doors, but he had scarcely got beyond the shop with the wreaths when a small female figure emerged from the darkness.
>
> "Are you the person I spoke to on the telephone?"

INSPECTOR AND MME MAIGRET AT HOME: A LITTLE EXCURSION

We first meet Maigret on April 15, 1913, in *La Première enquête de Maigret* (*Maigret's First Case*). Jules is a young policeman newly married to Mme Maigret, "a big, fresh girl, the kind we see only in *pâtisseries* or behind the marble counter of *crémeries*." They have just moved into an apartment in a *petit-bourgeois* neighborhood near Place de la République.

After Maigret rises to the rank of commissioner in the Police Judiciaire, colleagues urge to him to move to a district befitting a man of his stature. But he and Madame remain in their apartment on the Boulevard Richard-Lenoir. The address (as we learn in *Maigret et son mort*) is No. 132. The Maigrets' third-floor apartment fronts on Boulevard Richard-Lenoir, with greenhouse-style windows overlooking the esplanade, the site of a colorful outdoor food market every Tuesday and Friday morning.

For Maigret, that lover of waterways, another attraction of the neighborhood is its proximity to the Canal Saint-Martin. The tree-shaded stretch of the canal with its footbridge arching over the locks is one of the moodiest spots in Paris. Pure Maigret.

Rue de Sévigné

MUSÉE CARNAVALET
Officially the Musée de l'Histoire de Paris, the Musée Carnavalet is a cornucopia of the city's history. Mme de Sévigné's apartment and Marcel Proust's cork-lined bedroom are its most famous literary attractions, but beyond them, one of its richest troves is its portraits of writers. The entrance is at No. 23.

MME DE SÉVIGNÉ
On October 7, 1677, Mme de Sévigné wrote to her daughter Françoise-Marguerite about her lease of the Hôtel Carnavalet:

> It is an admirable affair; there will be room for all of us and we shall have
> good air. As one cannot have everything, we will have to do without parquet
> and without the small fireplaces that are so much in vogue; but we have at
> least a beautiful courtyard, a beautiful garden, a beautiful neighborhood and
> good little "blue girls" who are very well behaved (the *enfants bleus* were the
> children in the convent school next door).

Mme de Sévigné lived in the Hôtel Carnavalet for nineteen years, until her death in 1696. Her presence is evoked in two rooms on the first floor, decorated in the style of the period and enlivened with portraits of her family, friends, of the famed letter-writer herself, pretty and plump with alert eyes and a hint of a ready smile on her lip, and of Françoise-Marguerite, the principal recipient of her mother's letters starting in 1671, when she moved to Provence with her husband the Count of Grignan.

Mme de Sévigné knew personally almost everyone who mattered in the political, social, and literary worlds of the second half of the seventeenth century, from Louis XIV on down. Her letters provide commentary on the age that is direct, witty, chatty, and refreshingly low on sentimentality. Her eye for significant detail in descriptions of people,

Mme de Sévigné, portrait by Claude Lefèbvre

places, and dress is exceptional. She was a close friend of Mme de Maintenon, Louis XIV's morganatic wife, best friends with Mme de La Fayette and La Rochefoucauld, and a regular at the salons of Mme de Rambouillet, Mlle de Scudéry, and Mme de Sablé. But her high social position and famed moral rectitude did not keep her from visiting Ninon de Lenclos's racy salon on Rue des Tournelles, even though Ninon had slept with both her husband and son.

Mme de Sévigné's great love for her daughter and her candid, often humorous airing of family concerns (amusement mingled with alarm about her son Charles's entanglements with actresses, for example) personalize the letters, whose style is the epitome of the seventeenth-century's unsurpassed elegance of expression.

OTHER WRITERS AT THE CARNAVALET

Other writers whose portraits hang in the museum include Voltaire, Alphonse de Lamartine, Alfred de Musset, Théophile Gautier, and busts of Victor Hugo and Alexandre Dumas *père*. There is also a painting of Chateaubriand's muse Mme Récamier on her chaise longue, by François Gérard.

THE EARLY TWENTIETH CENTURY

The large exhibit on Parisian writers in the early twentieth century features the reconstituted bedrooms of Marcel Proust, Countess Anna de Noailles, and Paul Léautaud. Eccentrics all, they did much of their writing in bed.

The dominant figure is Proust, whose cork-lined bedroom combines furnishings from his last three apartments. The principal item of furniture is the brass bed in which he slept as a child, wrote *In Search of Lost Time*, and died. Many objects that he used regularly, such as his famous fur-lined overcoat and his walking stick are also on display.

Anna de Noailles, a very successful poet in the early twentieth century, gave her friend Marcel the idea of lining his bedroom with cork, as she had done on Rue Scheffer. In her reconstituted bedroom, a jolly yellow fabric with vertical blue stripes hides the cork.

Paul Léautaud, novelist, poet, and writer for the magazine *Mercure de France* from 1893 until the Occupation, was best known as a straight-shooting theater critic during his lifetime, but is now appreciated primarily for his *Journal littéraire*, a brilliant and utterly uninhibited chronicle of the literary and theatrical life of Paris, which he wrote from his debut at the *Mercure* to his death six decades later.

Like many writers of his time, Léautaud was a notorious misogynist, but could not do without women. Nor, it seems, could they do without him. At eighty-one he was juggling affairs with two women, but dumped them both for a girl of sixteen.

In his later years he lived like a *clochard* in his house in suburban Fontenay-aux-Roses, surrounded by three hundred stray cats and a hundred stray dogs, although his bedroom here gives no hint of what it must have been like when he shared it with up to twenty-four cats.

Rue Pavée

HÔTEL DE LAMOIGNON

The tall, handsome Hôtel de Lamoignon at No. 24 rue Pavée is one of the oldest houses in the Marais, built in 1584 for Diane de France, the legitimized daughter of Henri II. Guillaume de Lamoignon, the first president of the Parliament of Paris, bought the building in 1658 and held a salon attended by Mme de Sévigné, La Rochefoucauld, Boileau, Racine, and other *grand siècle* literati.

By the time Alphonse Daudet lived here in the 1860s and 1870s, the building had gone to seed like the rest of the Marais, but his regular guests on Wednesday evenings included Flaubert, Turgenev, Gautier, Zola, and Edmond de Goncourt. Daudet's novelist son Léon (later Proust's champion at the Académie Goncourt) was born here in 1867. As a little boy, he nicknamed Flaubert and Goncourt the "the giants" because they were so tall. In his memoir *Paris vécu*, Léon recalls his mother making him memorize the opening line of Flaubert's *Salambo* ("C'était à Mégara, faubourg de Carthage, dans les jardins de Hamilcar") and recite it for the author. When he did, Flaubert would "catch hold of me and lift me in his strong arms, and I would see in close-up his Vercingetorix moustache and his large shiny cheeks."

The hôtel houses the Bibliothèque historique de la Ville de Paris, a library specializing in the history of Paris. Though access to the collection is for researchers only, the public is free to enter the lobby, from which the reading room with its superb painted Louis XIII ceiling is visible.

Rue Vieille-du-Temple

BEAUMARCHAIS

Of all the amazing characters in eighteenth-century Paris, few if any could match Pierre-Augustin Caron de Beaumarchais, whose life reads like a picaresque novel. Born Pierre-Augustin Caron in 1730, the son of a clockmaker in Les Halles, he became clockmaker to the king at twenty-one, musical tutor to Louis XV's children, royal financier, pamphleteer, philosopher, legal expert, secret agent, arms dealer, nobleman, publisher of the complete works of Voltaire at a time when they were officially banned in France, theater owner, champion of the rights of authors, and dramatist, writing two of the finest and most politically important plays of the eighteenth century, *Le Barbier de Séville* (*The Barber of Seville*) and *Le Mariage de Figaro* (*The Marriage of Figaro*).

Pierre-Augustin Caron de Beaumarchais, portrait by Jean-Marc Nattier

On October 6, 1776, Beaumarchais signed a lease on the Hôtel des Ambassadeurs de Hollande at No. 47 rue Vieille-du-Temple, where he set up a gun-running operation to the American rebels. When he first heard about the rebellion in London in the spring of 1775, Beaumarchais had written to young Louis XVI, urging him to capitalize on England's distress by helping them fight "*la tyrannie anglaise.*" Louis eventually agreed, authorizing a trading company to secretly purchase and ship arms. In the spring of 1777, Beaumarchais shipped enough canons, rifles, gunpowder, and other supplies to equip twenty-five thousand men, which would prove crucial to the Americans' first victory, the defeat of Burgoyne at Saratoga.

Throughout this time, Beaumarchais remained involved with the theater, spearheading the creation of an association to protect playwrights. During the Comédie française's highly profitable run of the *Barber of Seville* in 1775, the actors took all the receipts, leaving him only a modest fixed fee. In 1777 Beaumarchais and colleagues launched a long and eventually successful series of legal actions to establish their literary rights. The Société des Auteurs Dramatiques remains a leading force in French theater to this day.

In 1778 Beaumarchais wrote the greatest French comedy of the eighteenth century, *The Marriage of Figaro*, but the government, fearful of the play's mockery of exorbitant aristocratic privileges, refused to allow it to be performed. Finally, after six years of royal foot-dragging, *Figaro* opened at the Théâtre de l'Odéon, a triumphant success.

Three years later, in 1787, Beaumarchais bought a large piece of land fronting what is now Nos. 2 through 20 on Boulevard Beaumarchais, where he built an Italianate villa and magnificent gardens. He died in 1799 and was buried in a simple, nonreligious tomb in his garden. In 1825, his remains were transferred to the Père-Lachaise Cemetery.

A vigorous bronze statue of Beaumarchais stands in the little triangle on Rue Saint-Antoine at the foot of Rue des Tournelles.

The Northern Marais

Since its opening in 1985, the Musée Picasso at No. 5 rue de Thorigny has been one of Paris's most popular attractions, but few who flock to it are aware that another towering genius also has ties to this building.

One of the Marais's most magnificent mansions, the Hôtel Salé was built at enormous expense in the mid-seventeenth century by Pierre Aubert de Fontenay, a *nouveau riche* who made his fortune collecting salt taxes for the king (hence the name of the building, *salé* meaning "salty"). After the Marais went out of fashion, the building fell to ever more mundane uses. In its incarnation as a boys' school, it entered literary history: Balzac was one of its students.

YOUNG BALZAC

For reasons never made public, though there are clues in his writing that it had something to do with sex, Honoré Balzac was expelled from school in his native Touraine at the age of fourteen. To complete the academic year, his parents sent him to the Institut Ganser-Beuzelin in the Hôtel Salé. Except for a brief hiatus, Balzac boarded here from 1813 to 1816, and would spend almost a decade in the Marais.

Young Honoré Balzac

In his autobiographical novel *Louis Lambert*, Balzac describes his brutal experience at the Touraine boarding school where he was sent at the age of eight, in 1807. Though the school was only forty miles from his home in Tours, Balzac's mother came to see him just twice in his six years, and he was never brought home for holidays. He was a lonely boy, a dreamer, incapable of following orders, for which he was sentenced to long periods in the *cachot*, a solitary confinement closet. Once delivered to the freedom of Paris, however, Balzac was seized by the conviction that he was destined do something great.

In 1814 the Balzac family moved to Paris, settling in the apartment house still standing at No. 122 rue du Temple. There Honoré met a friend of his grandmother, Mlle de Rougemont, who had known Beaumarchais. Fascinated by the phenomenal life of this man from humble family origins like his own, who had died only days before he was born, Balzac pressed the old lady for every anecdote, every conversation she could remember.

Balzac received his *baccalauréat* in September 1816 and enrolled in law school, but spent far more time auditing literature courses at the Sorbonne than attending law lectures. After becoming an apprentice clerk in a law office where a spirited group of young men worked, Balzac came alive. A natural actor, he kept his young colleagues in stitches with his word play and stories—a bit too much for the management at times. One morning the chief clerk sent a note to his house saying, "M. Balzac is asked not to come in today, because there is a great deal of work to do." But Balzac was also a great listener, and the dramas unfolding in his coworkers' lives inspired in him what André Maurois called "the dreadful poetry of life."

When Balzac's family moved to the country in 1819, he convinced his parents to support him for a trial period: He would attempt to become a writer.

The Southern Marais

RABELAIS

In the mid-sixteenth century, François Rabelais lived on Rue des Jardins-Saint-Paul, most likely at No. 8. The street was named for a medieval garden running along the outer face of Philippe Auguste's twelfth-century wall, across the street from Rabelais's home. A large section of the wall with two of its round towers remains. It stands nine meters high and runs about a hundred meters from Rue Charlemagne toward the Quai des Célestins.

In *Pantagruel*, published in 1532, Rabelais made fun of the ancient ramparts, which were still the first line of defense on the Left Bank. Panurge says:

> Oh, how strong they are! They're just the thing for keeping goslings in a
> coop. By my beard, they are pretty poor defenses for a city like this. Why, a
> cow could knock down more than twelve foot of them with a single fart.

In his final years, Rabelais lived on a sinecure, the salaries from two curacies at churches in which he seems never to have set foot. He died at his house on Rue des Jardins-Saint-Paul on April 9, 1553, at about sixty years of age, and was buried in the local cemetery of Saint-Eloï. The cemetery was closed in 1791 to clear land for real estate development, but unlike the Cimetière des Innocents in Les Halles, from which the skulls and bones were transferred to the Catacombs before construction began, houses were built over the remains. So Rabelais's unquiet ghost still roams the Marais.

MME DE SÉVIGNÉ

The Rue des Lions-Saint-Paul was named either for the lions in Charles V's menagerie at the Hôtel Saint-Pol or for the painted tableau of his pets over the main gate. With the exception of one contemporary building that blends nicely into the streetscape, all the *hôtels* on this block-long street were built between the sixteenth and the eighteenth centuries. Mme de Sévigné lived in the house at No. 11 from 1645, the year after she married the Marquis de Sévigné, to 1650, the year before he was killed in a duel. Her son Charles was born here in 1647 and her daughter Françoise-Marguerite in 1648. Mme de Sévigné's house has the best preserved façade on the street, and there is a lovely interior courtyard.

JAMES MORRISON, POET

On July 3, 1971, at five in the morning, Jim Morrison died in the bathtub of a borrowed fourth-floor apartment at No. 17 rue Beautrellis. He was twenty-seven. The cause of death was undoubtedly the huge quantities of opium he was snorting, but his girlfriend Pamela Courson (or Mrs. Morrison, as she sometimes called herself) convinced the police that he was not a drug user and had a serious heart condition. The medical examiner listed cause of death as heart attack and identified him as "James Morrison, Poet." Rumors began flying in the American community the very morning of Morrison's death: that he had OD'd in the toilet of a rock club and his body had been carried to the apartment; that he was offed by J. Edgar Hoover; that he was not dead, but faking it. Amazingly, none of the army of police officials and emergency rescue-squad members who saw the corpse recognized the rock icon, nor did the man who came every day to keep the body packed in dry ice because of the city's heat wave.

A friend who had been walking with Jim in Père-Lachaise Cemetery a few weeks earlier told Pamela that the singer had expressed the hope of being buried there someday. She agreed with the suggestion. When Pamela and the friend went to an undertaker, he informed them that it would be almost impossible to find a plot in that very crowded burial ground. But when the friend mentioned that James Morrison was a famous young writer, the undertaker found a plot right away. The hush-hush burial took place on July 7. The cemetery has not been the same since.

L'Arsenal

The huge Renaissance mansion of the Arsenal at No. 1 rue de Sully, with its main entrance on Boulevard Henri IV, was built in 1594 for the duc de Sully, the Grand Master of the Royal Artillery.

In 1757, when the Marquis de Paulmy received permission to install his vast library of books, manuscripts, maps, and prints, he opened it to researchers and men of letters. Three decades later, the comte d'Artois, Louis XVI's youngest brother, bought the building and enlarged the collection. After the Revolution, the Directoire made the Bibliothèque de l'Arsenal a national library. Young Balzac conducted research at the library during the early 1820s when he was living nearby, and in 1824 poet Charles Nodier, godfather to the Romantic poets, began his twenty years as its director. Nodier held a weekly salon where Lamartine, Hugo, de Musset, de Vigny, Dumas, Sainte-Beuve, and other young writers of the budding movement gathered on Sunday evenings to talk and recite their works. The library can be visited, but access to its collections is limited to accredited researchers.

MME DE SÉVIGNÉ AT THE ARSENAL

The long-running trial of Nicolas Fouquet, Louis XIV's disgraced superintendent of finances, was held at the Arsenal in the early 1660s. Mme de Sévigné, a close friend and firm believer in his innocence, wrote in her letter of November 27, 1664, to her cousin Pomponne:

> I must tell you what I have done. Just imagine, some ladies suggested that I
> should go into a house that looks straight at the Arsenal, so as to see our poor
> friend return. I saw him coming from quite a distance. M. D'Artagnan was
> by his side and fifty musketeers behind, at thirty or forty paces. He looked
> very preoccupied. When I saw him my legs trembled and my heart beat so
> fast that I felt quite faint. As he drew near to us on the way back to his cell,
> M. D'Artagnan nudged him and pointed out that we were there. So he bowed
> to us and took on that gay expression you know so well. I don't think he recognized me, but I confess I felt strangely moved when I saw him disappear
> through that little door.

Almost two centuries later, M. D'Artagnan became the model for Alexandre Dumas's illustrious cape-and-sword hero.

Rue de Lesdiguières

BALZAC

In 1819, when Balzac was twenty, his parents rented him a *mansarde* in a house at No. 9 rue de Lesdiguières, by the Place de la Bastille, for his trial period as a writer. Here he began writing pulp romance novels under such high-flying *noms de plume* as Lord R'Hoone (an anagram of Honoré) and Horace de Saint-Aubin. Between work sessions he prowled the neighborhood:

> Listening to these people, I could take in their lives. I felt the rags on their
> backs, I walked in their broken down shoes. Their desires, their needs, every-
> thing passed into my soul.

When his two-year period was up, he moved in with his family in suburban Villeparisis, where he met his mother's friend Mme Laure de Berny, with whom he began his first important love affair. At forty-five, she was twenty-two years older than Balzac and two years older than his mother. Their affair continued until her death in 1837 and inspired his novel *Le Lys dans la vallée* (*The Lily in the Valley*), published in 1836. The melodramatic fare Balzac was churning out now failed to reward him with the literary distinction he craved. After reading one of his plays, François Andrieux of the Académie française said, "The author should do anything except literature."

At this point in his life, nobody except Balzac and his adoring sister Laure still believed that he would become a successful writer—much less the one who would revolutionize the French novel.

La Bastille

So vivid is the ancient fortress-prison in our imaginations, thanks largely to Charles Dickens, that we can't help feeling disappointed the first time we emerge from the Bastille Métro station, scan the wide cobblestone expanse, and not see it. "Where is it?" we wonder. Then, because we know perfectly well that it is gone, "Where was it?"

Demolition of the Bastille began days after the mob seized it in 1789. Within three years, every block of its eighty-foot-high walls and eight round towers had been carted away, many of them used for the construction of the Pont de la Concorde. A plaque on the wall above the Café Français at No. 3 place de la Bastille shows an outline of the fortress superimposed on a street map of the southwestern corner of today's Place de la Bastille,

The Bastille in the 18th century

and a wide row of rosy gray paving stones set into the sidewalk and streets traces the line of its walls.

By the time the mob stormed it, the four-hundred-year-old fortress had long outlived its military value. Louis XVI's finance minister had proposed tearing it down because it was a waste of money even as a prison. Among the Bastille's inmates had been Montgomery, the Scottish knight who accidentally killed Henri II, Nicolas Fouquet during his three years of investigation and trial, and, most intriguingly, the Man in the Iron Mask, imprisoned from 1698 to his death in 1703.

Speculation abounds, but no solid proof of the man's identity has ever surfaced, nor has the reason he had to wear the mask (which was black velvet, not iron). The first person to speculate about him in print was Voltaire, who talked to some of the jailers while he himself was a guest of the establishment fourteen years after the man's death. Voltaire hints at a resemblance to somebody famous, but doesn't name names.

Alexandre Dumas immortalized the famous prisoner in *Le vicomte de Bragelonne* (*The Man in the Iron Mask*), the last of his *Three Musketeers* novels. In his version, the man is Louis XIV's unwanted twin brother.

VOLTAIRE

Voltaire was imprisoned here twice. His first stretch began at the age of twenty-three, when he was locked up on orders of the Prince Regent, Philippe II, duc d'Orléans, for writing satirical verses about him. During his eleven-month stretch, from May 1717 to April 1718, he wrote the *Henriade*, an epic poem about Henri IV, and worked on *Oedipe*, a tragedy that became a hit at the Théâtre-Français after he was released. It was during this stay in the Bastille that François-Marie Arouet invented the pen name of Voltaire, but how or why he chose it, nobody knows.

Voltaire, portrait by
Nicolas de Lagrillière

Upon his release Voltaire was granted an allowance by the Regent, who received this thank-you note in reply:

Je remercie Votre Altesse de ce qu'elle veut bien se charger
de ma nourriture, mais je la prie de ne plus se charger de
mon logement.

(I thank Your Highness for keeping me in food, but I pray
him not to concern himself any more with my lodging).

Eight years later, he was back behind bars.

One night at the opera the young Chevalier de Rohan-Chabot made the mistake of mocking Voltaire, who proceeded to make a laughingstock of him. Unable to match wits, the chevalier sent a pack of thugs to give his adversary a thrashing. Voltaire was enraged, not so much by the beating he took as by the indifference of his *soi-disant* friends in the aristocracy, none of whom would denounce a member of their own class. To avenge this humiliation, Voltaire bought a sword and began taking lessons in preparation for a duel. When the Rohan-Chabots got news of the plan, they persuaded the duc de Bourbon to lock Voltaire up to protect their kinsman, a notorious coward. His stay this time was short, from April 17 to May 11, 1726. By now a respected man of letters, he garnered strong public outcry in his favor, convincing the government to release him quickly, but on one condition: that he go into exile immediately. He agreed and crossed over to England.

THE MARQUIS DE SADE

In 1784 the Marquis de Sade, forty-four at the time, was transferred to the Bastille from the Château de Vincennes, where he had already spent seven years for indulging in the sexual practices named after him. "The Divine Marquis" lived well: His cell was draped with tapestries; he dined on oysters, pâtés, pigeon, and truffled chicken; drank wine from his estate in Provence; and he scolded his wife when his fresh fruit, cakes, and jam failed to arrive on time. And he could write to his heart's content. But on July 4, 1789, annoyed at the governor, the Marquis de Launay, for forbidding him to take his daily walk on the roof, he created a public disturbance by using a funnel normally used for evacuating urine into the moat as a megaphone to shout from his window to passersby on Rue Saint-Antoine. According to the police report:

He assembled many people, spewed invectives about the governor, invited
the citizens to come to his rescue, and cried that they wanted to slit his throat

. . . At one in the morning the jailers seized him and transported him to
Charenton.

If he had kept his mouth shut, the mob would have liberated him ten days later, free to go back to his civilian pursuits.

During the storming of the Bastille practically everything was trashed or burned, including Sade's 600 books and the manuscripts left in his cell when he was whisked off to the insane asylum. But during the demolition a certain Arnoux Saint-Maximin discovered a scroll in a secret compartment in the wall of Sade's cell. The twelve-meter-long roll of twelve-centimeter (4.5-inch) squares of paper, pasted together and covered with Sade's microscopic handwriting was the manuscript of *Les Cent Vingt Journées de Sodome* (*The 120 Days of Sodom*), perhaps the most pornographic novel ever written.

Saint-Maximin sold the scroll to a collector whose descendents sold it to a publishing house in Germany, where it first came out in German translation in 1904, with a translation into French the same year. The book first did not appear in its original French until 1935, but even then was an expurgated version. The full text as it flowed from Sade's quill in his cell was not published legally until 1965.

DICKENS

In Dickens's *A Tale of Two Cities*, Mme Defarge, the wife of Faubourg Saint-Antoine wine shop owner Jacques Defarge, is the most fiery ringleader:

> Madame Defarge, still heading some of her women, was visible in the inner
> distance, and her knife was in her hand. Everywhere there was tumult, exul-
> tation, deafening and maniacal bewilderment, astounding noise, yet furious
> dumb-show.
> "The Prisoners!"
> "The Records!"
> "The secret cells!"
> "The instruments of torture!"
> "The Prisoners!"

In the actual storming of the Bastille, the defenders put up a good fight, killing more than eighty attackers and wounding almost ninety, with only one defender killed. But to avoid further bloodshed, the Marquis de Launay elected to surrender the Bastille and its seven insignificant prisoners after mob leaders promised safe conduct for him and his staff of Swiss guards and superannuated soldiers. Instead, the mob cut off the marquis's head and paraded it about on a pole.

Dickens credits Mme Defarge with the deed:

. . . suddenly animated, she put her foot on his neck, and with her cruel knife—long ready—hewed off his head.

In real life, an apprentice chef named Desnot did it with his pen knife.

Place de la Bastille

Although the mother of all revolutions has no monument to commemorate it at the spot where it started, there is a memorial for a far lesser upheaval four decades later. La Colonne de Juillet, the July Column, poking up from the cobblestone vastness of Place de la Bastille, honors Parisians who lost their lives in the Revolution of July 1830, which toppled Charles X, the last Bourbon king, and brought his cousin Louis-Philippe to power.

Place de la Bastille in about 1840, the "stovepipe" and the elephant

HUGO

Victor Hugo watched the July Column going up in the early 1830s, when he was a neighbor at the Place des Vosges. A "gigantic stove adorned with a stovepipe," he called it. The elephant it replaced was another story. This giant plaster and wood model of an elephant, built in 1812, was to be the centerpiece of a magnificent fountain dreamed up by Napoléon, but the empire collapsed before the elephant could be bronzed. The poor pachyderm was removed from its base to make way for the "stovepipe" and shunted to the edge of the Place de la Bastille, near where the Opéra is now. Punished for decades by wind, sun, and rain, the aged eyesore moved Hugo deeply. In *Les Misérables* he wrote:

In that open and deserted corner of the Square, the broad front of the colossus, his trunk, his tusks, his size, his enormous rump, his four feet like columns, produced at night, under a starry sky, a startling and terrible outline. One couldn't tell what it meant. It was a sort of symbol of the force of the people. It was gloomy, enigmatic, and immense. It was a mysterious and mighty phantom, visible standing by the side of the invisible specter of the Bastille.

In one of the most touching scenes in the novel, the resourceful street urchin Gavroche takes two little lost boys he finds wandering on Rue Saint-Antoine into the comfy nest he has built for himself in the belly of the beast, protected from the rats infesting the structure by a cage made of copper mesh appropriated from the Jardin des Plantes. The little boys are the brothers Gavroche did not know he had.

When the elephant was finally demolished in 1846, armies of rats swarmed from the ruins and terrorized the district for weeks.

La Bastoche

In the early twentieth century "La Bastoche" was the slang term for the low-life area of Bastille, with its pimps and prostitutes, rough dance halls, and bougnats, Auvergnat holes-in-the-wall selling coal and cheap booze. Bar- and club-lined Rue de Lappe, its main night-life street, is still jumping, including a survivor from La Bastoche's heyday, Le Balajo, a popular dance hall opened in 1936.

In Somerset Maugham's novel *The Razor's Edge*, the narrator takes a group of upper-class American friends to a dive on this street:

> Men danced with podgy boys with made-up eyes; gaunt, hard-featured women danced with fat women with dyed hair; men danced with women. There was a frowst of smoke and liquor and of sweating bodies. The music went on interminably and that unsavoury mob proceeded round the room, the sweat shining on their faces, with a solemn intensity in which there was something horrible.

Père-Lachaise Cemetery

With more than three-hundred-thousand Parisians in residence, Père-Lachaise is truly a city of the dead. The moody park laid out as a *jardin à l'anglaise* takes full advantage of the hilly contours of its 105-acres, its mossy tombs and cobblestone walks shaded by more than five thousand trees. Named for Louis XIV's confessor Father François d'Aix de la Chaise, who retired here when it was a Jesuit retreat, the property was acquired by Napoléon and opened as a cemetery in 1804.

To publicize the new cemetery, then outside the city limits, the directors hit upon a scheme to enhance its prestige: acquiring the remains of illustrious figures and reburying them. So, in 1817, with much pomp and ceremony, the remains of the celebrated medieval lovers Abélard and Héloïse were buried in a cloister-like tomb, and the unlikely authentic remains of Molière and La Fontaine were placed in side-by-side mausoleums.

The next writer to be transferred was Beaumarchais, moved in 1825 from the tomb on his estate near the Bastille.

BALZAC

The first great writer to be buried at Père-Lachaise when he died was Balzac, in 1850. As a fledgling novelist, the cemetery was his favorite place for recreation. "I rarely go out," he wrote his family, "but when I do wander, I go cheer myself up in Père-Lachaise." He later used it as the setting for one of the towering scenes in French literature, the ending of *Le Père Goriot*, in which Rastignac, standing alone at the grave of the pathetic old Goriot after the body has been lowered into the ground, issues his challenge to Paris:

> Rastignac walked a few steps to the highest part of the cemetery, and saw Paris spread out below on both banks of the winding Seine. Lights were beginning to twinkle here and there. His gaze fixed almost avidly on the space that lay between the column of the Place Vendôme and the dome of the Invalides; there lay the splendid world that he had wished to gain. He eyed that humming hive with a look that foretold its despoliation, as if he already felt on his lips the sweetness of its honey, and said with supreme defiance,
> "It's war between us now!" ("A nous deux, maintenant!")
> And by way of throwing down the gauntlet to Society, Rastignac went to dine with Madame de Nucignen.

THE LAST HALF OF THE NINETEENTH CENTURY

A simple pillar marks the grave of Gérard de Nerval, who committed suicide in 1855 at age forty-six. Alfred de Musset died at the same age two years later, ill and depressed, writing little over his last fifteen years. A willow was planted by his grave, fulfilling a wish he expressed in an early poem.

On December 20, 1897, Émile Zola, one of the pallbearers for Alphonse Daudet, was hissed by bystanders during the funeral procession for his pro-Dreyfus sympathies. Despite his political differences with Daudet and his *antidreyfusard* family, Zola delivered a lovely graveside eulogy for his old friend. Less than a month later he published "J'accuse!"

THE TWENTIETH CENTURY

When Oscar Wilde died at his seedy hotel in Paris in 1900, he was so deeply in debt that he was buried in a low-rent cemetery south of the city. Nine years later his loyal friend Robbie Ross finally managed to pay off the debts and purchase a plot at Père-Lachaise, where the remains were transferred. Ross commissioned Jacob Epstein to create Wilde's rather Pharaonic monument, installed in 1914.

Guillaume Apollinaire, who died of the Spanish flu in 1918, is commemorated by a tall rough-granite gravestone carved by his Cubist friend Serge Férat.

Raymond Radiguet was buried here in December 1923, dead at the age of twenty, nine months after the publication of his masterpiece, *The Devil in the Flesh*.

Marcel Proust's spot is hard to find in the Proust family's burial site, as it was designed for his eminent father Dr. Adrien Proust, who died in 1903. The bronze portrait on the tomb is of Dr. Proust. Jeanne, Proust's adored mother, died two years later. Marcel was buried here in 1922, fame finally arriving toward the end of his life.

Gertrude Stein, a fixture of American expatriate Paris from 1903 to her death in 1946, is buried alongside her partner, Alice B. Toklas, who died in 1967.

Poet Paul Eluard, a militant Communist from the late 1920s onward, died in 1952 and was buried in a section reserved for notable Communists near the Mur de Féderés, the wall where the last survivors of the Communard forces were lined up and shot on May 27, 1871.

Colette was interred on August 7, 1954, after a grand state funeral in the Cour d'Honneur of the Palais-Royal, held there because the Catholic Church refused to give her a religious service.

Richard Wright died in December 1960, thirteen years after choosing exile in Paris. His ashes are stored in the columbarium, Box 848, in the southeast corner, where there is a wall plaque in his honor.

After Jim Morrison's burial on July 7, 1971, his grave became the most unquiet one in the cemetery, thanks to some of his cult-like followers. A guard is on duty to protect it and the surrounding tombs from the graffiti—"The Lizard King lives!" "We're waiting for you, Jim!"—scrawled all over them in the early years.

Georges Perec, the amazingly inventive author of *La Vie: mode d'emploi* (*Life: A User's Manual*) and eight other novels, died of bronchial cancer in 1982, four days short of his forty-sixth birthday. His ashes are in Box 382 on the south side of the Columbarium.

THE HEART OF THE RIGHT BANK

The heart of the Right Bank, the core of modern Paris, runs from the Hôtel de Ville to the Place de la Concorde, and takes in the whole city center within the Grands-Boulevards, from Concorde to République.

The heart of the heart, so to speak, is La Ville, "the Town," as it was known in the Middle Ages, the first part of mainland Paris to be settled after the Norman invasions ceased and Parisians felt safe to settle outside their island fortress of La Cité. La Ville was first settled in the tenth century by boatmen who created a port near the current site of Hôtel de Ville. La Ville expanded quickly, and by the end of the twelfth century had become so prosperous that Philippe Auguste decided to protect it with nine-meter-high ramparts enclosing what today are the neighboring quarters of Hôtel de Ville, Châtelet, and Les Halles.

Hôtel de Ville-Châtelet-Les Halles

Place de l'Hôtel de Ville was originally known as the Place de Grève, named after the sloping bank (*grève*) to the port. In the Middle Ages, workers would "*faire la grève*," shape up for a job here. This was also the main site for public executions. Huge, raucous crowds would watch victims hanged, beheaded, burned alive, or, in the bloodcurdling method used to punish exceptionally heinous crimes, drawn and quartered.

CLAUDE LE PETIT

In his collection of satirical ballads, *Paris ridicule*, Claude Le Petit plays on the river's proximity to the execution site:

> Certes, Grève, après maint délict
> Vous estes, pour mourir, un lict
> Bien commode pour les infasmes,
> Car ils n'ont qu' à prendre un batteau
> Et, d'un coup d'aviron, leurs âmes
> S'en vont en Paradis par eau.

> (Certainly, Grève, you are a very convenient bed for villains,
> after many offenses, to die,
> since they only have to take a boat,
> and with a stroke of an oar,
> their souls go to Heaven by water.)

Paris ridicule is a posthumous work, because a stroke of bad luck led to Le Petit's own ride to Heaven. While Le Petit was out of his room one day, a breeze came up and blew some of his verses out the window, which were found by a priest who was passing by. Scandalized by one called "Le Bordel des muses" ("The Whorehouse of the Muses"), a satire of the Holy Virgin, he ran straight to the authorities, who wasted no time arresting

Vieux-Paris

Vue de l'Hôtel de Ville de Paris, sous Louis XV,
où l'on voit dans l'éloignement le Pont Marie
et le Pont de bois dit le Pont Rouge

18th century rendering of the Hôtel de Ville, the place where executions took place, and the port

the poet. The court ordered that Le Petit's right hand be chopped off and he be burned alive, the blasphemous poem with him. But the executioner showed mercy, strangling him before throwing him on the fire. Le Petit died on September 1, 1662, at twenty-four.

Thanks to a Dutch friend who honored his promise, *Paris ridicule*, Le Petit's most important work, was published four years after his death.

CHÂTELET

Place du Châtelet is named for a little fortress built in 1130 to protect the bridge to the royal palace on the Île de la Cité, but expanded over the centuries to become a huge ungainly structure with a half dozen conical towers and numerous wings. This was the seat of the provost, the chief law enforcement officer of Paris, along with the civil and criminal courts of the city, its main prison, debtors' prison, and morgue. It was the most feared spot in Paris until Napoléon had it demolished in 1802. A marble plaque at No. 12 avenue Victoria shows where it stood.

François Villon appears to have been locked up in the Grand-Châtelet four times. The first, in 1455, was for killing a priest in a knife fight, for which he was eventually exonerated. The second was for theft the following year, for which he was banished from Paris. After a general amnesty allowed him to return, Villon was held briefly in 1462 on suspicion of another theft but released, and was arrested again the same year for taking part in a brawl in which an emissary of the Pope was killed. Villon was tortured, convicted of murder, and sentenced to be hanged. In his cell he wrote "La Ballade des pendus" ("The Ballad of the Hanged Men"):

Frères humains, qui après nous vivez,
N'ayez les cueurs contre nous endurcis . . .

(Brothers among us who live on after us
Harden not your hearts against us . . .)

His sentence was reduced on appeal to ten years' banishment from Paris, from which he never returned.

The other literary giant locked up in the Grand-Châtelet was Molière, in debtors' prison. After the Illustre-Théâtre's money-losing first year, 1643-1644, creditors took the company to court. As security for the theater's debts, the court chose to jail Molière, the youngest member of the troupe at twenty-three, presumably because his father was a well-to-do merchant. Molière entered the prison on August 2, 1645, but was released only three days later because of his youth. He and his partners, the Béjarts, gave up on Paris three months later and went on the road.

GÉRARD DE NERVAL

In the decades after the Grand-Châtelet was torn down, the surrounding tangle of shabby little streets and alleys remained. Among them was the Rue de la Vieille-Lanterne, a cul-de-sac now buried beneath the Théâtre de la Ville. On the icy morning of January 26, 1855, Gérard de Nerval was found hanging from a lamp post in this alley.

Gérard de Nerval in 1854, photograph by Nadar

The previous night he had left a note for the aunt with whom he had been living since his release from Dr. Blanche's mental clinic in Passy three months earlier. It read: "Don't wait for me this evening, because the night will be black and white."

Despite Nerval's long history of mental illness, Théophile Gautier and other close friends refused to believe it was suicide. A gentle man of forty-six, Nerval had been suffering from psychological disturbances for fifteen years, several times requiring stays at mental clinics, but through it all he continued to write the luminous prose and poetry which led Proust to rank him among the handful of greatest writers of the nineteenth century, and whose vision—"the seeping of dream into real life"—led André Breton to cite him as a precursor of Surrealism.

At the time of Nerval's death, the first part of his masterpiece "Aurélia," a dazzlingly lucid account of the phantasmagorical life he led during his states of dementia, was running in *La Revue de Paris*, and the second part, pages of which were found in his pocket, was scheduled to appear three weeks later.

He is buried at Père-Lachaise Cemetery.

In the garden of the Tour Saint-Jacques, across Avenue Victoria from the Théâtre de la Ville, is a memorial to Nerval, a granite stele and a smooth boulder next to it inscribed with his poem "El Desdichado," "The Disinherited One," a quote from which T. S. Eliot used in *The Waste Land*:

Je suis le ténébreux—le veuf—l'inconsolé,
Le prince d'Aquitaine à la tour abolie:
Ma seule étoile est morte—et mon luth constellé
Porte le Soleil noir de la Mélancolie

(I am the man of shadows—the widower—unconsoled,
the prince of Aquitania, in the abandoned tower:
My only star is dead—and my starred lute
Carries as its emblem the Black Sun of Melancholy)

Les Halles

By 1135 the primitive food market on the Place de Grève could no longer cope with the town's needs. Louis VI ("Louis the Fat") had it transferred to Les Champeaux, "the little fields," a bit to the north, where the Forum des Halles is now. At the end of the century Philippe Auguste built two vast wooden halls for shelter. From these early structures Les Halles got its name.

JEAN-JACQUES ROUSSEAU IN LES HALLES

Chased from France in 1762 for the individualist approach to religion he espoused in *Émile, ou de l'éducation*, Rousseau returned to Paris eight years later and in 1771 took a little third-floor flat on the market street Rue Plâtrière, renamed Rue Jean-Jacques Rousseau two decades later. There is a plaque where his house stood, at No. 52.

Rousseau supported himself and his longtime mistress Thérèse Levasseur, whom he had married two years before his return, by copying sheet music. But his real work was the soul-searching autobiography *Confessions*, begun after his archenemy Voltaire publicly revealed that Rousseau had fathered five children and abandoned them to a foundling home. Rousseau felt he needed to explain his behavior and he wrote a massive apologia with a rationale for every step in his life. His readings at the salons of Mme Geoffrin and other great ladies had them in tears.

Rousseau's central philosophical idea, first advanced in 1750, was in response to the question "have the arts and sciences contributed to the improvement of morals?" His

Jean-Jacques Rousseau,
by Quentin de la Tour

answer was a resounding NO. Rousseau asserted that man is basically good, but the arts and sciences have corrupted him by creating an artificial and vicious world in which society heaps riches and privileges on people who own property and inflicts misery on those with none. To Voltaire, Diderot, and other leading Enlightenment thinkers, Rousseau's theory of "natural man" was not only simpleminded, but it contradicted everything they believed in: human progress through intellectual achievement. And as Rousseau's detractors enjoyed pointing out, his basic source of income, copying music, was artistic; and though he attacked the theater as a corruptor of morals, he wrote numerous operas, ballets, and plays. His *Pygmalion* was a hit at the Comédie-Française in 1775.

With all intellectual Paris against him, Rousseau was pleased to accept the offer of a house in the country in the spring of 1778, particularly with Voltaire now in town. On May 20 he moved to rural Ermenonville as the guest of the Marquis de Girardin.

ZOLA'S LES HALLES

The explosive growth of Paris after the Revolution convinced Napoléon III that a radical modernization of the market was needed. "Make me umbrellas," he told the architect Victor Baltard. Between 1852 and 1870, ten airy pavilions of cast iron and glass—a new architectural technique at the time—went up, ushering in Les Halles' most glorious period.

Published in 1873, *Le Ventre de Paris* (*The Belly of Paris*), the third novel in Zola's Rougon-Macquart series, captures this era marvelously well. One can dip into the novel practically anywhere and come up with sharply observed passages such as the following, about a charming fruit vendor and her products:

> The cherries looked like the red kisses of her bright lips; the silky peaches were not more delicate than her neck; to the plums she seemed to have lent the skin from her brow and chin; while some of her own crimson blood coursed through the veins of the currants. All the scents of the avenue of flowers behind her stall were but insipid beside the aroma of vitality which exhaled from her open baskets and falling kerchief.

In 1969 the government relocated the market to Rungis, near Orly Airport, to relieve central Paris of the massive traffic congestion around Les Halles. The graceful Baltard pavilions were torn down and replaced by today's giant multilevel shopping mall, which sells everything but the fresh meat, fish, fruit, vegetables, butter, and eggs that had been sold here since the days of Charles the Fat.

Molière Country

YOUNG MOLIÈRE

Molière was born in Les Halles in the Pavillon des Singes, "the monkey house," named for a bas-relief on the façade showing seven simians in an orange tree. His father Jean Poquelin was a prosperous *tapissier du roi*, an upholsterer to the king, and *valet de chambre ordinaire du roi*, one of the honorary valets who prepared the king's bedchamber. Molière's birthplace is marked by a plaque on the house at No. 96 rue Saint-Honoré, which replaced "the monkey house" in 1802. (Note that another house nearby at No. 31 rue du Pont-Neuf displays a bust of Molière and a plaque that claims, incorrectly, he was born there in 1620.)

Molière was baptized Jean-Baptiste Poquelin at the church of Saint-Eustache on January 15, 1622, and grew up in the neighborhood. As the eldest son he was due to inherit the family business, but it did not appeal to him, nor did law school, where his father sent him as an alternative. As Molière's friend La Grange said, he "chose the profession of actor because of the invincible passion he had for the theater"—that and a passion for an actress, Madeleine Béjart, the beautiful and talented eldest daughter of a family of actors. They met in 1640, became lovers, and with the Béjarts and others founded the Illustre-Théâtre on Rue Mazarine in 1643: The following year he adopted his stage name. After losing money in Paris for two years in a row, the troupe had to go on the road.

MOLIÈRE'S BIG BREAK

For the next thirteen years the company scratched out a living as itinerant players in the South of France, where they often crossed paths with Italian *commedia dell'arte* troupes and fell in love with their improvisational style of comedy. Molière began writing imitative sketches. These were surefire crowd-pleasers in the provinces, but when the troupe finally had a chance to perform for Louis XIV, they chose to put on a tragedy, as prestige in the French theater lay in that genre.

The performance took place on October 24, 1658, in the Salle des Caryatides in the Sully Pavilion of the Louvre, with Molière playing the tragic hero in Pierre Corneille's *Nicodème*. Louis, then twenty, was not moved.

In a desperate attempt to save the evening, the troupe put on Molière's comic sketch *Le Docteur amoureux*, with Molière again in the lead. A contemporary wrote:

> He was every bit a comedian from his foot to his head. He seemed to have many voices, all speaking in him, and with step, a smile, a wink, and a nod of the head, he could say more than the most eloquent speaker could have said in an hour.

The king was so amused that he gave Molière and company a playhouse in the palace.

The company's first offerings in its new venue—all tragedies—were flops. But in November 1659 they had a hit with *Les Précieuses ridicules*, Molière's satire of young gentlewomen made silly by their devotion to pretentious language (though he took the precaution of making the learned ladies provincials rather than *parisiennes*). The play made Molière the talk of the town.

When his younger brother Jean died in 1660, Molière had to assume the title of *tapissier du roi* and *valet ordinaire du roi* so the family would not lose the inherited offices. The positions gave him the chance to develop a personal relationship with the king, which would prove useful at several critical moments in his career.

One occurred almost immediately when, without prior notice, the royal superintendent of buildings began demolishing the Salle du Petit-Bourbon, where the company had been playing, in preparation for new construction. With the troupe suddenly homeless, Molière appealed to the king. Louis gave him Cardinal Richelieu's old theater in the Palais-Royal.

MOLIÈRE AND COMPANY AT THE PALAIS-ROYAL

The Théâtre du Palais-Royal stood at the corner of Rue Saint-Honoré and Rue de Valois, where a plaque on the wall of the Palais-Royal marks its site. The theater was a wreck when the troupe took it over in the fall of 1660, with half of the roof rotted away, but it was ready for business the following January. The first play in the new theater was a flop: *Dom Garcie de Navarre*, the only tragedy Molière would write.

His true talent was confirmed by *L'École des femmes* (*The School for Wives*), a smash hit at the end of 1662. Molière's sophisticated verse, bright play of ideas, and believable characters lifted the play to an artistic plane never before seen in French comedy, but academics and theatrical rivals berated him for violating the classical rules differentiating tragedy and comedy, and the *dévots*, the archconservative faction of the Church, tried but failed to have the play banned as immoral. Then Molière's enemies began spreading rumors about his marriage.

Earlier in 1662 Molière had married Armande Béjart, then twenty, the youngest child of the Béjart family. His enemies claimed that she was the daughter of Madeleine, his former mistress, not Madeleine's much younger sister, as the family maintained, and therefore the marriage was quasi-incestuous. Some went farther, alleging that Molière had married his own daughter. Modern research indicates that Madeleine was indeed Armande's mother, but by another lover, the comte de Modène.

The longest and bitterest fight of Molière's career was over *Tartuffe*, his black comedy about a domineering con man masquerading as a *dévot*. After its premiere in 1664 the real-life *dévots* pressured Louis XIV into banning further performances. They scored another victory the following year by having *Dom Juan* banned as well.

Molière received solid support during this painful period from his friends La Fontaine,

Boileau, and young Racine, whose first play he produced. The four became frequent drinking companions until December 1665, when Racine suddenly withdrew a play in rehearsal at Molière's theater and gave it to the rival Théâtre de l'Hôtel de Bourgogne. It was an act of treachery Molière never forgave.

Molière, by Pierre Mignard

Shortly afterwards, he rented a hideaway in rural Auteuil as a refuge from his woes (which were marital as well as professional—Armande was rumored to be having an affair), where he wrote *Le Misanthrope*, about a man whose contempt for humanity leads him to withdraw from the world.

In 1667 Molière tried again with a rewritten, retitled version of *Tartuffe*, but it was banned after one performance. At last, on February 5, 1669, the play opened in a version authorized by the king and went on to become the most successful first run of any play in the company's history.

Sometime in the early 1670s Molière returned to Armande at their home on Rue Saint-Thomas-du-Louvre, their discord resolved, as evidenced by her pregnant state when they moved to a big new apartment on Rue de Richelieu in October 1672.

MOLIÈRE'S DEATH

In *Le Malade imaginaire*, the tyrannical hypochondriac Argan is convinced that everyone hates him and wishes him dead. To dissuade him, the servant Toinette talks him into playing dead in order to witness his wife's inconsolable grief:

Argan: Isn't there any danger in counterfeiting death?
Toinette: No, no. What danger would there be?

Argan slumps in his chair and plays dead.

On the evening of February 17, 1673, while playing Argan, Molière suffered a convulsion, but managed to disguise it from the audience and complete the show. When she realized that her husband was truly in distress, Armande, who was playing Argan's daughter, had him carried across the garden of the Palais-Royal in Argan's chair to their home, where he began coughing blood. She immediately sent to their parish church of Saint-Eustache for a priest to hear Molière's renunciation of his life as an actor, needed for burial in sacred ground. The curate refused her request. Before she could locate a sympathetic priest, Molière died, apparently of a tubercular hemorrhage.

The house in which he died stood at No. 40 rue de Richelieu, where there is a plaque. Across the street is the Fontaine Molière, a voluptuous nineteenth-century memorial designed by Visconti.

MOLIÈRE'S BURIAL

Armande hastened to Versailles and appealed directly to Louis XIV for a Christian burial for her husband. Shortly afterward, the archbishop ordered the pastor of Saint-Eustache to bury Molière, but discreetly, at night, with no funeral Mass, only two priests in attendance, and as the *tapissier du roi* Jean-Baptiste Poquelin, not as an actor.

On the night of February 21, 1673, Armande, the troupe, and many friends followed the funeral procession, torches in hand, from Rue de Richelieu to the Cemetery of Saint-Joseph, off Rue Montmartre, to pay their respects to France's greatest man of the theater.

The Palais-Royal

LA MAISON DE MOLIÈRE

In the 1780s Louis-Philippe duc d'Orléans (nicknamed "Philippe Egalité" for his egalitarian political views, but a big spender deeply in debt) turned real estate developer, hiring Victor Louis to build three large apartment buildings with arcades lined with boutiques, restaurants, cafés, and two theaters surrounding a central garden, just as we see the Palais Royal today.

The two theaters are still in service. The Théâtre du Palais-Royal is of little literary interest, having specialized in light comedies and operettas since it opened in 1785, but the Théâtre-Français is enormously important. Completed in 1790, this gem of a Doric-style theater, all gilt and red velvet, with 892 seats, has been the home of the Comédie-Française since 1799. Its entrance is at No. 2 rue de Richelieu.

Molière never played this theater, having died long before it was built, but because the Comédie-Française was an outgrowth of his old troupe and his plays have always been the most frequently performed, it is known as "the House of Molière."

The armchair in which he was carried home after his fatal attack in 1673 is displayed in a glass case in the upper lobby.

BALZAC'S PALAIS-ROYAL

In the early decades of the nineteenth century the Palais-Royal was a mecca for libertine living. Balzac, that insatiable explorer of the "ocean" of Paris, used it often as a setting in the *Comédie humaine.*

In *Le Père Goriot,* set in 1819, Delphine sends Rastignac into one of the Palais-Royal's gambling dens to bet her last hundred francs to "either lose it all or bring me back six thousand francs." After an old man at the table explains the rules of roulette, Rastignac bets on twenty-one, his age. To everyone's amazement, he wins seven thousand francs on two spins of the wheel.

Another Balzacian hero visits a gambling house in *La Peau de Chagrin (The Wild Ass's*

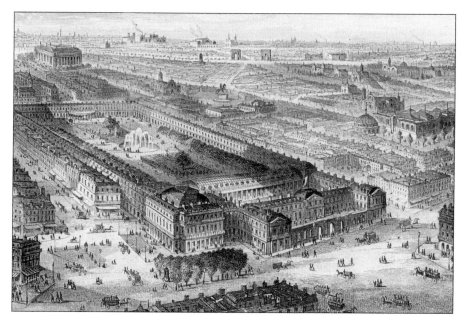

The Palais-Royal in the 19th century, the theater of the Comédie-Française in foreground

Skin), but the outcome is far different. A brilliant student, now twenty-six, desperately poor with no foreseeable means of achieving his extravagant dreams of wealth and power, Raphaël de Valentin has decided to bet the little money he has left, and if he loses, to commit suicide. Luck is not with him. After losing his last *sou*, he heads for the Pont-Royal "lost in a daze of meditation similar to that which used to fasten on criminals as the tumbrel conveyed them from the Palais de Justice to the Place de Grève, toward the scaffold reddened with the blood shed there since 1793."

The Balzac character most closely linked to the Palais-Royal is *Lost Illusions*'s Lucien de Rubempré. Recently arrived from Angoulême in 1821, the "great man in embryo" goes to the Palais-Royal hoping to find a publisher for his collection of delicate poems *Les Marguerites*. There Lucien's mentor, the venal theater critic Lousteau, introduces him to the book publisher Dauriat, who is also a mogul in the far more lucrative trade of journalism. He grudgingly agrees to read Lucien's poems. That night, on a dare, Lucien knocks off a cleverly flattering review of a play, making his name overnight in that sleazy craft. When he returns to the Palais-Royal a week later, Dauriat tells him that he has rejected *Les Marguerites*—for his own good:

> "Yes, Monsieur, you'll get more money from me in the next six months for the articles I shall ask from you than you would from your unsaleable poetry."
> "But what about my reputation as a writer?" cried Lucien.
> Dauriat and Lousteau burst out laughing.
> "God save us!" said Lousteau. "The man still has his illusions."

HENRY JAMES

In 1836 Philippe Egalité's son, the "citizen king" Louis-Philippe, ordered the gaming houses closed and the prostitutes expelled. Overnight, the Palais-Royal slipped into the faded gentility that characterizes it to this day. By the late 1860s, the period in which *The American* is set, it was respectable enough for a Jamesian hero:

> The place was filled with people, the fountains were spouting, a band was playing, clusters of chairs were gathered beneath all the lime trees, and buxom, white-capped nurses, seated along the benches, were offering to their infant charges the amplest facilities for nutrition. There was an easy, homely gaiety to the whole scene, and Christopher Newman felt that it was most characteristically Parisian.

Over a drink at a café, Newman confides to his old business acquaintance Tom Tristram his reason for abandoning his obsessive money-making pursuits in America: "I have come to see Europe, to get the best out of it I can. I want to see all the great things, and do what the clever people do." That includes, "if the fancy takes me, to marry a wife."

In 1875, James, then thirty-two, moved to Paris, renting an apartment at No. 29 rue Cambon, near Place Vendôme. He supported himself by writing a series of sketches for the New York Tribune—"Paris through Fresh Eyes," the paper billed them—while finishing his first novel, *Roderick Hudson*, and starting *The American*. The following year he moved to London and finished the novel.

THE GRAND VÉFOUR

During the same period, the old comrades Flaubert, Turgenev, and Edmond de Goncourt used to dine regularly at the Grand Véfour, inviting the younger writers Zola and Daudet, then in their thirties, to join them. "Les Dîners des Cinq" was a revival of "Les Dîners Magny," held twice monthly in the 1860s at the Left Bank restaurant of the same name. The first group had been sadly diminished by the deaths of Théophile Gautier, Sainte-Beuve, and Goncourt's younger brother Jules, while George Sand, a sometime partic
ipant, had retired to Nohant. The five nicknamed their new get-togethers *"le dîner des auteurs sifflés"*—the dinner of authors who have been hissed—all having written at least one play that died an ignominious death.

Opened in 1784, the Grand Véfour at No. 17 rue de Beaujolais is one of the most glamorous and highly rated restaurants in Paris, with prices to match. Hugo, Balzac, George Sand, the Palais-Royal neighbors Colette and Jean Cocteau, André Malraux, and Jean-Paul Sartre and Simone de Beauvoir were among the countless writers who dined amid its splendid gilt and wood-paneled décor. Drawings by Cocteau decorate the menus, the ashtrays are modeled on George Sand's hands, and brass name plaques of famous diners are fixed to the tables.

COLETTE

Colette lived a few steps from the Grand Véfour building twice, from 1927 to 1930 and from 1938 until her death sixteen years later. Both apartments were at No. 9 rue de Beaujolais, where there is a plaque in her honor.

Colette and her husband
Maurice Goudeket in their
Palais-Royal apartment

The first period began four years after the breakup of her marriage to Henry de Jouvenel, who left her when he found out that Colette had seduced his sixteen-year-old son Bertrand—she was fifty-four when it started—an affair that went on for three years. She sublet a friend's *entresol* studio, the view of the garden blocked by the arcades, expecting to stay only a month, but ending up keeping "the tunnel" for three years. During this period she wrote *La Naissance du jour* (*Break of Day*), her reflections on ageing and the renunciation of love, and her classic memoir about her mother, *Sido*.

In 1938 Colette leased a spacious apartment upstairs with a superb view of the garden. Now she had "Paris de ma fenêtre." At sixty-five, she was happily married to her devoted third husband, Maurice Goudeket, but the first truly peaceful time in her life quickly turned anxious when France and Germany went to war the next year, and all the more so during the Occupation, when her deepest concern was for Maurice, who was Jewish. He was arrested in December 1941 and interned at Compiègne, but because the German ambassador's wife was a fan of Colette's, she managed to get him released after two months. He lay low in the country until the Liberation.

Nonetheless, this was a productive period for Colette. *Le Pur et l'impur* (*The Pure and the Impure*), her observations and analyses of sexual relationships, particularly between women, came out in 1941. She also wrote her famous story "Gigi" and her chronicles *Journal à rebours* and *Paris de ma fenêtre*, which reveal the hardships of daily life during the Occupation.

The war finally over, she was elected to the Académie Goncourt.

In her final decade, Colette was a fat old lady half crippled by arthritis, but loved by the French people and respected by fellow writers from Gide to Simone de Beauvoir, who called her "a formidable goddess-mother."

In a 1948 meeting set up by Cocteau, Truman Capote, then twenty-four, went to pay his respects:

> She received me in her bedroom. I was astonished. Because she looked precisely as Colette ought to have looked. And that was astonishing indeed.

Jean Cocteau in 1941

Reddish, frizzy, rather African-looking hair; slanting, alley-cat eyes rimmed with kohl; a finely made face flexible as water . . . rouged cheeks . . . lips thin and tense as wire but painted a really brazen hussy scarlet.

Refused a religious funeral by the Church when she died in 1954, she was saved by the French government, which put on a magnificent State service in the Cour d'Honneur of the Palais-Royal. Colette is buried at Père Lachaise cemetery.

In 1996, a small square on the Rue Saint-Honoré side of the Comédie-Française was christened Place Colette.

JEAN COCTEAU

At the end of 1940, six months into the Occupation, Jean Cocteau moved to an entresol flat around the corner from his friend Colette at No. 36 rue de Montpensier, where there is a plaque in his honor. Despite his fame as a relentlessly self-promoting artist, poet, collaborator of Satie, Milhaud, and Stravinsky, playwright of *La Voix humaine*, *La Machine infernale*, and *Les Parents terribles*, novelist of *Les Enfants terribles*, and avant-garde film maker of *Le Sang d'un poète*, Cocteau, then fifty, was constantly broke because of his opium addiction. But with the support of Jean Marais, the astonishingly handsome actor half his age who became his lover in 1937, Cocteau was well on his way to kicking his habit.

Cocteau felt a good deal of empathy with the occupiers ("The honor of France may one day lie in the fact that it refused to fight," he wrote in his journal on May 5, 1942), and he had few qualms about cultivating professional contacts among the collaborationists. Yet he was not afraid to make waves in support of a friend, as he did for Max Jacob, fighting to get him released from the Nazi detention center at Drancy. He almost succeeded, but sadly, the frail, elderly poet contracted bronchial pneumonia there and died.

In 1943, Jean Genet brought him the manuscript of his first novel, *Notre Dame-des-Fleurs* (*Our Lady of the Flowers*), which so awed Cocteau that he immediately made arrangements to get it published. The following year he saved Genet from life imprisonment as a career criminal after his thirteenth felony conviction. "You don't lock up Rimbaud," he told the court.

After the war, Cocteau escaped being charged with collaborationist activities because the prosecutors failed to fit his actions into their categories for indictable crimes.

In 1946 he launched his triumphant postwar career as a movie director with *La Belle et la Bête*, a huge hit starring Jean Marais. In the money at last, he bought a country home with Marais the following year in Milly-la-Fôret southwest of Paris, where he spent most

of his time from then on. His success in films continued with *Les Parents terribles*, *Orphée*, and *Le Testament d'Orphée*. He was elected to the Académie française in 1955 and died eight years later at the age of seventy-four.

Four years after his death, Cocteau's name was published on a list of Grand Masters of the Priory of Sion, said to be a secret brotherhood founded in Jerusalem in 1099. The Priory of Sion was later revealed to be an elaborate hoax, but Dan Brown spun it with resounding success in *The Da Vinci Code*, with "Jean XIII Cocteau" mentioned a number of times to lend the far-fetched story a touch of verisimilitude.

On and Off Rue des Petits-Champs

VIDOCQ IN THE GALERIE VIVIENNE

One of the most glamorous and best preserved of Paris's early nineteenth-century *passages couverts*, the Galerie Vivienne (main entrance at No. 4 rue des Petits-Champs) is where the flamboyant Eugène-François Vidocq established the first private detective agency. The grand sweeping staircase in the gallery at No. 13 leads up to the suite where his *bureau de renseignements* was located from 1833 to his retirement in 1847.

A career criminal and escaped convict, Vidocq was appointed the first chief of La Sûreté, the secret police brigade set up by Napoléon in 1811, where he created a remarkably efficient network of fellow ex-criminals and snitches to ferret out evildoers in underworld *milieux*. He later did investigative work for Balzac, who used him as a model for Vautrin, the arch-criminal who ends up as chief of La Sûreté in *La Comédie humaine*. Hugo also found him fascinating and based aspects of Jean Valjean on him.

Edgar Allan Poe, never having set foot in Paris, did not know Vidocq in person, but he knew a good deal about him, having translated parts of Vidocq's *Mémoires* for an American magazine. So it was no mere whim that brought Poe to set "The Murders in the Rue Morgue" on "one of those miserable thoroughfares which intervene between the Rue de Richelieu and the Rue Saint-Roch," an imaginary street in this neighborhood, and make his sleuth, C. Auguste Dupin, a Frenchman. Published in 1841, the story launched a new literary genre, the private-eye story.

LAUTRÉAMONT AND MALDOROR ON RUE VIVIENNE

Little is known about the life of the reclusive comte de Lautréamont other than that his real name was Isadore Ducasse, that he was born in Uruguay of a mother who committed suicide, and that he attended *lycée* in France, died young, and left a masterpiece behind him, *Les Chants de Maldoror*. This series of five hallucinatory prose poems is so gruesome in places that even he was horrified by what his unfettered imagination had dictated. Maldoror is a grotesque, profoundly evil, dazzlingly brilliant being of mythic dimensions who lives in a murky den on or near Rue Vivienne and spreads terror through Paris at night.

> Shutters are closed with a slam, and the inhabitants bury themselves under their blankets. One would think that the bubonic plague had broken out. Thus, while the greater part of the town is getting ready to plunge into the revels of night, the Rue Vivienne is suddenly frozen in a kind of petrifaction. Like a heart which has ceased to love, the life has gone out of it. But soon the news of the phenomenon spreads to other parts of the populace, and a grim silence hovers over the august capital. What has happened to the gas-lamps? What has become of the street-walkers? Nothing . . . dark and empty streets! A screech owl, its leg broken, flying in a rectilinear direction, passes over the Madeleine and soars up toward the Thrône, shrieking: Woe to us.

Lautréamont's last known addresses are all in this general area—Rue Notre Dame-des-Victoires, Rue Vivienne, and lastly No. 7 rue du Faubourg-Montmartre, where he died on November 24, 1870, most likely of tuberculosis, at the age of twenty-four. As no one claimed the body, he was buried in a common grave in Montmartre Cemetery.

A little plaque by the door of the apartment house where he died quotes Maldoror:

> Qui ouvre la porte de ma chambre funéraire? J'avais dit que personne n'entrât. Qui que vous soyez, éloignez-vous.

> (Who opens the door of my funerary chamber? I said that no one enters. Whoever you may be, go away.)

STENDHAL ON RUE DE RICHELIEU

In 1821 the Austrians, then masters of northern Italy, expelled Stendhal from Milan as a suspected spy. He had left France six years earlier because the restored Bourbon monarchy wanted no truck with a former high-level bureaucrat in Napoléon's Empire. Having fallen in love with Italy as a boy lieutenant in Napoléon's army (and in love then and later with a number of Italian women), Stendhal settled in Milan, where in 1815, at the age of thirty-two, he decided to take a shot at writing, publishing studies of Mozart and Hayden that year, and adopting the *nom de plume* of Stendhal (his real name was Henri-Marie Beyle) two years later.

Stendhal (Henri Beyle), portrait by Pierre Joseph Dedreux Dorcy

Having become *persona non grata* in his adopted city, he moved to Paris, where he spent most of the 1820s. Stendhal lived in three houses on Rue de Richelieu, all long gone, at No. 45, No. 61, where there is a plaque, and No. 69, where he wrote *Le Rouge et le noir*.

Published in 1830, *Le Rouge et le noir* is a masterpiece, but to a literary world swept up in Romanticism, Stendhal's unheroic treatment of the hero Julien Sorel, his desensationalizing of inherently dramatic scenes such as Julian's execution, and his colloquial writing style, were the opposite of what readers wanted. "I shall be understood in 1880," he predicted, rightly so. By then *Le Rouge et le noir* was acclaimed as one of the great novels of the century.

With the overthrow of Charles X, the last Bourbon king, in 1830, Stendhal was finally able to return to the civil service. He would spend the following eleven years working at consulates in Italy.

On leave in Paris in 1838, he holed up in his room at No. 8 rue Caumartin, where in a period of fifty-two days he wrote *La Chartreuse de Parme* (*The Charterhouse of Parma*), an exhilarating five-hundred-page epic of adventure, intrigue, and romance. Many readers—Balzac, Henry James, and Gide were among them—believe it is superior to *Le Rouge et le noir*.

Stendhal returned to Paris gravely ill in 1841 and died the following year at the Hôtel de Nantes on Rue Neuve-des-Petits-Champs (now No. 22 rue Danielle-Casanova). He is buried in Montmartre Cemetery.

WALTER BENJAMIN AT THE BIBLIOTHÈQUE NATIONALE

Until 1996, when the eleven million volumes of the French national book collection were moved to the new Bibliothèque Nationale François Mitterrand on the Left Bank, all writers in need of research (Stendhal among them) went to the original Bibliothèque Nationale, established in the seventeenth century. Open to the public for exhibits and to researchers for its special collections, its main entrance is at No. 58 rue de Richelieu.

Walter Benjamin

This is where Walter Benjamin, that extraordinary jack of intellectual trades—philosopher, social historian, literary critic, translator, travel writer—worked on *Passagen-Werk*, or *The Arcades Project*, his vast, uncompleted study of what he called "Paris, Capital of the Nineteenth Century." This work, combined with the tragic nature of his death, would make him a cult figure after the war.

A German Jew and a Marxist, Benjamin left his native Berlin a month after Hitler came to power in 1933, stayed with friends in Spain and Denmark (with Bertolt Brecht at his house of exile), and finally settled in his dream city of Paris, where he scratched out a living on a small stipend from a New York foundation and writing for magazines. His main focus, however, was the *Arcades Project*, his exhaustive study of the social, cultural, and economic life of Paris in the nineteenth century, starting at the dawn of the century with the creation of the *passages couverts*. More than a hundred of these skylight-covered walking streets lined with shops, precursors of the modern consumer society, were built in the heart of the Right Bank, drastically changing the commercial and street life of the city and stimulating the culture of *flânerie*, aimless but alert strolling, of which Baudelaire, one of his key subjects, was a champion.

After war was declared in September 1939, the French detained Benjamin as a German national and assigned him to a "camp for voluntary laborers." In poor health because of a heart condition, he collapsed several times on the 150-mile march to his camp in Nevers. Adrienne Monnier and Jules Romains managed to get him released in November. Friends offered to help him escape Europe, but he refused. He went back to work at the library.

But after France fell to the Nazis the following year, he fled to the south, managed to secure a visa to the United States, and on September 26, 1940, joined a small group of refugees making the arduous crossing of the Pyrenées. When the group arrived in the Spanish town of Port Bou, the Guardia Civil told them their papers were invalid and they would have to go back to France. Sick and exhausted, the frail forty-eight-year-old Benjamin, whose brother Georg had already been "accidentally electrocuted" in a concentration camp, chose to take his own life rather than risk falling into the hands of the Gestapo.

After the war, writer Georges Bataille revealed that Benjamin had given him one thousand pages of notes for the *Arcades Project* to hide in the library. He turned them over to Theodor Adorno, who worked tirelessly to get his old friend Benjamin's works—including a number of finished sections of the *Arcades Project*—into print.

CÉLINE IN THE PASSAGE DE CHOISEUL

Louis-Ferdinand Céline (*né* Destouches) grew up in this congenial *passage* at No. 40 rue des Petits-Champs, where his mother owned a lace and lingerie shop with family quarters upstairs, first at No. 67, where they moved in 1899, when Louis-Ferdinand was five, and from 1904 to 1907 at No. 64. Thanks to an inheritance from Céline's grandmother (whose first name he would later use as his *nom de plume*), they then moved to a bourgeois apartment two blocks away at No. 11 rue Marsollier.

In Céline's *Mort à credit* (*Death on the Installment Plan*) the hero Ferdinand lives as a boy in the Passage des Bérésinas, clearly based on the Passage de Choiseul, which he sees as "an unbelievable pesthole":

> It was made to kill you off, slowly, but surely, what with the little mongrels'
> urine, the shit, the sputum, the leaky gas pipes. The stink was worse than
> the inside of a prison. Down under the glass roof the sun is so dim you can
> eclipse it with a candle.

Here Ferdinand undergoes a brutal, impoverished, culturally deprived childhood with a spineless father whose repressed rage is constantly on the verge of exploding, and sometimes does. In reality, Céline's childhood was comfortably *petit-bourgeois*; an only child with a room of his own, and by all evidence he had a calm and affectionate relationship with his parents. But, as Gide pointed out, "It is not reality which Céline paints, but the hallucinations reality provokes."

His first novel, *Journey to the End of the Night*, had created a sensation in 1932, almost winning the Prix Goncourt and racking up outstanding sales. He considered *Death on the Installment Plan*, published in 1936, a superior work and a sure thing for the Goncourt. Instead, most critics scoffed at it, sales were poor, and it was not even nominated. Céline's nasty side now began to come out. His first anti-Semitic work, *Bagatelles pour un massacre*, was published the next year, to great success. Others were soon to follow.

THE PRIX GONCOURT

In France, people who know nothing about the Goncourts, or even much about literature, all know the name, thanks to the prize Edmond de Goncourt created. At his death in 1896, he left funds for the establishment of the Académie Goncourt, a committee of ten novelists charged with awarding an annual prize for the best new work of prose fiction published during the previous year. The first was in 1903.

The most important winner, both for the author and for the credibility of the prize, was Marcel Proust for *A l'ombre des jeunes filles en fleur* (*Within a Budding Grove*) in 1919. Other famous winners include André Malraux for *Man's Fate* in 1933, Simone de Beauvour for *The Mandarins* in 1954, and Marguerite Duras for *The Lover* in 1984. The only writer to win twice was Romain Gary, for *Les Racines du ciel* (*The Roots of Heaven*) in 1956, and nineteen years later, under the false identity of "Émile Ajar," for *La Vie devant soi* (*The Life Before You*). Only one writer has refused the prize, Julien Gracq in 1951, because he hated the intrusion of "fiduciary values" in literature. Winning the Goncourt guarantees sales of four hundred thousand books on average.

Every November since 1914, the committee has met at Restaurant Drouant at No. 18 rue Gaillon, at Place Gaillon, an elegant eatery founded in 1870, to select the winner.

The biggest scandal took place in 1932 when two votes previously pledged to Céline's *Journey to the End of the Night* were switched at the last minute, the prize going instead to a long-forgotten novel called *Les Loups* by Guy Mazeline. So strongly had Céline been assured of victory that he came in person to join the press and the spectators awaiting the announcement on Place Gaillon. Though his failure to win was a shock, the *scandale* generated enormous publicity for a first-time novelist, helping sell fifty thousand copies in the first two months alone.

On and Off Rue de Rivoli

It is difficult to imagine this part of Paris as it was in the late eighteenth century. Rue de Rivoli did not exist; the Louvre was such a wreck that Louis XVI was thinking of tearing it down; the large Marsan Pavilion had yet to be built. On the other hand, Catherine de Médicis's massive sixteenth-century Tuileries Palace, destroyed by the Communards in 1871, still stood at the eastern end of the Tuileries Gardens.

The Louvre opened as an art museum in 1793 after the Revolution, but by then the vast rambling structure, long abandoned by royalty, had been taken over by squatters. Napoléon chased out the interlopers, refurbished the building, completed the Cour Carrée, and built the Marsan Pavilion along Rue de Rivoli, which he also created, supervising the projects from his residence in the Tuileries Palace. Napoléon III, who also lived there, completed the Louvre as his uncle had envisioned it.

This was the Louvre as Henry James and his characters knew it.

HENRY JAMES

In the opening scene of *The American*, set in the waning years of the Second Empire, Christopher Newman, "a powerful specimen of an American" only a few days into his first trip to Paris, meets the deviously charming young artist Mlle Noémie Nioche in the Salon Carré of the Louvre and buys the *Madonna* by Murillo she is copying. His plunge into the ways of the French is about to begin.

The Ambassadors, a late-period masterpiece published in 1903, is set almost entirely in Paris, and the Louvre is again a fruitful place for James's characters to meet. The Grande Galerie is where Lambert Strether arranges to meet Little Bilham, Chad Newsome's amiable but difficult-to-read friend, inviting Maria Gostrey along to help him size up the young man.

"Oh, he's all right—he's one of *us*!" Miss Gostrey, after the first exchange, soon found a chance to murmur to her companion; and Strether, as they proceeded and paused, as a quick unanimity, between the two seemed to have phrased itself in half a dozen remarks—Strether knew that he knew, almost immediately, what she meant, and took it as still another sign that he had got his job in hand.

THE TUILERIES PALACE AND TUILERIES GARDENS

In Flaubert's *Sentimental Education*, Frédéric Moreau and his friend Hussonnet wander though the Tuileries Palace during the Revolution of 1848, watching the mob demolish everything it can get its hands on. They see Louis-Philippe's throne tossed out the window and crash into the garden:

> An explosion of frenzied joy followed, as if, in place of the throne, a future of boundless joy had appeared; and the mob, less out of vengeance than from a desire to assert its supremacy, smashed or tore up mirrors, curtains, chandeliers, sconces, tables, chairs stools—everything that was moveable, in fact, down to albums of drawings and needlework baskets. They were the victors, so surely they were entitled to enjoy themselves.

After escaping the madhouse, Frédéric and Hussonnet repair to the Tuileries Gardens, where they spot "a big fellow walking briskly along between the trees with a musket on his shoulder. A cartridge belt was strapped around his red tunic, and a handkerchief was wound round his forehead, under his cap."

It is Dussardier, who, unlike his apathetic friends, has plunged into the armed revolt:

> Throwing himself into the arms of his friends, he cried:
>   "Oh, how happy I am, my dear fellows!"
>   He was incapable of saying another word, he was so breathless with joy and fatigue.

Dussardier would be killed three years later protesting against Louis-Napoléon's *coup d'état*.

In the character of Frédéric Moreau, Flaubert created the prototype of the modern anti-hero. Like Frédéric, Flaubert was not politically *engagé*. To Sartre he represented "the exact opposite of my own conception of literature: a total disengagement and a certain idea of form, which is not what I admire." To Flaubert, the writer should be "like God in the universe: omnipresent but invisible."

PLACE DE LA CONCORDE

In the mid-eighteenth century the city fathers decided to honor Louis XV, then known as the *Bien-Aimé*, by turning a wasteland adjoining the Tuileries Garden into the most impressive square in Europe. By the end of Louis's reign nineteen years later, however, the *Bien-Aimé* had become the *Mal-Aimé*, having squandered the state's coffers, lost all France's colonies, and lived a dissolute life with Mme de Pompadour, Mme du Barry, and countless other mistresses. In 1792, the mob pulled down Louis's equestrian statue in the Place de la Concorde, and the square was renamed Place de la Révolution.

A guillotine was set up the following January, and Louis XVI was beheaded. Over the next two years, 1,343 heads would roll on this spot, including those of Marie-Antoinette, Mme du Barry, Danton, Robespierre, Saint-Just, and most memorably in fiction, Sidney Carton in Dickens's *A Tale of Two Cities*. Having taken the condemned man Charles Darnay's place in the Conciergerie prison, he mounts the scaffold knowing that his life has not been a waste after all:

> It is a far, far better thing that I do, than I have ever done; it is a far, far better rest that I go to than I have ever known.

RUE DE RIVOLI

Napoléon began work on Rue de Rivoli and its arcaded buildings, the part running along the Tuileries, in 1811, though the full length of the arcades was not completed until the midcentury. With their delightful views over the Tuileries, the hotels along this street became very popular with tourists, particularly the English. Still one of Paris's most elegant hostelries, the Meurice at No. 228 was the first choice of British visitors. As William Thackeray noted in his *Paris Sketch Book* of 1840:

> Here you will find apartments at any price: a very neat room, for instance, for three francs daily; an English breakfast of eternal boiled eggs, or grilled ham; a nondescript dinner, profuse but cold; and a society which will rejoice your heart. Here are young gentlemen from the universities; young merchants on a lark; large families with nine daughters, with fat father and mother . . .

In Huysmans's 1884 novel *A rebours*, the hero Des Esseintes orders his carriage to stop at Galignani, Paris's oldest English-language bookshop, at No. 224, where he picks up a Baedeker guide to London. On a whim, the decadent aesthete has decided to venture out of the artificial paradise he has created, and is on his way to catch the boat-train to England. Before entering the Gare Saint-Lazare, however, he stops at a British pub across the street, where he soaks up enough ersatz London atmosphere to satisfy his wanderlust. He gets in his carriage and goes back home.

PARIS. — *Perspective du Jardin des Tuileries et de la Rue de Rivoli*

The Tuileries and
Rue de Rivoli

Coincidentally, Oscar Wilde and his bride arrived on their honeymoon at the Hôtel Wagram at No. 208 on May 29, 1884, only two weeks after *A rebours* came out. Wilde was shaken to the core by this "guidebook of decadence" beckoning him toward a life totally at odds with his new role as the husband of the elegant Constance Lloyd. In *The Picture of Dorian Gray*, Dorian reads "a poisonous book" given to him by Lord Henry Wotten. During Wilde's sodomy trial in 1895 it was identified as *A rebours*.

GEORGE ORWELL

In one of the wilder episodes of *Down and Out in Paris and London*, Orwell writes about his experience as a dishwasher in a luxury hotel (not named in the book, but in real life the elegant Hôtel Lotti around the corner on Rue de Castiglione), where there was "a secret vein of dirt, running through the great garish hotel like the intestines through a man's body:"

> It was amusing to look around the filthy little scullery and think that only a double door was between us and the dining room. There sat the customers in all their splendour—spotless table-cloths, bowls of flowers, mirrors and gilt cornices and painted cherubim; and here, just a few feet away, we in our disgusting filth. For it really was disgusting filth. There was no time to sweep the floor until evening, and we slithered about in a compound of soapy water, lettuce leaves, torn paper and trampled food.

Place Vendôme

The epitome of late-seventeenth-century urban development, Place Vendôme was designed by Jules Hardouin-Mansart in 1686. The splendid façades on the octagonal square were built right away, but it took forty years for all the buildings behind them to be completed. Most were private residences of bankers and financial speculators, most notoriously John Law, the bursting of whose "Mississippi Bubble" in the 1720s ruined countless investors. The buildings are now occupied by government offices, banks, upscale boutiques, and the Ritz.

THE RITZ

Now a synonym for luxury and high living ("puttin' on the ritz,"), the word originated as a family name, that of César Ritz, the Swiss hotelier who opened his establishment on the Place Vendôme in 1898. He guaranteed the hotel's success by hiring Auguste Escoffier, a man renowned for his *haute cuisine*, as the chef. The Ritz, at No. 15, was home to the duchesse de Gramont, the Maréchal de Lautrec, and Voltaire's friend the Marquis de Valette, among others.

PROUST

The Ritz was Proust's favorite place for a night on the town in his later years. He even kept a suite, preserved in its Louis XV style. Proust would arrive around midnight, roam the lobby in his fur-lined overcoat, observe people in the public rooms, get together with friends, and soak up the gossip from the omniscient *maître d'hôtel* Olivier Dabescat, the model for his counterpart Aimé at the Grand Hôtel de Balbec in *In Search of Lost Time*. He also flirted with a young waiter named Henri Rochat, who moved into his apartment on Rue Hamelin. Proust loved the iced beer introduced by the hotel and famously sent his driver Odilon to fetch some as he lay on his death bed.

FITZGERALD

Scott and Zelda Fitzgerald spent more time at the Ritz bar than was good for them during their five stays in Paris between 1924 and 1931, when Zelda's mental collapse put her in a sanitarium. But Fitzgerald put the Ritz to superb fictional use in his novel *Tender is the Night* and in his story "Babylon Revisited," published in 1931. In it, Charlie Wales has returned to Paris after a year and a half of sobriety to gain custody of his daughter Honoria, who is in the care of his dour sister-in-law Marion, the girl's legal guardian, since his wife's death. He finds the mood of the city very different from what it had been before the Crash, when he was one of those Americans on the *années folles* binge. Now, "the stillness in the Ritz bar was strange and portentous. It was not an American bar any more—he felt polite in it, and not as if he owned it. It had gone back into France."

Place Vendôme

HEMINGWAY

During the final days of the Occupation in August 1944, Ernest Hemingway and his band of irregulars "liberated" the wine cellar of the Ritz. That bit of history, along with the *grand cru* publicity value of the Hemingway name, got him a bar named in his honor.

Though the Ritz does not appear in Hemingway's works from the 1920s, he wrote about the period in his memoir *A Moveable Feast*, a quarter of which is devoted to trashing the memory of his long-dead friend Fitzgerald, the first person to invite him to the Ritz when he was too poor to afford it:

> Many years later at the Ritz bar, long after the end of World War II, Georges,
> who is the bar chief now and was a *chasseur* when Scott lived in Paris, asked
> me, "Papa, who was this Monsieur Fitzgerald that everyone asks me about?"

Georges puzzles over the mystery of why he remembers Hemingway, who was too poor to come often, but can't remember Fitzgerald, who was said to be a regular. The scene ends with him telling Hemingway, "You write about him as you remember him, and then if he came here, I will remember him."

"We will see," Papa responds.

OBELISK PRESS

Englishman Jack Kahane's Obelisk Press became famous in the 1930s as a publisher of English-language books too hot for companies in Britain and America to handle, most notably Henry Miller's *Tropic of Cancer*, published by Obelisk in 1934. Other steamy titles included Miller's *Black Spring* and *Tropic of Capricorn*, Anaïs Nin's *The House of Incest*, Lawrence Durrell's *The Black Book*, and reprints of Radclyffe Hall's lesbian tearjerker *The Well of Loneliness* and Frank Harris's four mind-numbing volumes of sexual confessions, *My Life and Loves*.

But Kahane also craved literary respectability. He published deluxe editions of his idol James Joyce's *Pomes Penyeach* and *Haveth Childers Everywhere*, and a fragment from *Work in Progress* (*Finnegans Wake*), as well as Richard Aldington's novel *Death of a Hero* and Cyril Connolly's *Rock Pool*.

Obelisk's address, No. 16 place Vendôme, also testifies to his yearning for respectability: It was quite literally a front. The entrance from the stylish square opened into a long, narrow corridor leading to a little room in the back.

HARRY'S NEW YORK BAR

Just around the corner from the Place Vendôme via the Rue de la Paix is Harry's New York Bar at No. 5 rue Daunou, or SANK ROO DOE NOO, as a sign in the window says. Opened by the American jockey Ted Sloan in 1911, the bar did a land-office business with American army officers and ambulance drivers during World War I, but when Sloan ran into financial difficulty in 1923 he sold it to bartender Harry MacElhone, a New Yorker. Hemingway claimed that Harry invented the Bloody Mary for him in the 1940s, supposedly because the tomato juice, Worcestershire and Tabasco sauces would hide the scent of alcohol from his girlfriend Mary Welsh. Actually, the drink was invented around 1920, most likely at this bar, but probably not by Harry. He certainly was a friend of Hemingway, however, starting in the 1920s, seconding him at boxing matches in Montmartre and holing up in the bar afterwards to rehash the events.

Another of the establishment's claims to fame: George Gershwin composed "An American in Paris" on the piano downstairs during his long stay in Paris in 1928.

Among the many other writers who warmed to the bar's clubby male atmosphere were Fitzgerald, Sinclair Lewis, Noël Coward, Ian Fleming, and, surprisingly, Jean-Paul Sartre, who discovered bourbon and hot dogs here.

The Grands-Boulevards

The word boulevard derives from a military term, the Old Dutch *bolwerc*, or bulwark, and here refers to medieval ramparts that stood along this route. Louis XIV had them torn down in the late seventeenth century and replaced by a string of broad thoroughfares along the northern edge of the city from the Bastille to the Madeleine. The heyday of the Grands-Boulevards lasted a full century, from the 1820s through World War I. The Boulevards des Italiens, named for an Italian troupe that set up shop at the Opéra-Comique in 1782, was the most popular with high society and writers. Balzac, Dumas,

Nerval, Gautier, Baudelaire, Flaubert, Zola, Maupassant, and Proust are but a few of the writers who frequented the many cafés and restaurants on this short stretch of the Boulevards between Rue de la Chausée d'Antin and Rue de Richelieu. The names of the establishments are legendary, but none remain, except on the printed page.

In *Swann's Way*, after a missed communication, the amorous hero searches feverishly for Odette one night, rushing to the Maison Dorée, Tortoni, and the Café Anglais, while his coachman scours the other cafés. Returning "with a haggard air" to his coach, Swann bumps into a young woman walking toward him. Odette! She could not find a table at Prévost, she tells him, and supped in a secluded nook at the Maison Dorée instead. Their chance meeting breaks the ice. A memorable carriage ride follows.

THE GRAND HÔTEL

One of the few buildings of literary interest remaining from the great days of the Grands-Boulevards is the appropriately named Grand-Hôtel. Paris's first modern luxury hotel, it opened in 1862, covering the large triangular block bounded by Rue Scribe, Rue Auber, and the Boulevard des Capucines.

In July 1870, in Zola's *Nana*, a strange group of women—Nana's fellow courtesans—have gathered in a hotel room to witness her gruesome death from smallpox. Meanwhile, outside in the street, the Parisians are rejoicing about France's declaration of war on Prussia:

> The darkness was deepening, and in the distance gas-lamps were lighting up
> one by one. Meanwhile the curious faces could be seen at the windows, while
> under the trees, the human flood swelled from one minute to the next, till it
> ran in one enormous stream from the Madeleine to the Bastille . . . Among
> the jostling, scattering groups, a band of men in workmen's caps and white

smocks appeared, uttering a regular cry which had the rhythmical beat of hammers on an anvil.

"To Berlin! To Berlin! To Berlin!"

THE CAFÉ DE LA PAIX

The only café remaining from the great days of the Grands-Boulevards is the Café de la Paix. Opened in 1872, it wraps around the corner of Boulevard des Capucines and Rue Auber, across from the Opéra de Paris. Countless writers have patronized this sumptuously decorated belle époque-style establishment.

In "My Old Man," one of Hemingway's first published stories, the twelve-year-old narrator often sits with his father, a jockey, on the terrasse of the café. The story originally appeared in *Three Stories and Ten Poems*, published in Paris by Robert McAlman's Contact Editions in 1923. Although the print run was only three hundred copies, it became an important stepping stone for the novice writer, because Edward J. O'Brien, the editor of *Best Short Stories*, selected it for his prestigious annual anthology that year.

THE OPÉRA DE PARIS

Construction of Charles Garnier's vast, outlandishly ornate opera house began in 1862, but soon came to a halt when underground springs flooded the site. Eight months were required to pump out the water and build a giant watertight dam around the foundations. The building took more than a decade to complete, interrupted by the Franco-Prussian War and the Commune, and was finally inaugurated in 1875.

The subterranean water fostered a myth that there was a lake under the opera house. In Gaston Leroux's novel *The Phantom of the Opera*, published in 1911, Erik, the hideously disfigured genius who has convinced almost everyone that a ghost haunts the Opéra de Paris, dwells in a house he has built on an island in the lake. Here he sequesters Christine Daaé, the lovely singer he kidnaps, with a mirrored torture chamber to destroy anyone who dares try to rescue her.

THÉÂTRE DES VARIÉTÉS

The booming theater district of the nineteenth century stretched from the Boulevard Montmartre to the Boulevard du Temple, "le Boulevard du Crime" brought to life so brilliantly by Marcel Carné and Jacques Prévert in their film *Les Enfants du paradis*. Of the theaters from the era still in operation, the Théâtre de la Porte Saint-Denis and the Théâtre de la Renaissance among them, the Théâtre des Variétés is the one with the richest literary history. Opened in 1807, this pretty Greek Revival playhouse at No. 7 boulevard Montmartre put on such hits as Alexandre Dumas's *Keen*, starring Frédérick Lemaître, in 1837 and the stage adaptation of Henri Mürger's *Scènes de la vie de bohème*, the source of Puccini's *La Bohème*, in 1849.

Gérard de Nerval haunted the Théâtre des Variétés in the mid-1830s because of his obsession with a bit-part actress named Jenny Colon. She would be unknown today if Nerval had not based one of his "*filles de feu*," the faithless Aurélia, on her in his magical stories "Sylvie" and "Aurélia."

In the opening scene of Zola's *Nana*, he introduces all the main characters at the opening night of a musical called *The Blonde Venus*, in which an eighteen year-old girl makes two brief appearances. "She had no talent at all," says Zola, "but that didn't matter, because she had something else." By "flaunting her nakedness with a cool audacity, sure of the sovereign power of her flesh," she ends up stealing the show . . . and showing herself as a natural for her real career as a courtesan:

> A wave of lust was flowing from her as from a bitch in heat, and it had spread
> further and further until it filled the whole house . . . And Nana in front of
> this fascinated audience, and those fifteen hundred beings crowded together
> and overwhelmed by the nervous exhaustion which comes toward the end
> of a performance, remained victorious by virtue of her marble flesh, and that
> sex of hers which was powerful enough to destroy this whole assembly and
> remain unaffected in return.

MONTMARTRE

This hill, the highest in Paris, topped by the bulbous white basilica of the Sacré-Coeur, is famed for its army of artists and charming, steep, winding streets. The Butte is just one of Montmartre's five literary neighborhoods. The other four—Lower Montmartre, La Nouvelle Athènes, Place de Clichy, and Batignolles—each have their own offbeat literary history.

La Butte de Montmartre

The place to start exploring is the top of the hill, where Gérard de Nerval, its first literary resident, wrote in his book of essays *La Bohème galante*:

> Here there are windmills, cabarets, rustic pleasances, quiet little streets lined
> with cottages, farms and half-wild gardens, meadows diversified with min-
> iature precipices and springs gushing from clayey soil, oases of verdure in
> which goats frolic under the watchful eye of the little girls, sure-footed as
> mountaineers, who mind them.

Enchanted though he was by Montmartre's rustic charm, Nerval wasn't there as a tourist. He had been committed to a mental clinic in March 1841, arranged by his friend Théophile Gautier, who was concerned about a severe attack of the dementia which had been plaguing Nerval off and on for several years. Dr. Esprit Blanche's establishment was in the Folie Sandrin, the handsome eighteenth-century mansion at No. 22 rue Norvins, where a plaque commemorates the doctor and his famous patient. While in treatment, Nerval wrote a "journal of madness," which later evolved into his dazzling story "Aurélia." After eight months in Dr. Blanche's care, Nerval emerged feeling healthy and lucid, and far from renouncing his "illness," he believed that his hallucinations were poetic visions. He felt, as did his friends, that he was possessed by a divine madness: "*Ici a commencé pour moi ce que j'appellerai l'épanchement du songe dans la vie réelle*" ("Here began for me what I would call the outflow of dream into real life").

VERLAINE AND RIMBAUD

In the summer of 1871, after Paul Verlaine, then twenty-seven, lost his job as a civil servant at the Hôtel de Ville, he and his young wife, Mathilde, moved into the home of her bourgeois parents, the Mauté de Fleurvilles on Rue Nicolet. The house is still standing, at No. 14, where a Ville de Paris plaque tells what happened, but without the darker details.

Ironically, it was Verlaine's mother-in-law who urged him to invite Arthur Rimbaud to

Verlaine and Rimbaud at the left in Henri Fantin-Latour's *Un Coin de Table*, 1872, Musée d'Orsay

stay with the family. This cultivated lady, a former piano student of Chopin and Debussy's teacher at the time, was thrilled by the verses mailed to her son-in-law by the unknown poet. "Come, dear great soul," Verlaine wrote, believing he was addressing a mature man. But Arthur Rimbaud was less than seventeen when he knocked on their door on September 10, 1871, and a rude, coarse, unkempt boy at that.

Rimbaud, who despised all bourgeois attitudes, responded to Mme Mauté's and Mathilde's well-meaning but patronizing reception with grunts. But Verlaine, after reading *Le Bateau ivre* and hearing the "devilishly seductive" boy Rimbaud expand on his vision of the poet as a seer, was ready to follow him anywhere. So "Rimbe" and "Verlomphe" embarked on what Rimbaud called "a long, immense, and reasoned disordering of all the senses" in quest of a new, visionary poetic language, with absinthe as their holy sacrament. Their outrageous behavior alienated them not only from the family, but from Verlaine's circle of poet friends, the "Vilains Bonshommes," who were considered the most avant-garde poets of their time, although Rimbaud found them hopelessly conventional and made no secret of his contempt.

A month after Rimbaud's arrival, M. Mauté returned from a long hunting trip and ordered the disruptive boy out of the house. But the family's season in hell was just beginning.

One night Verlaine returned home drunk, beat the pregnant Mathilde, and tried to set her hair on fire. Later he flung his three-month-old son Georges against the bedroom wall. Miraculously, the baby was unhurt. Outraged, M. Mauté threw his son-in-law out of the house. Verlaine moved into the room he had rented for Rimbaud in Montparnasse, but when Mathilde threatened divorce, he returned to her at Rue Nicolet, and Rimbaud went home to his mother in Charleville, by the Belgian frontier.

After a few months of impeccable behavior, Verlaine came home one night with stab wounds in his thighs. The boy was back.

In July 1872 the two poets left Paris, first travelling to Belgium, then England, then back to Brussels where, on July 19, 1873, Verlaine shot Rimbaud with a revolver, luckily only grazing his wrist. The court sentenced Verlaine to two years in prison.

Rimbaud took off for the Middle East and North Africa, never to write poetry again. His work, barely known to begin with, was forgotten. But in 1884, after Verlaine published some of Rimbaud's poems, which he knew by heart, in his book *Les Poètes maudits*, France began awakening to the genius of the wild boy from Charleville.

Max Jacob in front of the Bateau Lavoir

AT THE BATEAU-LAVOIR

The Bateau-Lavoir was a ramshackle cluster of wooden buildings with dirt-cheap artist's studios, so nicknamed by Max Jacob after the washerwomen's barges on the Seine. He called it "the central laboratory of modern art," because young Picasso worked here from 1904 to 1912, as did Modigliani, Braque, Jean Gris, and Kees van Dongen at various times. The original structure burned to the ground in 1970, but a replica was constructed at its site, No. 13 place Émile-Goudeau, with memorabilia from its heyday in a display window.

Max Jacob, poet, art critic, and painter, met Picasso at his first show in Paris in 1901, and was the first writer to take an interest in his work. In the winter of 1903-1904, Picasso met another kindred spirit, Guillaume Apollinaire, whom he introduced to Jacob. Apollinaire brought his fellow poet and art critic André Salmon into the circle, and the three became

Marcel Aymé's Walker-through-Walls, sculpture by Jean Marais

musketeer-like champions of the new art. Apollinaire wrote his first article about Picasso in 1905 and published the first book-length study of Cubism eight years later.

In 1909, after Jacob had a radiant vision of Christ and the Virgin in his sad little room at No. 7 rue Ravignan, he converted to Catholicism, with Picasso acting as godfather at the baptism. Jacob practiced the faith devotedly for the rest of his life (though not without guilt over his homosexuality). Still Jewish in the eyes of the Nazis, however, he was arrested on February 24, 1944, at the monastery where he lived in Saint-Benoît-sur-Loire and taken to the detention center in Drancy outside Paris, where he died of pneumonia two weeks later.

GERTRUDE STEIN

In the autumn of 1905, art connoisseur Leo Stein bought a water-color by Picasso, and his friend Henri-Pierre Roché, later the author of *Jules et Jim*, took him to meet the artist at the Bateau-Lavoir. After Leo introduced Picasso to his sister Gertrude, the Steins began collecting his work, and Picasso and his mistress Fernande Olivier became fixtures at their Saturday evenings at No. 27 rue de Fleurus.

Picasso soon asked Gertrude to sit for a portrait. Over that winter and the following spring she made the long trek from Montparnasse to his studio no less than ninety times. After the last sitting, Picasso scraped the face off the canvas in frustration and left for his summer in Spain. When he returned in the fall of 1906, his vision transformed by the African and primitive Iberian sculpture he had been absorbing, and with no further sittings, he painted a mask-like face, very different in style from the body. When people remarked that she did not look like her portrait, he said, "She will." He was right, as Man Ray's photograph of Stein sixteen years later would prove.

MARCEL AYMÉ

A few steps up Rue Ravignon is the narrow, block-long street where Marcel Aymé's delightful story "Le Passe-muraille" ("The Walker-through-Walls") begins:

> There lived in Montmartre, on the third floor of No. 75 *bis* rue d'Orchampt,
> an excellent man named Dutilleul who possessed the singular gift of being
> able to walk through walls without experiencing any discomfort.

After becoming aware of his gift, this timid clerk can't think of anything much to do with it. But the insufferable highhandedness of his superior at the ministry gives him an idea:

he pokes his head through the wall of the boss's office and shouts "Sir, you are a scoundrel, a blockhead and a mountebank," repeating the intrusion again and again until the man is carted off to a madhouse.

After that, Dutilleul becomes a veritable Arsène Lupin. He robs banks and jewelry shops, leaves notes as "the werewolf," and becomes a celebrity, albeit an anonymous one, all over France. Everything goes fine until an encounter with a ravishing blonde on Rue Lepic changes his life. Swept up in love, he makes a careless blunder and ends up in a most uncomfortable position, as depicted in the sculpture by Jean Marais at Place Marcel Aymé showing the excellent man struggling to emerge from a wall.

Aymé lived in the apartment house at No. 26 rue Norvins (now No. 2 place Marcel Aymé) from 1934, the year after his first big success with *La Jument verte* (*The Green Mare*), until his death in 1967. His popularity during his early period came from animal fables treated with an ironical modern eye. *Les Contes du chat perché* (*The Wonderful Farm*) remains popular with children worldwide.

Louis-Ferdinand Céline in the early 1930s

During the Occupation, Aymé hobnobbed with reactionary and anti-Semitic writers and artists in Montmartre. He published in anti-Semitic magazines, but since his pieces did not deal with race or politics, unlike those of his friend Céline, he was not charged with collaboration.

After the war, in his novel *Uranus* and his collection of stories *Le Vin de Paris* (*The Wine of Paris*), Aymé wrote about the vicious and cowardly behavior of the French during the Occupation and the post-war purge of collaborators, genuine or falsely accused. Work during his last two decades was dominated by theater (his play *Clérambard* was a hit in Paris and New York) and film adaptations of his stories.

CÉLINE

In August 1929 Dr. Louis-Ferdinand Destouches, who practiced medicine in the nearby industrial suburb of Clichy, moved to a top-floor apartment No. 98 rue Lepic, where he lived for a decade, first with the American dancer Elizabeth Craig, who left him in 1933, and then with another dancer, Lucette Almanzor, who later became his wife. He spent his nights writing the explosive novel *Voyage au bout de la nuit* (*Journey to the End of the Night*), published in 1932 under his pen name, Louis-Ferdinand Céline. In this brilliant, misanthropic, scatological, exuberantly written work, his alter ego Bardamu's stream of consciousness narrative rockets along on the rails of the three-dot technique (…) Céline invented. Though the novel was based on his experience as a soldier in World War I, his travels in colonial Africa and big-city America, and his medical practice, it is hallucinatory in style. In one section, Bardamu leads the showgirl Tania up to the Place du Tertre where it dawns on him as they settle into a café that all the people on the square are dead. The ghosts take to the sky:

> Twisting and turning, the phantoms pour from all directions, the ghosts of a thousand heroic battles . . . They pursue, they challenge, they charge one another, centuries against centuries. For a long while, the north is cluttered with their abominable mêlée. The bluish horizon detaches itself, at last the day rises through the big rent they've made in the night while escaping.

The book became a best seller, made Céline famous, and brought him enormous critical esteem. But after the commercial and critical failure of his next book, *Mort à credit* (*Death on the Installment Plan*), he wrote his first anti-Semitic work, *Bagatelles pour un massacre,* predicting a war instigated by the Jews in which the naïve French would be led to the slaughter.

In December 1939, with the *drôle de guerre* under way, Céline gave up his apartment and volunteered as a physician on a French Navy transport. After a collision with a British ship put it out of service, he and Lucette moved back to Montmartre, to a fourth-floor flat at No. 4 rue Girardon, and he took a job at another clinic.

During the Occupation, Céline socialized with Nazi officials and collaborationist writers, and published anti-Semitic articles. In June 1944, a week after D-day, he fled with Lucette and their cat Bébert to Germany, where his eight-month stay included a stint as house doctor at the castle of Sigmaringen, with the *crème de la crème* of French collaborationist officialdom gathered around Marshal Pétain. Just over a month before the German surrender, he managed to escape to Denmark, where he had deposited a cache of gold.

When the French issued an extradition request at the end of 1945, the Danish government arrested Céline, holding him under surveillance, but he managed to prolong his stay in Denmark through legal maneuvers until 1951, returning to France only after he had been granted an amnesty. This amnesty was based, officially, on the Médaille Militaire he won for bravery under fire in World War I.

Céline's first five novels after the war were ignored by the press, which treated him as a pariah. Ironically, the one that returned him to critical and commercial success, *D'un château l'autre* (*Castle to Castle*) in 1957, was based on his bizarre experiences in Germany and Denmark. But the taint of anti-Semitism, which never faded, remains difficult for admirers of his writing to reconcile with his work.

When Céline died in the Paris suburb of Meudon on July 1, 1961, his death went largely unnoticed, overshadowed as it was by Hemingway's suicide the following day.

TRISTAN TZARA

La Maison de Tristan Tzara, the clean Modernist house cut into the wooded hillside at No. 15 avenue Junot, is far from what one might expect of the founder of a movement that he described as:

Freedom: Dada Dada Dada, a roaring of tense colors, and interlacing of opposites and of all contradictions, grotesques, inconsistencies: LIFE.

Launched in wartime Zürich, then a hotbed of draft dodgers, political rebels, and intellectuals, Dada was a wild, anarchic, nihilistic, radically anti-art, anti-establishment, and outrageously playful movement (its very name is nonsense). But its aim was dead serious: to demolish the political and cultural past of the Western world.

Tzara was twenty when he and his friends began publishing their magazine *Dada* in 1916. Born Sami Rosenstock in a remote town in Romania, this small dandyish poet with a monocle had the words, the charisma, and the ability to shock that catapulted the movement to international fame.

In 1921 Tzara moved to Paris to join early Dadaists Marcel Duchamp, Francis Picabia, and Man Ray with their new supporters André Breton, Louis Aragon, and Philippe Soupault, who took part in Dada's public manifestations of disgust. But two years later the new boys broke with Tzara and launched their own Surrealist movement.

Tristan Tzara, on the left, the word DADA on his forehead, at a 1920 Dadaist get-together

In the spring of 1924 he met a young Swedish art student named Greta Knutson at La Cigale in Montmartre, where his play *Mouchoir de nuages* was on the boards. It was *le coup de foudre*, love at first sight. Greta's wealthy family gave the newlyweds the money to build a house. The couple hired Adolf Loos, one of the great figures in Modernist architecture, who designed two austere cubes one atop the other, completed in 1926. After the marriage broke up seven years later, Tzara left the house and settled in Saint Germain-des-Prés. For all his many accomplishments during the course of his life—highly regarded poetry, perceptive studies of primitive and modern art, support of the Republicans during the Spanish Civil War, distinguished Résistance leader during World War II—he could never outgrow his image as the youthful "father of Dada."

He died in 1963 and is buried in Montparnasse Cemetery.

THE LAPIN AGILE

During the late nineteenth and early twentieth century, this colorful cabaret at No. 22 rue des Saules was a popular spot with Guillaume Apollinaire, André Salmon, Max Jacob, Francis Carco, Pierre Mac Orlan, and Roland Dorgelès, whose outstanding war novel *Les Croix de bois* (*Wooden Crosses*) was edged out for the 1919 Prix Goncourt by Proust's *A l'ombre des jeunes filles en fleurs* (*Within a Budding Grove*) by only two votes.

In 1910 Dorgelès, who hated what the painters at the Bateau-Lavoir were doing to art, came up with an idea for exposing them to ridicule. He tied a paintbrush to the tail of the cabaret owner's pet donkey, Lolo, dipped its tail into pots of paint, and held a canvas for the beast to slap colors on. He entitled the result "And the Sun Went Down over the Adriatic" and submitted it to the Salon des Indépendents as a "futurist" painting. It received favorable notices and sold for four hundred francs.

Looking just as it did when Utrillo made his innumerable paintings, the Lapin is still jumping, with jolly cabaret songs performed nightly by talented youngsters.

Lower Montmartre

Lower Montmartre is the garish sex and entertainment district at the foot of the Butte, along and around Boulevard de Clichy. The Moulin Rouge, the Folies Pigalle, the Elysées Montmartre, sex shops, sex shows, bars, and clubs dominate the area, with Place Blanche and Place Pigalle the twin hubs of activity.

Until 1860 the Wall of the Farmers General ran down the middle of the boulevard, where the esplanade is now. With the toll wall demolished, the area became Paris's main place for *louche* entertainment. In Maupassant's *Bel Ami*, published in 1885, Georges Duroy's bourgeois mistress Mme de Marelle makes him take her to La Reine Blanche, a dance hall at Place Blanche on the site of today's Moulin Rouge, where "she held tightly to his arm, scared and pleased, casting delighted glances at the whores and the pimps."

On November 28, 1906, Colette put on a show called *Rêve d'Égypte* at the Moulin Rouge with her very butch cross-dressing lover Missy, the marquise de Belboeuf, as her partner. Wearing a man's suit and pith helmet, Missy played the role of an archeologist who discovers a remarkably curvaceous mummy and removes the bands of cloth. When Colette emerged from the wrappings seemingly nude, Missy kissed her on the lips.

The riot police had to be called in to clear the house.

THE POPE OF SURREALISM

On January 1, 1922, André Breton, then twenty-five, and his bride Simone settled into a studio overlooking Place Blanche. Except for the five years he spent in America during and after World War II, he remained in this unremarkable building at No. 42 rue Fontaine until his death forty-four years later. It would become the center of the Surrealist revolution.

For the first time in seven years, Breton had a place of his own rather than a cot in an army barracks or a room in a cheap hotel. He could afford it thanks to his job as advisor to collector Jacques Doucet on manuscripts and artworks, and to the allowance Simone received from her affluent parents. For himself, Breton collected works by his friends Max Ernst, Francis Picabia, Man Ray, and Marcel Duchamp, along with paintings by Picasso,

Braque, and De Chirico. He also began assembling his amazing wall of masks and fetishes from Africa and Oceania now owned by the Centre Georges Pompidou's Musée d'Art Moderne.

Breton's routine was a model of regularity: work all day at Doucet's archive (now kept at the Bibliothèque Sainte-Geneviève); between 6:30 and 7:30 hold court at the Café Cyrano on Place Blanche; dine with fellow Surrealists at a cheap restaurant or at his place; and after dinner, play games and psychological experiments. His favorite literary game was the "cadavre exquis": words were written at random on folded sheets of paper, circulated around the room, and without knowledge of what words were written on them, the group collectively created phrases. The name of this game came from one of its first results: "Le cadavre exquis boira le vin nouveau" ("The exquisite corpse will drink the young wine"). The Surrealists also practiced hypnosis as an aid to attaining their goal of "psychic automatism in its pure state."

THE HARLEM OF PARIS

In the 1920s there were so many African American musicians playing in the jazz clubs along Rue Fontaine and its tributaries that this part of Lower Montmartre became known as "The Harlem of Paris." In 1924 Langston Hughes, the future poet laureate of the Harlem of New York, then twenty-two, took a job as a busboy at Le Grand Duc, at the corner of Rue Fontaine and Rue Pigalle. One of his first published poems was called "Jazz Band in a Parisian Cabaret":

> Play that thing, Jazz band!
> Play it for the lords and ladies,
> For the dukes and counts,
> For the whores and the gigolos,
> For the American millionaires,
> And the school teachers
> Out on a spree . . .

TOP Colette and Missy in a stage performance, 1906

BOTTOM Young Langston Hughes

The Surrealists, particularly Philippe Soupault, were fascinated by jazz. While many audiences enjoyed the upbeat music as a novelty, he saw it as a liberating new musical form, its improvisation a musical counterpart of the free-flowing spontaneous technique of automatic writing. In Soupault's 1927 novel *Le Nègre* the narrator spends night after night at the Tempo-Club in quest of his hero, the Afro-Caribbean drummer and drug dealer Edgar Manning.

The Surrealist Adventure, with Louis Aragon, André Breton, Philippe Soupault and Raymond Queneau, in the 1920s

Jean Cocteau also loved jazz, but for its explosive energy rather than for its musical qualities. He used to sit in (badly) on drums.

The Harlem of Paris was popular with white American writers as well, including the man who invented the phrase "the Jazz Age," F. Scott Fitzgerald. In 1925, Fitzgerald made friends with Ada "Bricktop" Smith, the redheaded African American hostess at Le Grand Duc who later became the owner of Bricktop's, the era's most successful club. Cole Porter also became a friend and wrote "Miss Otis Regrets" for her. Fitzgerald later said, "My greatest claim to fame is that I discovered Bricktop before Cole Porter."

In "Babylon Revisited," Fitzgerald's recovering alcoholic Charlie Wales takes a look at some of his old haunts, including Bricktop's, "where he had parted with so many hours and so much money," and in Hemingway's *The Sun Also Rises*, Jake Barnes and Lady Brett Ashley dance at Zelli's, another popular jazz club.

DIVINE MEETS DARLING

In Jean Genet's novel *Our Lady of the Flowers,* a prisoner named Jean fantasizes at night in his cell about a transvestite named Divine, her lover and pimp Darling Daintyfoot, and other extraordinary characters. The main story takes place in Montmartre, where Divine is a hooker. On her first night in the district, at three in the morning, as she gets up from a bench on the almost deserted esplanade at Place Pigalle, a tipsy young man bumps into her. After a "bantering and dangerous conversation," she takes him to her garret on Rue Caulincourt. The next morning, having figured out that he must be a pimp, she fears that he will beat and rob her. But encouraged by the successful night they had in bed, she takes a risk:

> Without quite knowing where the adventure would lead, rather as a bird is
> said to go into a serpent's mouth, she said, not quite voluntarily and in a kind
> of trance: "Stay," and added hesitantly, "if you want to."
> "No kidding, you feel that way about me?"
> Darling stayed.

L'ASSOMMOIR

The Goutte d'Or district on the eastern fringe of Montmartre has absorbed wave after wave of desperately poor immigrants—Italian, Polish, Jewish, now North African. Before them all came the rural French, who are the subject of Émile Zola's novel *L'Assommoir,* set in the 1850s and 1860s. The title comes from an old slang term for a shop selling rot-gut booze. Place de l'Assommoir, a small, desolate modern square, is named for the novel.

Gervaise, a pretty but lame young woman from Provence who has been dumped by her unfaithful lover, works as a laundress in the public washhouse, scratching out a living for herself and her two young children. Her lackluster neighbor Coupeau, a roofer, marries her, and she starts to save money to open a laundry shop of her own. But when Coupeau falls from a roof and is incapacitated, she has to spend all her savings on his medical care, his booze, and on supporting the family. Zola allows Gervaise one moment of happiness when the blacksmith Goujet loans her the money she needs, no strings attached. Her shop prospers and becomes a cozy social center:

Gervaise with her bucket, title page of Émile Zola's *L'Assommoir*

> She enjoyed putting her iron down for a minute and going out to the doorway to beam at the street at large, bursting with the shopkeeper's pride in her own little bit of pavement. The Rue de la Goutte d'Or belonged to her, and so did the streets nearby and all the neighborhood. Standing there with her white bodice, bare-armed and with her fair hair blowing loose from the flurry of work, she could crane her neck and take in with a glance left and right to each end of the street, the whole scene, people, houses, road, and sky.

"I wanted to depict the inevitable downfall of a working-class family in the polluted atmosphere of our urban areas," said Zola. Soon enough, Gervaise is drawn to her destruction, ending up a half-crazed alcoholic and starving to death behind the staircase of her tenement house.

Zola portrayed the poor not as saints, but as complex characters capable of viciousness as well as good. In so doing he angered the Left, who liked to think of the poor as simple, good-hearted folk crushed by those in power. From the Right came outrage about the violent scenes, such as a fight between Gervaise and Virginie in the washhouse, the sordid sexuality, and the crude slang. The controversy made Zola, only moderately well-known at the time, the most talked-about writer in France. Published in 1877, *L'Assommoir* became a landmark in literary history, confirming the dominance of the naturalist school, with him its unquestioned leader.

MONTMARTRE CEMETERY

Incongruously, one of the most important cemeteries in Paris is in Lower Montmartre. Toward the end of his life, Heinrich Heine had a dream about it:

> It was a bright and early morning and I was walking in the cemetery at Montmartre, where I proposed to be buried one day—it's quiet and you're

not disturbed nearly so much as you are at Père Lachaise. The tombstones were gleaming in the rising sun, and lo! in front of every tombstone stood a pair of highly polished shoes, women's or men's, according to whether the sleepers down below were married women, spinsters, or men. It was like a big hotel where the bootblack goes from door to door as soon as it is light and neatly and carefully places the footwear where it belongs. All the occupants of the grave were still fast asleep, but there was a magnificent shine on the polished boots, as if they had been polished by angels, and the whole picture seemed to say, "Yes, we shall rise again and begin a new life."

An abandoned limestone quarry at the foot of the Butte de Montmartre, this terrain became a dumping ground for victims of the Revolution and was consecrated as a cemetery in 1825.

The first celebrated writer buried here was Stendhal, born Henri-Marie Beyle, who died in 1842. A bronze medallion portrait of him is set into the red marble gravestone. Heine followed fourteen years later, a white marble bust atop his tomb, which is inscribed with lines of his verse. Heine's loyal French wife, Mathilde, is with him.

Over the next forty years, a number of other leading writers checked into Heine's "hotel": poetess Marceline Desbordes-Valmore; *Scènes de la vie de bohème* author Henri Mürger; Alfred de Vigny; Théophile Gautier; Alexandre Dumas *fils*; and Edmond and Jules de Goncourt.

The comte de Lautréamont (*né* Isadore Ducasse), author of *Les Chants de Maldoror*, died during the Prussian siege of Paris in 1870, at twenty-four. No one claimed the body, and he was buried in a common grave.

Émile Zola was buried here a few days after his death in 1902. Six years later his remains were transferred to the Panthéon. The original tomb is now a memorial. Mme Zola and Zola's two children by his mistress Jeanne Rozerot, Dr. Marguerite and Dr. Jacques Zola, are buried here.

In Genet's *Our Lady of the Flowers*, Divine is accompanied to her grave by "the girl-queens and the boy-queens, the aunties, fags and Nellies," and, showing up late, Darling Daintyfoot.

The entrance to the cemetery is at the end of Avenue Rachel, off Boulevard de Clichy.

La Nouvelle Athènes

GEORGE SAND

The cradle of the Romantic movement, "La Nouvelle Athènes," as its developers christened it, was the western half of today's Ninth Arrondissement, sloping gently uphill from the Grands-Boulevards to Lower Montmartre. The great actors Talma and Mlle Mars, the painter Géricault, along with many other artists, pioneered the district in the early nineteenth century.

After they wintered in Majorca (because of Chopin's health) and spent the summer in Nohant, George Sand and her lover returned to Paris in the fall of 1839, renting separate domiciles at No. 16 (today No. 20) rue Pigalle, a quiet rural street at that time. Chopin took an apartment in the main house and Sand took twin pavilions at the rear of the garden, where she lived with her children, eleven-year-old Solange and sixteen-year-old Maurice, who was studying painting with Delacroix. Sand's friend Balzac described her house:

George Sand, etching by Desmadryl after the 1838 painting by Auguste Charpentier now in the Musée de la Vie Romantique

> The salon where she receives is full of superb Chinese vases that are filled with flowers. The furniture is green. There is a cabinet full of curiosities, pictures by Delacroix, her portrait by Calamatta. Chopin is always there. The piano is magnificent. She smokes cigarettes and nothing else. One climbs to her apartment by a straight ugly staircase. Her bedroom is brown, her bed is two mattresses on the floor *à la turque*.

This was a happy time for Sand and Chopin. He liked her children, and they him. Sand, six years his elder, gave Chopin the motherly attention he needed, and the music he was producing thrilled her. As was her habit, Sand wrote from midnight to dawn, with no let-up in her staggering literary flow.

In 1842 the ménage moved to the Square d'Orléans, a secluded London-style private square entered at No. 80 rue Taitbout (and open for the public weekdays only). Sand's and Chopin's studios were kitty-corner across the courtyard, hers at No. 5, above the coach entrance, and his on the ground floor at No. 9. Thanks to Sand's friend Charlotte Marliani, who opened her large apartment at No. 7 nightly to Sand's and Chopin's circle of writers, artists, and musicians, their social life was very exciting. Among the regulars were Balzac, Delacroix, the exiled Polish poet Adam Mickiewicz, Heinrich Heine, the actress Marie Dorval, and Pauline Viardot, a brilliant young singer who took piano lessons from Chopin. The heroine of *Consuelo*, one of Sand's most successful novels, was based on Pauline.

For Chopin, the nine years he spent with Sand were the most productive of his life, composing most of his greatest works during the period. They broke up in 1847 and both left this lovely square.

THE MUSÉE DE LA VIE ROMANTIQUE

At the height of the Romantic period, Dutch-born painter Ary Scheffer's weekly salon at No. 16 rue Chaptal drew *le Tout-Paris* of the intellect and the arts. Neighbors George

Sand, Chopin, Géricault, and Delacroix were regulars. Other guests included Liszt, Rossini, Pauline and Louis Viardot, and Turgenev.

Scheffer was one of the most successful painters of his time, due largely to his post as art teacher to Louis-Philippe's children. When their father unexpectedly came to the throne in 1830, the king made Scheffer the official court painter.

In 1855 Scheffer talked Charles Dickens into sitting for a portrait, much to Dickens's regret. He was in Paris writing a novel under a tight deadline and the long sittings drove him crazy. "I can scarcely express how uneasy and unsettled it makes me to sit, sit, sit, with *Little Dorrit* on my mind," he wrote his friend Foster. And when the portrait was finished, Dickens didn't think it was a good likeness.

Ary Scheffer's home and studios are now the Musée de la Vie Romantique. The ground floor of the house is devoted to George Sand, whose salon has been reassembled as it was in Nohant, including her glamorous 1838 portrait by Auguste Charpentier. Another room displays her letters, manuscripts, first editions, and quite skillful artwork.

RUE DES MARTYRS

In the early 1850s Baudelaire made the Brasserie des Martyrs, at No. 9 rue des Martyrs, his headquarters. He had been living nearby on Rue Pigalle, translating Poe's stories and writing critiques of music and art. Other habitués were his photographer friend Nadar, Gustave Courbet, and Henri Mürger, whose *Scènes de la vie de bohème* had launched the bohemian vogue a few years earlier.

Edmond and Jules de Goncourt also lived nearby, on Rue Saint-Georges, from 1849 to 1863. In their *Journal* entry of May 18, 1857, they described the brasserie as "a tavern and a cavern of all the great men without a name, of all the bohemias of petty journalism."

In November that same year, young Alphonse Daudet arrived from his native Languedoc. He lived with his elder brother on the Left Bank, but was captivated by this place. In his memoir *Trente ans de Paris*, he wrote:

> It would take a volume to describe the Brasserie table by table. Here, the thinkers' table—dark hair, beards trembling, an acrid odor of tobacco, cabbage soup, and philosophy. Farther on, dark blue jackets, berets, animal cries, jokes, witticisms; over here, the artists, painters and sculptors . . . And here now are the women, former models, faded beauties, with strange names like Titine de Barancy and Louise Coup-de-Couteau.

One of those beauties was Marie Rieu, a former model twice Daudet's age who became his mistress, and inspired the character of young Jean's mistress Fanny in *Sapho*, the author's *roman à clef* about his early years in Paris.

Rue de Martyrs was also noted for its lesbian bars and eating establishments. In Zola's *Nana*, the heroine and her friend Satin dine at Laure Piédfer's *table d'hôte*:

> This Laure was a lady of fifty whose swelling contours were tightly laced
> by belts and corsets. More women came in one after another, and each one
> craned up to reach over the saucers piled on the counter to kiss Laure on the
> mouth with tender familiarity while the monstrous creature tried with tears
> in her eyes to divide her attentions as to make nobody jealous.

Colette and her cross-dressing lover Missy, the Marquise de Belboeuf, used to cruise the bars on this street, picking up young showgirls and taking them back to Missy's *garçonnière* for parties of a very private nature.

TURGENEV AND THE VIARDOTS

In 1843 Ivan Turgenev, then twenty-five, met and fell under the spell of the twenty-two-year-old Spanish contralto Pauline Viardot-Garcia at the Saint Petersburg Opera. She was a homely woman, but one of the most charismatic divas of her time. Turgenev also met her husband, French impresario Louis Viardot. Twenty years Pauline's elder, he was open-minded about her affairs. It is not known for certain whether Turgenev's love was ever consummated. If so, it was probably for only a brief period in 1848, when he suddenly began addressing her as "beloved angel" and "the only most loved" in his letters.

An odd sort of ménage developed, with Turgenev living with or in close proximity to the Viardots in France and elsewhere in Europe, where all his major works, including *A Sportsman's Sketches* and *Fathers and Sons*, were written, far from his native Russia.

Ivan Turgenev,
photograph by Nadar

From 1871 until his death twelve years later he lived with the Viardots in their townhouse at No. 50 *bis* (then No. 48) rue de Douai, still there, with a plaque. On the ground floor was a large music room where Pauline held her weekly salon. Turgenev lived in a four-room suite on the top floor. To hear Pauline sing during the day, he had an acoustical tube installed between the music room and his study. She called it "Turgenev's ear."

At one of Pauline's musical evenings in 1875, Turgenev met a young American writing his first novel. The following Sunday he took Henry James to the Rue du Faubourg Saint-Honoré to meet his best friend, Gustave Flaubert.

UBU ROI

Alfred Jarry became famous overnight, on December 11, 1896, when his play *Ubu Roi* premiered at the Théâtre Nouveau at No. 15 rue Blanche. The first word set off a riot: "*Merdre!*"

It was the first time the M-word had been spoken onstage. Pandemonium reigned for a quarter of an hour before the audience quieted down and the performance could go on, though shouting flared up throughout.

The hero Père Ubu is a comic monster par excellence. Urged on by his Lady Macbeth-like wife Mère Ubu, this obese, cartoonishly grotesque, amoral captain in King Wenceslaus's royal guard slaughters his master, becomes King of Poland, and goes on to commit all manner of other ludicrously heinous deeds in this and two further plays, *Ubu Cocu* and *Ubu enchaîné*. A new word entered the French language: *ubuesque*, meaning cowardly and cruel.

William Butler Yeats was in the audience. "Feeling bound to support the most spirited party," he cheered for the play. But, as he recounted in his *Autobiography*:

> . . . that night at the Hôtel Corneille I am very sad, for comedy, objectivity, has displayed its growing power once more. I say, after S. Mallarmé, after Verlaine, after G. Moreau, after Puvis de Chavannes, after our own verse, after the faint mixed tints of Conder, what more is possible? After us the Savage God.

The absurdist bomb thrown onto the Parisian stage in the era of ethereal Symbolism, gritty naturalism, and the "well-made play," made the twenty-three-year-old Jarry a hero of the *avant-garde*. In coming decades he would become a patron saint of the Dadaists, the Surrealists, and the Theater of the Absurd.

ZOLA IN LA NOUVELLE ATHÈNES

In 1874, when his *Rougon-Macquart* cycle of novels was beginning to draw attention, Émile Zola moved with his wife Alexandrine from working-class Batignolles to No. 21 rue Saint-Georges. Three years later they moved to No. 23 rue Ballou (then rue de Boulogne) where other naturalist writers—Huysmans, Céard, Maupassant—sought him out. In 1878, thanks to his best seller *L'Assommoir*, Zola bought a house on the Seine in Médan. From this point on, he and Alexandrine spent half their year in the city and half in the country.

In 1888 Zola, then forty-eight, fell in love with Jeanne Rozerot, a pretty twenty-one-year-old laundress at the house in Médan. He rented her an apartment in Paris, at No. 66 rue Saint-Lazarre. The following year they had a daughter, and two years later, a son. Zola, who doted on Jeanne and their children, did all in his power to keep the affair secret, but in 1891 an anonymous letter-writer tipped Alexandrine off. In a rage, she smashed up Jeanne's apartment. Luckily, Jeanne and the children were out at the time. The affair continued, and Alexandrine managed to live with it, but an undercurrent of tension between her and her husband remained.

In 1889 the Zolas moved to the three-story town house at No. 21 *bis* rue de Bruxelles. It was here that Zola drafted *J'Accuse*, his open letter to the French president accusing the army of framing the innocent Captain Dreyfus for treason. Published in Georges Clemenceau's newspaper *L'Aurore* on January 13, 1898, the polemic electrified the nation and brought the disparate groups supporting Dreyfus together into a strong, cohesive movement. It also made Émile Zola enemy number one of the ultranationalist supporters of the army and the Church.

On the night of September 29, 1902, with the Dreyfus Affair dragging on, Zola died of carbon monoxide poisoning in his sleep. Alexandrine would have died too, but she passed out while trying to get out of bed and fell to the floor, where the concentration of gas in the air was thinner. The police ruled the death accidental.

In 1953 the Paris newspaper *Libération* published a letter from a M. Hacquin claiming that he *knew* Zola had been murdered because a close friend of his had been one of the killers. In a deathbed confession in 1927, this friend had described to Hacquin how he and others went up on the roof of Zola's house that night and blocked the exhaust vent with rags. Early the next morning they returned to remove the rags and dispose of the evidence.

Place de Clichy

Place de Clichy is the Times Square of Paris, though with drastically scaled down dimensions. A crossroad of seven streets, avenues, and boulevards, it features several cinemas, lights and billboards, a score of restaurants, bistros, and cafés, and a constant flow of people night and day. The big, lively *belle époque* Brasserie Wepler on the northeastern corner is hardly what might be called a literary café—but that was precisely its attraction to two writers who had no use for the polite world of literature, or the polite world at all.

CÉLINE AND MILLER

Though Louis-Ferdinand Céline was no regular café-goer, the Wepler was conveniently placed between his Montmartre apartment and the clinic where he practiced medicine in the industrial suburb of Clichy. In *Journey to the End of the Night*, the hero Bardamu finds himself at Place de Clichy at three turning points in his life, the first during the novel's opening scene at the outbreak of World War I, in which he leaps up from a table at the café and falls in with a passing regiment. The next thing he knows he's on a country road being shot at by Germans.

Coincidentally, in March 1932 Henry Miller and his sidekick Alfred Perlès moved to Clichy, where their apartment at No. 4 rue Anatole-France was a few blocks from Céline's clinic on Rue Fanny, making the wild men of French and American letters unwitting neighbors in this thoroughly unliterary spot. Céline had just finished his first novel, and Miller was just finishing his first, *Tropic of Cancer*, alternating between feverish bouts at his trusty Underwood and literary-erotic romps with Anaïs Nin. For a break, he would walk down Avenue de Clichy to the Wepler, keeping an eye out, as ever, for women:

LEFT Émile Zola, photograph by Nadar

RIGHT Place de Clichy around 1930, the Wepler is the big café to the right of the monument

Approaching the Place de Clichy toward evening I pass the little whore with the wooden stump who stands opposite the Gaumont Palace day in and day out. She doesn't look a day over eighteen. Has her regular customers I suppose. After midnight she stands there in her black rig rooted to the spot. Back of her is the little alleyway that blazes like an inferno.

Like the semi-fictionalized Henry of *Tropic of Cancer*, Céline's alter ego, Bardamu, also eyes the *péripatéticiennes*:

You've doubtless noticed the two prostitutes waiting at the corner of the Rue des Dames. They fill in the few weary hours separating deep night and early dawn. Thanks to them, life perseveres through the darkness. With their handbags chock-full of prescriptions, all-purpose handkerchiefs, and photos of children in the country, they are the connecting link.

Céline and Miller had much in common. Besides being first-time novelists living far from the literary heart of Paris and utterly unknown in those circles, they were old for literary beginners. Céline was thirty-eight when *Journey* came out in October 1932, and Miller was forty-two when *Tropic of Cancer* was finally released. And in the case of both writers, their success was *à scandale*.

When *Journey to the End of the Night* became a literary sensation, Miller was cheered by the similarities between Céline and himself, both personally and in the way they wrote. To him, Céline was one of that holy band of literary heroes—Rabelais, Villon, Boccaccio— "for whom shit was shit and angels angels."

Céline, whose English was excellent, read *Tropic of Cancer* when it came out and sent

Miller his congratulations, along with a bit of advice: "Learn to be wrong—the world is filled with people who are right—and that is why it disheartens so."

Batignolles

Like Montmartre, Batignolles was an independent village before being annexed to Paris in 1860. But unlike its hilly neighbor, Batignolles is flat and bare, its straight, narrow streets laid out in a grid. Small nineteenth-century working-class apartment houses predominate, their tall wooden shutters chipped and the paint faded.

VERLAINE

In 1851, at the age of seven, Paul Verlaine moved with his parents from his native Metz to No. 10 rue Nollet (then called Rue Saint-Louis), where they lived until the death of his father, a retired army captain, in 1865. Paul and his mother then moved around the corner to No. 26 rue Lécluse, where a plaque on the house commemorates the poet.

Verlaine was a scrawny, prematurely balding young man with dangerously violent tendencies, but his mother doted on him to the point of obsession—even though he beat her and twice threatened to kill her, knife in hand.

Inspired by Baudelaire's vision in *Les Fleurs du mal*, he began writing poetry at fourteen, published his first poem at nineteen, and his first collection, *Poèmes saturniens*, at twenty-two. He left Batignolles in August of 1870 when he married seventeen-year-old Mathilde Mauté de Fleurville. For her wedding present he composed a collection of poems called *La Bonne Chanson*. In "L'Écolière" ("Schoolgirl") the poet tells his young bride:

> Je t'apprendrai, chère petite,
> Ce qu'il te fallait savoir peu
> Jusqu'à ce présent où palpite
> Ton beau corps dans mes bras de dieu.

> (I will teach you things, my little girl,
> You did not need to know until now,
> When your lovely body
> Is trembling in my god-like arms.)

ZOLA AND THE IMPRESSIONISTS

Years before the Impressionists were first scornfully called "impressionists," young Émile Zola, introduced to their work by Paul Cézanne, his friend since *lycée* in Aix-en-Provence, became one of their most ardent supporters. In Zola's review of the Salon of 1866 he wrote with such enthusiasm about these avant-garde painters and their mentor Edouard Manet,

Frédéric Bazille's *L'Atelier de Bazille, Rue de la Condamine*, 1870, Zola on the staircase talking with Renoir. Painting at the Musée d'Orsay.

and savaged the Academic artists so harshly, that the magazine he was working for gave him the sack.

The following year Zola, then twenty-seven, moved from the Latin Quarter to Batignolles to be close to the revolutionary artists. Gathered around Manet were Renoir, Monet, Bazille, Cézanne for a time, and Fantin-Latour (though he was not of their *plein air* school). They met at the legendary Café Guerbois at No. 9 avenue de Clichy, steps away from the first of Zola's three residences in Batignolles, No. 1 rue Moncey (now Dautancourt). His friends Manet, Fantin-Latour, and Bazille all featured him in paintings, now at the Musée d'Orsay.

Besides his involvement with the painters, Zola also enjoyed his first success as a novelist in 1867 with *Thérèse Raquin,* and developed the plan for his "natural and social history of a family under the Second Empire," the *Rougon-Macquart* series of twenty novels. The first three, *La Fortune des Rougon, La Curée,* and *Le Ventre de Paris,* were written here.

In *L'Oeuvre* (*The Masterpiece*), the most personal of his novels, published in 1886, Zola's alter ego, the writer Pierre Sandoz, lives in a cottage on Rue Nollet, where he invites the painter Claude Lantier to dine with five other comrades from the early years of the *plein air* school and the Salon des Refusés. The uncompromising artist Lantier, modeled partly on Cézanne, has recently returned to Paris after working for several years in the country and looks forward eagerly to engaging in one of their passionate discussions, but the talk is no longer about art. It is all about success.

Claude felt plainly now that some link with the past was broken, and he wondered if they were really gone forever, those hectic friendly meetings he used to enjoy before anything had come between them and none had desired to monopolize all the glory. Today, the battle was on, and each man fighting greedily for himself. The rift was there, though barely visible as yet, which had cracked apart all the old sworn friendships and which would one day shatter them into a thousand pieces.

After seven years in Batignolles, Zola and his wife Alexandrine, whom he had married in 1870, moved down the hill to the relatively ritzy Nouvelle Athènes district.

THE BEAUX QUARTIERS

During the 1850s, Napoléon III and Baron Haussmann launched the development of "Les Beaux Quartiers," the whole west of today's Paris, which fanned out from the Place de la

Concorde all the way to the Bois de Boulogne and the northwestern fringes of the city. Sparsely populated when the development began, by the late nineteenth century most of the leading bourgeois and many aristocrats were living in the area, some in private mansions, but most in the six-story buildings with balconies on the second and fifth floors standardized by the baron. Imagine horse-drawn carriages on the broad tree-lined boulevards of the district, gas-lit at night, and you have the backdrop of the *belle époque* world brought to life by Émile Zola, Guy de Maupassant, and especially Marcel Proust, who lived almost all his life in a narrow slice of the Beaux Quartiers between the Champs-Élysées and the Parc Monceau. Proust stored the impressions which, in one of the most astounding feats of literary alchemy of all time, he would turn into the gold of *In Search of Lost Time*.

Proust Country

THE ALLÉE MARCEL PROUST

This pretty pebble walk winding through the lower gardens of the Champs-Élysées only a few blocks from his childhood home is where Proust used to play as a boy. In *Swann's Way*, the narrator finds it boring at first to be taken there by the nursemaid, but the place comes alive when Gilberte, the lovely, fickle daughter of Swann and Odette, enters the scene. One winter day, he has given up hope of her coming:

> And suddenly the sky was rent in two: between the punch-and-judy and the horses, against the opening horizon, I had just seen, like a miraculous sign, Mademoiselle's blue feather. And now Gilberte was running at full speed toward me, sparkling and rosy beneath a cap trimmed with fur, enlivened by the cold, by being late, by her anxiety for a game; shortly before she reached me, she slipped on a piece of ice and, either to regain her balance, or because it appeared to her graceful, or else pretending that she was on skates, it was with outstretched arms that she smilingly advanced, as though to embrace me.

THE PROUST FAMILY'S FIRST HOME

On September 3, 1870, newlyweds Dr. Adrien and Mme Jeanne Proust moved into the little Haussmann-style building at No. 8 rue Roy. He was thirty-six, his bride twenty-one. Less than a month later, Marcel was conceived. They remained in Paris throughout the German shelling of the city that winter, the anarchy of the Commune the next spring, and its decimation by the French army during "the Bloody Week" in May, because it was unthinkable for Dr. Proust to abandon his medical duties, and Mme Proust refused to leave his side. But once the fighting was over, and with her pregnancy advancing, they

Haussmann's Paris, seen from the top of the Arc de Triomphe

moved to the rambling country home of her uncle Louis Weil at No. 96 rue de la Fontaine in Auteuil to await the baby. After Marcel's birth on July 10, 1871, they moved back to their apartment, where they remained until Marcel's brother Robert was born two years later.

BOULEVARD MALESHERBES

Proust grew up in the Haussmann-style building at No. 9 boulevard Malesherbes, by the Madeleine, where the family moved in 1873. Their spacious first-floor apartment was on the interior courtyard, with windows overlooking the little street to the rear. Its elaborately molded walls and ceilings can be seen from the street, above the restaurant at No. 4 rue de Surène.

Marcel's father was a brilliant physician, the author of many books on public health. He was born in the village of Illiers near Chartres (the Combray of *In Search of Lost Time*) to a traditional middle-class French Catholic family of modest means, though he was an atheist, as was his wife Jeanne, *née* Weil, from a wealthy, cultivated, Parisian nonreligious Jewish family. Marcel was brought up in his father's family religion, but was far more attached to his mother, who awakened in him his passion for literature. He was a bit frail, but not chronically unhealthy until his first asthma crisis at the age of nine.

Proust attended the Lycée Condorcet, a short walk from home. The salons that he frequented as a young man were also within walking distance. He was a homosexual and grew into a gossip-loving aesthete, and a literary dabbler, with a groupie's avidity for the tiniest detail about the lives and loves of the aristocracy. He published a few sketches in newspapers and magazines and one book, *Les Plaisirs et les jours*, a collection of youthful stories and poems with a preface by Anatole France, watercolors by Madeleine Lemaire, and musical commentaries by Venezuelan composer Reynaldo Hahn, with whom he had his most intense amorous relationship as a young man. At the age of twenty-eight, when Proust moved to his next home, there was little to indicate that this "epitome of a bourgeois snob and a dilettante," as André Gide then considered him, would become a writer of any importance.

RUE DE COURCELLES

In October 1899, Proust moved with his parents to a huge apartment at No. 45 in the chic Parc Monceau neighborhood, as befit Dr. Proust's lofty standing. Proust's father died in 1903, followed by his mother two years later when he suffered a nervous collapse from the loss and was hospitalized for six weeks. Afterward, he spent several months in seclusion at the Hôtel des Réservoirs in Versailles. When his mother's will was read, he and his brother Robert were amazed to learn that they had inherited a fortune, since their parents had always claimed to be living at the limit of their means. Each inherited the equivalent of six million dollars in today's money, with an income of some $180,000 a year.

His brother having married and moved out, Marcel gave up the lease on this vast, expensive apartment laden with sad memories and moved to a place of his own.

NO. 102 BOULEVARD HAUSSMANN

On December 26, 1906, Proust took a *premier étage* apartment in this attractive nineteenth-century neoclassical-style building, which had been owned by his mother's late uncle Louis and was now the property of one of his aunts. He wrote to a friend, "It is a very ugly apartment, dusty, overhung by trees, everything I hate, which I have taken because it is the only one I have been able to find that Maman knew."

In his bedroom, where he spent virtually all his time, Proust had the windows overlooking the boulevard covered with heavy drapes, and settled into his constant battle between his asthma and his writing, though he later acknowledged that if he had not been ill, he would never have written *In Search of Lost Time*.

It was here in January 1909 that the incident which inspired the celebrated madeleine scene in *Swann's Way* took place. In real life, it was toast and tea, rather than madeleine and tea, that triggered the memories, and his housekeeper Céline Cottin served him the memory-jogging ingredients, not the narrator's mother, as in the book.

On the advice of his poetess friend Anna de Noailles he had his bedroom lined with cork in 1910 because of his sensitivity to noise. The only item of furniture Proust used was the bed, where he wrote, dozed, and talked with his housekeepers, first Céline Cottin, then Céleste Albaret.

By the end of 1912, he had completed *Du côté de chez Swann* (*Swann's Way*) and *Le côté de Guermantes* (*The Guermantes Way*), and had written a good deal of *Le Temps retrouvé*

(*Time Regained*). After rejections by a number of editors, including André Gide (much to Gide's later embarrassment), Proust signed a contract with Editions Grasset, paying the printing costs himself, a common practice for beginning novelists. *Swann's Way* came out in November of 1913, with the other novels scheduled for publication over the following two years. This became impossible because of the strict paper rationing imposed during World War I. Proust felt frustrated at first, but the delay was a godsend, giving him four unanticipated years to further develop the cycle. He greatly expanded the early version of *The Guermantes Way*, wrote *A l'ombre des jeunes filles en fleur* (*Within a Budding Grove*), and planned and wrote parts of other novels.

A month after the publication of *Swann's Way*, Proust suffered a shock second only to the death of his mother when Alfred Agostinelli suddenly left his service and without a word returned to his native Monaco. Proust had fallen in love with him six years earlier when he hired the then-teenager as a driver in Normandy, and then kept him on as a chauffeur and secretary. In May 1914 Agostinelli, who was training to become a pilot, was killed in a plane crash in the sea off Antibes. Proust poured his grief into the captivating character of Albertine.

When his aunt sold the building in 1919, Proust was forced to move, a terrible wrench for the invalid so secure in his cocoon.

Banque SNVB, which owns the building, opens Proust's former bedroom to visitors on Thursdays from 2:00 PM to 4:00 PM. The walls have been redone as they were when the cork panels were installed: corn yellow. Proust's famous bed is no longer here but can be seen in his reconstituted bedroom in the Musée Carnavalet. A plaque on the Boulevard Haussmann building commemorates Proust's residence.

PROUST'S FRIENDS AND MUSES

Proust began attending salons in 1889, the year he received his *baccalauréat* (with a first prize for French composition). His favorite salon was that of Geneviève Straus, the mother of his *lycée* classmate Jacques Bizet, at No. 134 boulevard Haussmann. This fascinating and highly cultivated lady was the daughter of composer Jacques Halévy, the widow of Georges Bizet, and wife of art collector Émile Straus, the chief counsel for the Rothschilds. Here Proust met a handsome, refined gentleman named Charles Haas, an art connoisseur, Franco-Prussian War hero, son of a Rothschild partner, and the first Jewish man to become a member of the supremely elite Jockey Club. Haas became the model for the look and style, though not the tormented love life, of Charles Swann. As for Mme Straus, she became one of Proust's most important inspirations for the bright, witty side of the duchesse de Guermantes.

Also in 1889 he began attending the star-studded salon of Mme Arman de Caillavet in the handsome Renaissance-style townhouse at No. 12 avenue Hoche, where he met his first established writer, Anatole France. He was Mme Arman's lover, she his despotic muse, locking him in his study and refusing to let him leave until he had completed his daily quota of text. She helped make him one of the most successful writers of his time (Académie Française in 1896, Nobel Prize in Literature in 1921). He became Proust's model for the writer Bergotte in *In Search of Lost Time*, Mme Arman de Caillavet one of his models for Mme Verdurin, and her son Gaston and daughter-in-law Jeanne for Saint-Loup and Gilberte.

When the Dreyfus Affair exploded, Anatole France became an active champion of the wrongly accused captain, as did young Proust, who solicited signatures on his behalf, even in high society circles hostile to Dreyfus.

In 1894, at artist Madeleine Lemaire's salon in her townhouse at No. 31 rue de Monceau, Reynaldo Hahn introduced Proust to Count Robert de Montesquiou. This exemplary *fin de siècle* dandy and sometime poet befriended Proust and later became, much to his displeasure, the principal model for the Baron de Charlus. On May 30 of that year, Montesquiou escorted Proust to the home of his cousin the Countess de Greffulhe, which stood at No. 8 rue d'Astorg. Proust's reception by this impeccably elegant lady at the pinnacle of French society opened the doors for him to other aristocrats' homes. The countess also became his main model for the look and bearing of duchesse de Guermantes, as her husband would become for all aspects of the insufferable duke.

But not all Proust's acquaintances were quite so respectable. Albert Le Cuziat, the former manager of a gay bathhouse he frequented on Rue Godot-de-Mauroy, opened a male brothel in 1916 in the Hôtel Marigny, a hostelry still in business at No. 11 rue de l'Arcade. Given Proust's adoration of his late mother, it seems strange that he gave Le Cuziat enough furniture from her apartment to equip the reception area and one of the assignation rooms. Albert Le Cuziat became the model for Charlus's devious factotum Jupien in *In Search of Lost Time*. Proust's visits were mainly for specialized gossip, not much, it seems, for the more banal offerings of the house.

Parc Monceau

In 1773 Louis-Philippe d'Orléans hired the painter-architect-writer Carmontelle to build him a large private garden in a stretch of countryside he owned on the Plain of Monceau. The result was a *jardin à l'anglaise* dotted with a pyramid, a pagoda, false medieval ruins, and other surprises. Haussmann's great landscape architect Alphand refurbished the park in the 1860s, and its discreet charms have been delighting the bourgeoisie ever since.

FLAUBERT'S SUNDAYS

Flaubert is often seen as a hermit, a sort of latter-day Saint Anthony struggling alone in the desert of his native Normandy, and indeed he did live most of his life and write most of his works there. But he also spent a great deal of time in Paris, particularly in the 1860s and 1870s, when he became a familiar figure at Princess Mathilde's salon and joined his fellow writers at the Magny dinners. He also did a staggering amount of research in libraries in Paris, particularly on *L'Éducation sentimentale* (*Sentimental Education*), which came out in 1869, the year he moved to an apartment on the fourth floor of the brick building at No. 4 rue Murillo overlooking the Parc Monceau. Here he began receiving fellow writers on Sundays: his most admired and beloved friend Ivan Turgenev, prickly Edmond de Goncourt, and young novelists Joris-Karl Huysmans, Alphonse Daudet, and Émile Zola. This was also where he began teaching his protégé Guy de Maupassant the craft of writing.

Gustave Flaubert,
photograph by Nadar

Much of the action in *Sentimental Education* takes place in the 1840s, with the political excitement reaching its peak during the Revolution of 1848. These were fiery times, but Flaubert's phlegmatic, constitutionally apolitical hero Frédéric Moreau sleepwalks through them, lost in his impossible love for Mme Arnoux. The naturalist writers—Zola, the Goncourts, and others—loved the uncompromising objectivity of this work and made it the cornerstone of their aesthetic. But the public was not ready for antiheroes. Novelist Henry Céard, a disciple of Zola, came to Rue Murillo to express his admiration for the novel. Flaubert was moved by the tribute, but, as Céard recounted in his memoirs, Flaubert said:

> "So you like it do you? All the same, this book is doomed to failure, because it doesn't do this." He put his long, powerful hands together in the shape of a pyramid. "The public," he explained, "wants works which exalt its illusions, whereas *Sentimental Education* . . ." And here he turned his big hands upside down and opened them as if to let his dreams fall into a bottomless pit . . .

Luckily, Flaubert was able to live well on his inheritance. But in the early 1870s, catastrophic investment of his capital by his niece's husband, who managed his estate, brought him to ruin. In 1875 he was forced to give up this apartment.

GUY DE MAUPASSANT

To the left of the Avenue de Courcelles gate and a few steps into the Parc Monceau stands a lively memorial to this dashing mustachioed writer, who lived in several places in the vicinity. Born in Normandy in 1850, his mother a childhood friend of Flaubert, Guy was an active young man with two all-consuming interests: sports and women. After school and the army (he served in the Franco-Prussian War) he drifted into a civil service job, but in his mid-twenties decided to become a writer, and Flaubert took him under his wing.

In 1876 or 1877 Maupassant contracted a virulent strain of syphilis. Eye and heart pains and migraines began attacking him as early as 1880, the year his great story "Boule de suif" came out. The standout in a collection of natural-ist stories by Zola and five disciples called *Soirées de Médan*, it catapulted him to fame. Driven to feverish activity by the early death he knew awaited him, Maupassant wrote all six of his novels (*Une Vie, Bel Ami, Mont Oriel, Pierre et Jean, Fort comme la mort,* and *Notre coeur*), more than two hundred stories, an enormous amount of journalism, and three collections of travel sketches during the following decade. He also lived the life of a seemingly carefree man about town and sailed the coasts of Normandy and the Mediterranean on his yachts *Bel Ami, Bel Ami II,* and *Bel Ami III*.

Guy de Maupassant, photograph by Nadar

In *Bel Ami*, after the hero Georges Duroy has made it big as a newspaper-man and seducer of women, he arrives at the park for a tryst with Mme Walter, his boss's wife:

As soon as he had greeted her, she said:

"What a lot of people there are in this garden."

He jumped at the opportunity.

"Yes, aren't there. Do you want to go somewhere else?"

"Where can we go?"

"Anywhere, in a cab for example. If you let down the blind on your side, you'll be well hidden."

"Yes, I'd prefer that, I'm terrified here."

"All right, meet me at the gate on the outer boulevard. I'll bring a cab."

And he hurried off. As soon as they had rejoined each other and she had carefully let down the blind on her side, she enquired:

"Where did you tell the driver to go?"

Georges replied:

"Don't worry yourself about that, he knows what to do."

The Plaine Monceau

COLETTE ON THE PLAINE MONCEAU

In 1897 Colette and her husband Willy moved from Rue Jacob to a sixth-floor apartment at No. 93 rue de Courcelles, on the broad plain stretching out to the north of the Parc

Monceau developed by Baron Haussmann for "the mushroom aristocracy," Zola's term for the Second Empire's *nouveaux riches.*

In *Claudine in Paris*, Colette's sprightly heroine is amazed to run into Luce, her dimwitted former schoolmate from Burgundy, in the fashionable Parc Monceau, and impeccably outfitted at that. Claudine accompanies her to a plush apartment on Rue de Courcelles, where she discovers that the lover paying the bills, the fat old bald man whose photograph she notices, is Luce's uncle, the widower of her deceased aunt. Claudine finds the arrangement "too modern for me."

In 1904, as their marriage was starting to unravel, Colette and Willy moved to No. 177 *bis* rue de Courcelles, taking the top two floors of the building. Two years later she left him and took up with the Marquise de Belboeuf, a rich cross-dresser known as Missy. In 1908 Missy bought and renovated a spacious townhouse at No. 25 rue Torricelli with an apartment for Colette on the ground floor and a duplex for herself upstairs. This was Colette's home base until she left Missy in 1911 for publisher Henry de Jouvenel.

BOULEVARD MALESHERBES

Ultrawide Boulevard Malesherbes, completed in 1866, was the main street of the new district. Zola's model for his courtesan's Renaissance-style mansion in *Nana* was that of the self-styled comtesse Valtesse de la Bigne at No. 98. *Née* Louise Delabigne, this gorgeous redhead from Normandy made her considerable fortune thanks to a series of wealthy admirers, one of whom, Baron de Sagan, financed the house. Valtesse had a rule: only men who could afford her would be allowed into her bedroom. When Dumas *fils* asked to see her famous bed, she told him, "No, it is not within your means, *mon cher maître.*" However, because she was sure his intentions were purely literary, she allowed Zola to enter it while he was researching *Nana.*

In the novel, having sold his last piece of land to satisfy Nana's insatiable need for money, Count Muffat rushes back from Normandy and, desperate to see her, bursts into her bedroom:

> . . . facing him, there was the gold and silver bed, shining in all the fresh splendour of its chasing, a throne wide enough for Nana to stretch out the glory of her naked limbs, an altar of Byzantine luxury, worthy of the omnipotence of her sex, which at that very moment lay openly displayed in the religious immodesty of an awe-inspiring idol. And beside her, beneath the snowy gleam of her bosom, amid her godlike triumph, there wallowed a shameful, decrepit thing, a comic and lamentable ruin, the Marquis de Chouard in his night-shirt.
>
> The Count had clasped his hands together and, shuddering from head to foot, kept repeating:
>
> "God! Oh, God!"

The man in bed with her is Muffat's father-in-law.

Valtesse's mansion at No. 98 is gone, replaced by an apartment house in 1904, but the town house next door at No. 100 was also designed by her architect Jules Février. Her fabulous bed still exists in the collection of the Musée des Arts Décoratifs.

DUMAS *PÈRE* AND *FILS* ON PLACE DU GÉNÉRAL-CATROUX

Called Place Malesherbes when it was created in 1862, this graceful square cut into four grassy triangles was renamed after World War II for an early supporter of Général de Gaulle. On the western lawn stands the liveliest memorial to any writer, Gustave Doré's sculpted tribute to Alexandre Dumas *père*, a life-sized bronze of the bulky author sitting atop the massive pedestal, a great clump of curly hair on his head, while below, a group of three readers is devouring one of his 646 books and D'Artagnan strikes a pose, sword in hand.

Alexandre Dumas *père*
photograph by Nadar

Despite Dumas's incredible success as a novelist and playwright, his extravagances and foolhardy business ventures left him deeply in debt late in life. In the mid-1860s, the prodigal father lived with his daughter at No. 107 boulevard Malesherbes or with his son Alexandre Dumas *fils* at No. 98 avenue de Villiers.

Dumas *fils* was a successful novelist and playwright, best known for *Camille*, but unlike his *père*, he managed his money. He called his father "a big child who I had when I was very young." Dumas *père* died in 1870 at his home in Puys, near Dieppe, at age sixty-seven.

A somber statue of Dumas *fils* by Saint-Marceaux stands in the eastern triangle.

MALLARMÉ'S TUESDAYS

Stéphane Mallarmé and his family moved to a small fourth-floor apartment close to the Lycée Condorcet, where he taught English, in 1875. The building still stands at No. 89 rue de Rome, where a plaque honors the poet. Five years later, he began holding his illustrious Tuesday evening salon, where Verlaine, Leconte de Lisle, Maeterlinck, Zola, Huysmans, Maupassant, and fledgling writers André Gide, Paul Claudel, and Paul Valéry were among those who gathered around his table, along with visiting foreigners Henry James, George Moore, Oscar Wilde, and Algernon Swinburne. Mallarmé's poetry ("The Afternoon of a Faun," "The Tomb of Edgar Poe") made him the acknowledged leader of the Symbolist school, but it wasn't until 1884 that he became known to the wider reading public, thanks to Verlaine's study of his work in *Les Poètes maudits*, and particularly to Huysmans's novel *A Rebours*, which describes the mysterious spell that Mallarmé's exquisite verse cast over the aesthete Jean des Esseintes.

Mallarmé lived here until his retirement from teaching in 1891, when he settled with his wife and daughter in their country house on the Seine at Pont de Valvins, now the Musée Stéphane Mallarmé.

GEORGES PEREC'S OULIPO MASTERPIECE

We cannot leave the Plaine Monceau without visiting, at least in our minds, the fictional street of Georges Perec's 1978 novel *La Vie mode d'emploi* (*Life: A User's Manual*). The house is on "Rue Simon-Crubellier," which Perec places in the quadrangle shared by Rue Médéric, Rue Jadin, Rue de Chazelles and Rue Léon-Jost, real streets near the Parc Monceau. The novel describes what we would see if the façade of a large Haussmann-style apartment house were stripped away, revealing, as in a doll's house, the people and objects inside in minute detail, with everything frozen at a single moment. As we traverse the house, the stories of the residents emerge bit by bit—the wealthy world-traveling amateur landscape artist Percival Bartlebooth, his servant Smantf, the jigsaw puzzle-maker Gaspard Winkler, Mme de Beaumont, the Altamonts, TV producer Remi Rorschach—until the narrative reaches its tragic dénouement at 8:00 PM on June 23, 1975.

One of the most brilliant French novels of the twentieth century, *Life: A User's Manual* is also the towering masterpiece of OuLiPo, the Ouvroir de Littérature Potentielle, or Workshop for Potential Literature, founded in 1960 by novelist Raymond Queneau and mathematician François Le Lionnais to explore "forms, new structures that could be used by writers in ways that please them," which the group achieved by inventing formal limitations, or "constraints." For example, Perec wrote one of his novels, *La Disparition* (*A Void*) without using "e," the most commonly used letter in the French language.

OuLiPo's games were anything but frivolous. Perec and his colleagues were turning their backs on a literary history that he characterized as "uniquely preoccupied by its grand uppercase letters (the Work, the Style, the Inspiration, the Vision of the World, the Fundamental Opinions, the Genius, the Creation, etc.)" and putting into practice a vision that considers writing "as practical, as work, as a game."

Perec was a strange, complicated, deeply alienated man, an orphan of World War II and the Holocaust. His Polish-born Jewish father was killed in combat in the French Army in 1940 and his mother deported to Auschwitz. In his 1975 memoir *W ou le souvenir d'enfance* (*W, or The Memory of Childhood*) he deals with the loss that haunted him daily. He died from cancer in 1982, just short of his forty-sixth birthday.

The Faubourg Saint-Honoré

BALZAC'S LAST HOME

When the aristocrats abandoned the Marais at the end of the seventeenth century, one of the prime areas they chose to resettle was the country village of Rouve, later incorporated into Paris as the Faubourg Saint-Honoré, just the sort of neighborhood where Balzac always dreamed of living.

In 1847 he bought and moved into a mansion on Rue Fortunée (now Rue Balzac) in anticipation of his marriage to his beloved Countess Hanska, a widow since 1841. His health had declined badly during her long period of obligatory mourning, as he drove himself at a furious pace to earn money to provide a suitable home for his aristocratic bride-to-be. Once in the mansion, he poured all his energy into renovating and furnishing it, doubling his debt to the equivalent of a million of today's euros in the process, secure in the knowledge that his wealthy wife would foot the bill.

In September 1848 he joined her in Russia, where, after receiving permission from the Czar, she married him on March 14, 1850. But Balzac had suffered a series of heart attacks the previous year, and his health deteriorated rapidly. In May, gravely ill from tuberculosis, he returned to Paris with his bride, and they moved into the house. He died here on August 18, 1850, at fifty-one.

Balzac the royalist and Victor Hugo the democrat were politically at odds, but during Balzac's final illness, Hugo showed himself to be a friend, visiting him twice on his deathbed and delivering a stirring graveside eulogy at Père-Lachaise Cemetery:

> Unbeknownst to himself, whether he wills it or not, with or without his consent, the author of the enormous, extraordinary work belongs to the powerful race of revolutionary writers.

The mansion was torn down in 1890, but there is a lovely secluded garden owned by the Rothschild Foundation, open daily, on the grounds where it stood. The entrance is at No. 22 rue Balzac, where a plaque honors fiction's greatest visionary.

FLAUBERT'S LAST HOME IN PARIS

In May 1875, depressed and financially ruined, Flaubert moved to a modest *pied-à-terre* at No. 240 rue du Faubourg Saint-Honoré. But as at Rue Murillo, he continued to receive his writer friends on Sundays. On December 12, 1875, a newcomer came to call: Henry James. He was thirty-two years old, a Paris correspondent for the *New York Tribune*, just completing his first novel, *Roderick Hudson*. To James, attending the salon made him feel as if he was entering "the councils of the gods."

Today Flaubert is a literary god, the founding father of the modern French novel, the writer who stripped the excesses of romanticism from the form, but his only commercial success was with *Trois Contes* (*Three Tales*) in 1877. It gave him some financial relief, but little emotional lift, as he was struggling with his last novel *Bouvard et Pécuchet*. Except for interruptions to write *Three Tales*, he wrestled with it daily from 1874 until his death six years later. "On some days I feel crushed by this burden," he told Turgenev in 1878. "It seems as if I have no more marrow in my bones, and I carry on like an old horse, worn out but courageous."

He died on May 8, 1880, at fifty-eight, with only the end of the final chapter of *Bouvard et Pécuchet* left to complete. The novel was published the following year with his four-page outline of how the book was to end.

Flaubert had planned to write a second book to be built around the *sottises* (stupid remarks) uttered in bourgeois society which he had been collecting for years. This *Dictionnaire des idées reçues* (*Dictionary of Received Ideas*), as he called it, was edited by friends and first published in 1882. It makes for mordantly funny reading:

ACADEMY, FRENCH Run it down, but try to belong to it if you can.
ACCIDENT Always "regrettable" or "unfortunate" (as if a mishap could ever
be a cause for rejoicing).
ACHILLES Add "fleet-footed": people will think you've read Homer.
ACTRESSES The ruin of young men of good family. Are terribly lascivious,
engage in orgies, run through fortunes, and end up in the workhouse. "I beg
to differ: some make excellent mothers!"

Avenue des Champs-Élysées

Paris's most famous avenue began as a tree-lined promenade for the aristocracy, an extension of the Tuileries Garden. Designed in 1667 by Le Nôtre, the Grand Cours was renamed the Champs-Élysées (Elysian Fields) in 1709, and was extended in 1724 to the top of the hill. Since Napoléon commissioned the Arc de Triomphe in 1806, the Champ-Élysées has been France's premier military parade route.

In Alphonse Daudet's story "Le Siège de Berlin" ("The Seige of Berlin"), which begins at the outbreak of the Franco-Prussian War, an old soldier moves into his granddaughter's

apartment overlooking the Champs-Élysées in order to have a good view of the French army's victory parade. To protect the doddering, octogenarian colonel from the truth, the people around him invent a fictitious military campaign with the French forces advancing inexorably toward Berlin. When he hears the blare of marching bands, he dons his uniform and steps out onto the balcony, only to see German troops marching down the avenue. The old man falls dead crying, "To arms! To arms! The Prussians!"

HEINE AND "LA MOUCHE"

The last years of Heinrich Heine were spent in a fifth-floor apartment overlooking the Champs-Élysées in the building that still stands at No. 3 avenue Matignon, where he is honored by a plaque. Other than yearning to hear the German language, "the loveliest and most euphonious in the world," he adapted quite well to his life in exile. George Sand, Théophile Gautier, and other French writers became friends for life. He wrote to a friend in Germany,

Heinrich Heine, drawing by Charles Gleyre

> If anyone asks you how I'm getting on here, tell them: "Like a fish in water." Or, rather, tell them that when one fish asks another fish how he's getting on, the reply is, "Like Heine in Paris."

However, early in his second decade of exile, a grave spinal disease, the result of a syphilitic infection, began to incapacitate him, and worsened steadily. The last time Heine went out was to witness the revolutionary uprising in February 1848. When a riot broke out, he took refuge in the Louvre and collapsed at the feet of the Venus de Milo. From then on, the "poor, unburied corpse," as he referred to himself, spent his days on a mattress on the floor with his books, papers, and journals scattered around him. Thanks to opium to lessen the pain, the care of his loyal wife Mathilde, and the visits of his many friends, Heine maintained his mental balance, and miraculously, he kept working to the very end, writing some of his finest poetry.

In June 1855, a mysterious young woman came to his apartment to deliver some sheet music from an admirer, a composer in Vienna. It was spiritual love at first sight. He begged her to come back, and she did, every day. She called herself Camilla Selden and was probably born in Prague, but nothing is known about her. Heine called her "La Mouche" because of a fly engraved on a signet ring she wore. He was enchanted by her way of pronouncing German when she read him poetry. On warm days in the fall, she would open the doors to the balcony above the Champs-Élysées, and he would lie propped up in bed watching the bustling life on the avenue below through opera glasses. He died on February 17, 1856, at the age of fifty-eight, after a quarter-century of exile in Paris.

SWANN AND ODETTE

In *Swann's Way*, during a carriage ride at night on the Champs-Élysées, Swann finally discovers a way to express the physical side of his love for Odette. When the carriage stops with a jolt and jostles her, he politely asks permission to readjust the *catleya* orchids in the opening of her décolleté dress, disordered by the impact. "She, who was not used to seeing men behave that way with her, said with a smile: 'No, not at all, that doesn't bother me.'" One thing leads to another . . .

But he was so shy with her that, having succeeded in possessing her that night by starting with arranging the *catleyas*, that either by fear of offending her, or fear of appearing in retrospect to have lied, or lack of boldness in devising a stronger form of demand than that one (which he could use again since it hadn't angered Odette the first time), he used the same pretext the following days.

LE FOUQUET'S

The most celebrated literary patron of this glamorous *belle époque* café, which opened in 1899, is James Joyce. "We dine in Fouquet's very frequently, in fact almost always," he wrote his son Giorgio in July 1934. Joyce could afford it thanks to the court decision in New York the previous December that cleared the way for his publisher to distribute *Ulysses* in America. He sat at the same table every evening and ordered the same menu (oysters, chicken with mushrooms or asparagus, and a cup of fruit or ice cream). He ate little, said little, smoked a lot, and drank several *pichets* of Muscadet.

The day after Christmas in 1937, he invited Samuel Beckett and Peggy Guggenheim to join him and his wife Nora for dinner. Beckett had met the flamboyant American heiress casually a few times before, but that night he ended up in her bed.

Place de l'Étoile

PLACE DE L'ÉTOILE AND *PLACE DE L'ÉTOILE*

Place de l'Étoile, named for the star-shaped array of streets running into it, the Arc de Triomphe in its center, tops the Champs-Élysées. In Patrick Modiano's novel *Place de l'étoile*, set during the World War II Occupation, the brilliant young Jewish writer Raphaël Schlemilovitch is approached by a German officer and asked, "Where is the Place de l'Étoile?" Raphaël points to the left side of his chest.

Published in 1968 when Modiano was twenty-two, *Place de l'étoile* is a kaleidoscopic work blending real and fictional characters. Freud, Proust, Captain Dreyfus, French Gestapo hit men, the collaborationist writers Brasillach and Drieu la Rochelle, Hitler and Eva Braun coexist in this giant literary carrousel gone wild. In it, Raphaël exposes Dr. Louis-Ferdinand Bardamu (the anti-Semite Louis-Ferdinand Céline) as "the greatest Jewish writer of all time."

Modiano was born in Paris in 1945, the son of an Italian Jewish father who hid out in the city during the Occupation, but eventually had to flee, and a Belgian actress mother. Modiano has two obsessions as a writer: Paris (he is an inveterate night walker, prowling every part of the city) and the Occupation. How did people in France, Jews and non-Jews, experience *les années noires*, those shame-filled years that haunt the nation's memory? *Rue des boutiques obscures, Livret de famille, Dora Bruder*, his screenplay for Louis

Malle's *Lacombe Lucien*—in virtually all his writings, he comes back again and again to this theme.

THE FITZGERALDS ON RUE DE TILSITT

> We were going to the Old World to find a new rhythm for our lives with a
> true conviction that we had left our old selves behind forever—and with a
> capital of just over seven thousand dollars.
>
> F. Scott Fitzgerald, *How to Live on Practically Nothing a Year,*
> *Saturday Evening Post,* September 1924

In April 1925 Scott and Zelda Fitzgerald and their four-year-old daughter Scottie moved to a furnished apartment a few steps from the Arc de Triomphe at No. 14 rue de Tilsitt, where they lived for almost a year. They were returning from a long stay on the Côte d'Azur, where Scott finished *The Great Gatsby* and Zelda had an affair with a French aviator.

Scott and Zelda Fitzgerald and their daughter Scottie on one of their many transatlantic crossings in the 1920s

The Fitzgeralds loved the high life—drinks (too many) at the Ritz, dinner at Prunier's—the kinds of establishment he brought to life so vividly in *Tender is the Night.* They were far more at home on the fashionable Right Bank than on the bohemian Left Bank. Even so, within days after his arrival, Fitzgerald made the trek up to Montparnasse to seek the up-and-coming young Ernest Hemingway, with whom he got together often after their awkward first meeting at the Dingo. But the visceral hostility between Ernest and Zelda was barely disguised when the Fitzgeralds hosted the Hemingways here.

Journalist William L. Shirer tells of Fitzgerald staggering into the *Chicago Tribune*'s Paris office to help him and his colleagues James Thurber and Eugene Jolas get the "goddam paper" to press (and then go out for a drink). Most evenings ended when they finally took Fitzgerald home in a taxi. One night when they poured Fitzgerald out of the cab in front of the Rue de Tilsitt house, Zelda shouted down from the balcony, "Scott, you bastard! You're drunk again!" He swore, "I'm sober, darling . . . really . . . I am . . . as . . . as sober . . . as . . . a . . . polar bear."

The Far West

PROUST ON RUE HAMELIN

Rue Hamelin is the colorless street in Chaillot where Marcel Proust lived from October 1919 to his death three years later. His apartment was on the fifth floor of the bland residential building (now a cozy hotel) at No. 44. In a note to Robert de Montesquiou, he called it "a wretched slum which barely holds my miserable pallet." But in *Monsieur Proust*, his devoted housekeeper Céleste Albaret's charming memoir, she says it was "just a picturesque joke" inspired by his nostalgia for the Boulevard Haussmann apartment. He expected his stay here to be temporary, but his steadily worsening health made it impossible to move.

It was here, on December 10, 1919, that his friend Léon Daudet came with wonderful news: *Within a Budding Grove* had won the Prix Goncourt. Now that Proust was famous, readers discovered the previously published *Swann's Way*, which convinced many that the prize was, if anything, six years overdue. Two further novels came out during his lifetime, *The Guermantes Way* and *Sodome et Gomorrhe* (*The Cities of the Plain*), and the remaining three novels of *In Search of Lost Time* were published within a few years after his death.

In September 1922, Proust's health began to decline rapidly. On November 18, he had Céleste send Odilon to the Ritz for iced beer. After he left, Proust told her, "Like everything else, it will come too late." A crisis set in. Céleste sent for his brother Robert and his personal physician, who rushed to his side just as Odilon came back. Ignoring the doctors, Proust said, "Thank you, my dear Odilon, for getting the beer." He slipped into unconsciousness and died at half past five that afternoon.

THE MAISON DE BALZAC

On the run from his creditors, Balzac took refuge in this "provisional shelter" at No. 47 rue Raynouard in rural Passy in November 1840, lying low until February 1847. Now the Balzac Museum, it is rich in objects from his life and work: his meticulously restored study; his famous coffee pot; his turquoise-studded cane; the superb marble bust by David d'Angers; and portraits of Eveline Hanska and his literary contemporaries Hugo, Dumas, and others.

Balzac leased the house under the name of "M de Breugnol," his housekeeper's name, Mme Breugiol, deliberately misspelled. To be allowed in, a caller had to give two passwords, "I am bringing lace from Bruges" and "The plum season has arrived." One feature of the house that he greatly appreciated was its exits on two roads. He even had an escape hatch cut into the floor of the parlor so that he could avoid creditors by slipping into the basement and out the back to Rue du Roc (now Rue Berton) to make his getaway.

Writing twelve to sixteen hours a day, he corrected the whole of the *Comédie humaine* for the collected edition and wrote more than twenty other books, which include the last volume of *Les Illusions perdues*, *Une ténébreuse affaire*, *Mémoires de deux jeunes mariées*, *La Rabouilleuse*, *Splendeurs et Misères des courtisanes*, *La Cousine Bette*, and *Le Cousin Pons*. As he wrote to his beloved Countess Eveline Hanska in Russia, "My arm has almost worn itself out from moving it around while I write."

The pace turned feverish starting in January 1842, when Mme Hanska informed him that her husband had died. Now that the way was open for them to marry, he wanted do so with a reasonably clean financial slate. By the end of 1845, thanks to his prodigious output, he had reduced his debt to 145,521 francs (the equivalent of about seven hundred thousand of today's euros), its lowest level in a decade. But overwork unquestionably hastened his death five years later.

Balzac's study in his museum-house on Rue Raynouard

DR. BLANCHE'S CLINIC

From his study window, Balzac looked down at the Hôtel de Lamballe, a grand but run-down mansion which stood in what is now the garden of the Turkish Embassy, at No. 17 rue d'Ankara. Balzac considered buying and restoring it for his beloved Eveline, but Dr. Esprit Blanche beat him to it. He purchased the house in 1847 and converted it into a mental clinic, sadly remembered for the fates of its two famous literary patients, Gérard de Nerval, who took his own life one icy night in 1855, and Guy de Maupassant, admitted after a suicide attempt on January 7, 1892, with an advanced stage of syphilis ravaging his brain. He died here the following year at forty-two years of age.

APOLLINAIRE

In 1909 Guillaume Apollinaire moved from Montmartre to Auteuil to be near his mistress Marie Laurencin, who lived with her mother. He first lived at No. 15 rue Gros, but when the Great Flood of 1910 made the building uninhabitable, he moved up the street to No. 37. On September 7, 1911, he was arrested there on suspicion of stealing the *Mona Lisa*. The police threw him in La Santé prison and threatened him with deportation (he was an Italian national). After five days of solitary confinement and *interrogation musclée*, he was released for lack of proof. Though he had nothing to do with the theft, newspapers kept attacking him to undermine his credibility as the leading expert on avant-garde art.

The following year, Marie Laurencin broke off their six-year affair. The pain inspired him to write his moving poem "Le Pont Mirabeau," named for the bridge nearby which had been the lovers' special tryst.

FRANÇOIS MAURIAC

The austere Art Deco building at No. 38 rue Théophile Gautier was François Mauriac's address from 1930 to his death forty years later, as the plaque notes. Born in Bordeaux in 1885, he came to Paris as a student in 1905 and stayed to become a writer, but returned frequently to his native Malagar, the setting for his strongest and most characteristic works. They include *Le Désert de l'amour* (*The Desert of Love*, 1925), *Thérèse Desqueyroux* (1927),

François Mauriac in 1951, a year before winning the Nobel Prize

and *Le Noeud de vipères* (*The Vipers' Tangle*, 1932) about the spiritual struggles of his heroes and heroines in the repressive bourgeois society of the small-town French Southwest, novels noted for their austere style and relentlessly tense atmosphere.

Mauriac was also a distinguished essayist and political journalist, a member of the Académie française, and, along with Gide and Malraux, one of the dominant figures in French literature in the 1920s and 1930s. He joined the Résistance during World War II and wrote for underground publications. Afterwards, as a dedicated Gaullist and Catholic, he was treated to endless attacks by the Leftist intellectuals of Saint Germain-des-Prés. Mauriac won the Nobel Prize in Literature in 1952. He died in Paris in 1970 at the age of eighty-four, and was buried in the modest cemetery in Vémars north of Paris, where he had spent much of the war and where there is a museum of his life and work.

MOLIÈRE AND FRIENDS

One block from the cheerful village-like Place Jean-Lorrain is the Auberge du Mouton Blanc at No. 40 rue d'Auteuil, a restaurant opened in 1938 on the site of a seventeenth-century inn of the same name. A plaque reads: "Long ago in this place the Auberge du Mouton Blanc received Molière, Racine, Boileau, La Fontaine, Ninon de Lenclos, La Champeslé."

Molière leased an apartment in the village in 1667 as refuge from domestic strife and professional aggravations. Religious conservatives were attacking him over *Tartuffe* and *Dom Juan*, Racine had betrayed him, Lully was conniving against him at court, and Armande, who remained in their apartment on Rue Saint-Thomas-du-Louvre, was rumored to be having an affair. True or not, there were serious strains in their marriage. Mirroring real life, the lover Alceste in *The Misanthrope*, asks his beloved Célimène to join him in his "*désert*," his refuge far from Paris. She refuses, saying:

> Moi, renoncer au monde avant que de vieillir,
> Et dans votre désert aller m'ensevelir!

> (Me, renounce the world before getting old,
> And go bury myself in your wasteland!)

Molière took rooms first at No. 2 rue d'Auteuil, and then at today's No. 62 rue Théophile Gautier, just a few steps away, which he kept until his death in 1673.

His friend Nicolas Boileau, who had a large estate in Auteuil (where a street is named for him) and Jean de La Fontaine (who has a street here) remained his loyal supporters and drinking companions to the end.

THE BOIS DE BOULOGNE

In 1852, Napoléon III gave the City of Paris the 2,200-acre former royal hunting forest

on the western edge of the city. It was in a shabby state, having been devastated by the forty thousand Russian and British troops who camped here after defeating Napoléon III's uncle in 1814 and 1815, then left to grow wild. Baron Haussmann transformed it into a *jardin à l'anglaise* on a grand scale, very much as we see it today. It became the most fashionable place in Paris for taking the air.

The Bois de Boulogne was one of Proust's favorite places to play as a boy, but this was also where he suffered his first, nearly fatal, asthma attack at the age of nine.

The Bois de Bologne as seen by the narrator at the end of *Swann's Way*

In *Swann's Way*, the Bois is the setting for crucial scenes in Swann's relationship with Odette and the "*petit clan*" of the Verdurins, and the novel ends with the narrator, now a middle-aged man, strolling through the park one November, nostalgic for the social world he knew, which has disappeared. The women he sees now are utterly lacking in the elegant simplicity of Mme Swann, upon whom he used to spy as a boy in the places where fashionable people took their promenades:

> The reality I had known no longer existed. It sufficed that Mme Swann did not appear, in the same attire and at the same moment, for the whole avenue to be altered. The places that we have known belong now only to the little world of space on which we map them for our own convenience. None of them was ever more than a thin slice, held between the contiguous impressions that composed our life at that time; remembrance of a particular form is but regret for a particular moment; and houses, roads, avenues are as fugitive, alas, as the years.

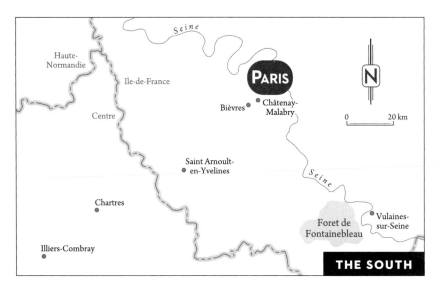

Haute-Normandie

Ile-de-France

Seine

PARIS

Bièvres • Châtenay-Malabry

Centre

Saint Arnoult-en-Yvelines •

Seine

Chartres •

Foret de Fontainebleau

Vulaines-sur-Seine •

Illiers-Combray •

N

0   20 km

THE SOUTH

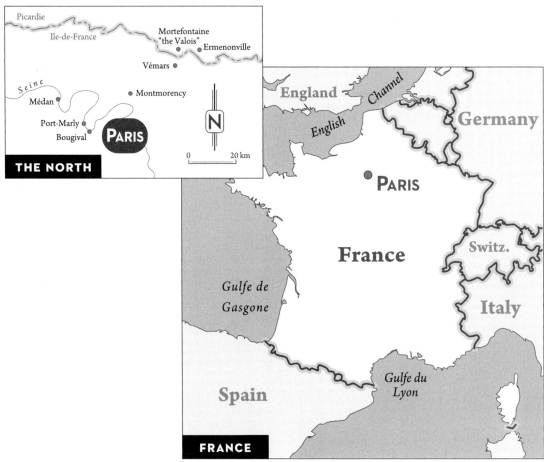

Picardie

Ile-de-France

Mortefontaine "the Valois" •

• Ermenonville

Vémars •

Seine

• Montmorency

Médan •

Port-Marly •

Bougival

PARIS

N

0   20 km

THE NORTH

England

English Channel

Germany

• **PARIS**

Switz.

France

Gulfe de Gasgone

Gulfe du Lyon

Spain

Italy

FRANCE

A Few Places Around Paris

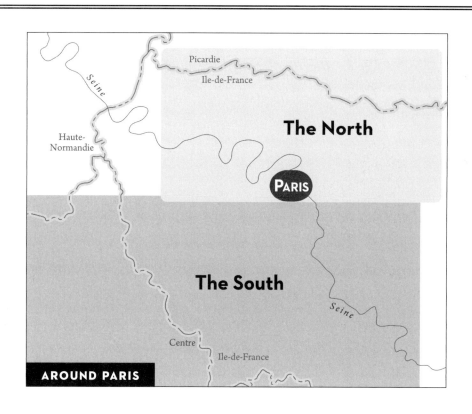

The Near North

JEAN-JACQUES ROUSSEAU IN MONTMORENCY

In April 1756, Jean-Jacques Rousseau, his mistress Thérèse, and her mother moved into L'Hermitage, a house owned by Mme d'Epinay near her château in Montmorency, twelve miles north of the city. "The solitary walker" was delighted with the lovely wooded countryside, and he launched into the most productive period of his life. Socially, however, things became complicated when Rousseau, then forty-four, fell madly in love with the comtesse d'Houdetot, his patroness's sister-in-law, who became his inspiration for the heroine in *Julie, ou la nouvelle Héloïse*. In the novel, the love letters that Saint-Preux sends to Julie are ones that Rousseau wrote to Sophie d'Houdetot. The letters from Julie to Saint-Preux are ones that Rousseau would have loved to have received from the countess, but did not.

On December 15, 1757, Rousseau burned his bridges with Mme d'Epinay and moved to a small house he rented nearby called Mont-Louis. It and its outbuildings now make up the Maison-Musée de Jean-Jacques Rousseau.

The original dwelling has the air of a charming little *maison de cure*. Thérèse's big iron cauldron hangs in the hearth. In Rousseau's bedroom is a pastel portrait of him, a gift from the artist, his friend Quentin de la Tour, acquired by the museum in 2007. What remains of the garden is dotted with lime trees and acacias. But the most touching place is the *donjon*, the tiny one-room cottage at the end of the garden where Rousseau could get all the privacy he needed.

In the four and a half years Rousseau lived in Montmorency, he published three of the most influential books of the eighteenth century: *Julie, ou la Nouvelle Héloïse*, the great precursor of the Romantic movement in literature; *Le Contrat social*, one of the ideological cornerstones of the Revolution ("Man is born free, yet everywhere he is in chains"); and *Emile, ou de l'éducation*, an approach to the education of children so radical that the Parliament of Paris condemned it for advocating a natural religion in which one's conscience is the judge. To avoid arrest, Rousseau fled Mont-Louis on June 9, 1762, and traveled incognito to Switzerland.

JEAN-JACQUES ROUSSEAU IN ERMENONVILLE

In the spring of 1778 Rousseau accepted the hospitality of another admirer, Marquis René de Girardin, and on May 26 moved with Thérèse to a little pavilion in front of the marquis's Château d'Ermenonville, thirty miles northeast of Paris. The marquis started renovating a thatch-roofed house in the orchard for them, but six weeks after his arrival, Rousseau died of a stroke at age sixty-six.

On July 4, he was buried in a torchlight ceremony on the Île des Peupliers, a tiny island in the main lake of the château's lovely park—now the 120-acre Parc Jean-Jacques

Rousseau—inspired by the marquis's reading of *La Nouvelle Héloïse*, and created by him a decade before Rousseau came to live in it. For the tomb the marquis commissioned a sepulcher by Hubert Robert, engraved with the words, "Here lies the man of nature and truth." It became a site of pilgrimage immediately.

Jean-Jacques Rousseau's room in his house in Montmorency

The sepulcher is empty. In 1794 the leaders of the Revolution ordered Rousseau's remains transferred to the Panthéon to be honored as one of the *grands hommes* of France, joining his archenemy Voltaire, already entombed there. (Voltaire always got the better of Rousseau, even in death: He lived almost two decades longer and beat him into the Panthéon by three years.) But if the trailblazing philosopher of nature could have had a say in it, he would have remained in his lovely resting place in the park.

GÉRARD DE NERVAL IN THE VALOIS

Another writer intimately linked to Ermenonville and its surrounding countryside is Gérard de Nerval, who grew up in the adjoining village of Mortefontaine, and was deeply influenced by the nature-loving side of Rousseau. Nerval, whose real name was Gérard Labrunie, was born in Paris in 1808, the son of a surgeon in Napoléon's army. His mother joined her husband on a campaign in Germany, and left him in the care of a wet nurse at seven months of age. Two years later she died of fever in Silesia without ever seeing her son again. He was raised by his great-uncle Antoine Boucher, a grocer in the village. As a boy, Gérard felt drawn to the site of an ancient Roman camp called the Clos de Nerval, from which he would take his *nom de plume*.

This land of mists, lakes, meandering streams, and shadowy forests affected his writing, most evidently in "Sylvie," one of the most enchanting prose pieces in all of French literature. In it, Nerval interweaves memories, dreams, and events, evoking the narrator's idealized love of three very different young women. Late one night at an ancient abbey in the heart of the Ermenonville forest, the narrator comes upon the performance of a medieval mystery play and is captivated by the sight of the angelic blonde Adrienne, his vision of feminine purity. As romantic today as in the pages of "Sylvie," the moody ruins of the twelfth-century Abbaye Royale de Chaalis are surrounded by a vast lawn with tree-shaded water basins and a splendid rose garden.

MAURIAC IN VÉMARS

François Mauriac first saw the Château de la Motte in 1913 when the budding novelist of twenty-eight visited his fiancée Jeanne's parents at their trim Second Empire mansion, today a few miles north of Charles de Gaulle Airport.

Though his deepest attachments were to the Bordeaux country where he grew up and where he set his most famous novels, Mauriac began feeling at home in Vémars during the Occupation. He kept a low profile, leaving the house only for Mass on Sunday and for the occasional walk in the woods, while writing for Résistance publications under his *nom de guerre* of Forez. As a Catholic and outspoken Gaullist, Mauriac was constantly under attack from the intellectual Left after the war. He was glad to put Saint Germain-des-Prés at a bit of a distance, although as one of the most brilliant and bitingly ironic editorialists of his day he was perfectly capable of defending his ideas.

Mauriac spent his last good days in Vémars at the end of August of 1970 before entering a hospital in Paris, where he died on September 1 at eighty-four years old. He and his wife are entombed in the cemetery at Vémars.

The municipality bought the Château de la Motte to save it from the wrecker's ball, and converted the sitting room into a small François Mauriac museum. It contains his ancient Remington, his personal library, and a fine collection of photographs, offering much insight into the life of this Gascon in the land of the Valois.

The Near West

IVAN TURGENEV'S DACHA IN BOUGIVAL

In 1874 Turgenev bought a property called Les Frênes (the Ash Trees) on the banks of the Seine in Bougival, twelve miles west of Paris. He gave his beloved Pauline Viardot and her husband Louis the handsome neoclassical villa already there, and the following year he built himself a tall, slim cottage on the wooded hillside above. He called it a "chalet," but everyone else called it a *"dacha."* He and the Viardots would spend August through November in Bougival, where he hunted and wrote, winter and spring in Paris, and in the summer he visited his vast estate in Russia, which had had five thousand souls when he inherited it from his mother. Turgenev, however, was an outspoken proponent of abolishing serfdom and even spent time in the Czar's jails for his views.

Turgenev was at the height of his glory both in Russia and France during his years at Bougival, where Flaubert, Maupassant, Henry James, Camille Saint-Saëns, and Edgar Fauré were among his many visitors.

The *dacha* is now a charming museum. His study overlooking the Seine, where he wrote his last works, *Virgin Soil* and *Poems in Prose*, and received his visitors, has been reconstituted, as has the bedroom where he died on September 3, 1883, at sixty-five, surrounded by Pauline and his friends.

Besides being one of the troika of greatest Russian novelists of the late nineteenth century, along with Tolstoy and Dostoyevsky, Turgenev was the driving force behind the translation of Russian literature into French and French literature into Russian, translating several of Flaubert's works himself. The museum is a treasure trove of both literatures.

ALEXANDRE DUMAS'S CHÂTEAU DE MONTE-CRISTO IN PORT-MARLY

The Three Musketeers, The Count of Monte Cristo, Queen Margot, and the sequel to *The Three Musketeers, Twenty Years After,* all published in 1844 and 1845, were so wildly successful that

Alexandre Dumas's
Château de Monte-Cristo

Dumas was able to buy five acres of land on a hillside overlooking the Seine in Port-Marly, and to realize his dream of building a château on his own scale—that is, larger-than-life.

Dumas's motto was *"J'aime qui m'aime"*—"I love whoever loves me"—and he meant it. He inaugurated his earthly paradise on July 27, 1847, with a party for six hundred guests. "Friends" kept flocking, but he turned no one away. The thought of this genial giant churning out pages to feed a mob of hangers-on appalled Balzac, himself a prodigal spendthrift. But Dumas thought he could write himself out of any hole.

Six months later, he was broke. His creditors forced him to sell the property the following year.

But the Château de Monte-Cristo remains. It is Renaissance in style with portraits of writers he admired on its elaborately sculpted façade. His own portrait resides above the front door, along with his family's coat of arms and the *"J'aime qui m'aime"* motto. On the grounds, amid springs and false grottoes, he also built a little Gothico-Savoyard pavilion called the Château d'If where he could isolate himself to write. Hilly footpaths thread the wooded park overlooking the Seine, where there is a labyrinth and a pond. Dumas, who was passionate about cooking and eating, stocked the pond with 2,500 fish and 1,200 fresh water shrimp.

If any proof should be needed of Dumas *fils*'s view of his father as "a big child I had when I was very little," the Château de Monte-Cristo is it.

LA MAISON D'EMILE ZOLA IN MÉDAN

The phenomenal success of *L'Assommoir* in 1877 gave Émile Zola the wherewithal to buy a "rabbit hutch," as he described it to Flaubert, on a small plot of land overlooking the Seine in Médan, eighteen miles west of Paris. He immediately started transforming the house, adding on to it as his income increased. *Nana* paid for one of the clunky wings, *Germinal* the other. As the "rabbit hutch" grew, so did his land holdings, eventually encompassing nine acres with a greenhouse, a palm garden, a farm with animals (rabbits included), and a small island in the Seine with a gazebo, where he entertained Turgenev, Edmond de Goncourt, Alphonse Daudet, his publisher Charpentier, and Henry James. From 1878 until his death twenty-four years later, Zola spent six months a year in Médan.

It is the house of a poor boy who has made it big and wants everyone to know it. Everywhere the visitor looks, he is struck by undeniable signs of wealth: the vast dining room with its *fleur de lis* ceiling; the enormous kitchen with its tiled floor and ceiling; the huge billiard room with the coat of arms; the breathtaking study with his motto *Nulla dies sine linea* (no day without a line) above the fireplace. It is here Zola wrote *Nana, Germinal, La Bête humaine*, and many other novels, turned out at a rate of almost one a year until the Dreyfus Affair took over his life. Here he also chaired gatherings of his Naturalist disciples Maupassant, Huysmans, and others, out of which came the 1880 collection of stories *Les Soirées de Médan*.

This house was also where Zola met Jeanne Rozerot, the pretty laundress who became his mistress, bore his two children, and rejuvenated him in the last fourteen years of his life.

MAURICE MAETERLINCK'S CHÂTEAU DE MÉDAN

In 1924 Maurice Maeterlinck bought this handsome fifteenth-century stone hunting lodge, which Ronsard and other poets of the Pléiade group frequented in the sixteenth century when their patron Jean Brinon was the owner. With its clean, aristocratic lines, the Château de Médan makes a striking contrast with Zola's nearby "*château démocratique.*"

The house was in ruins when Maeterlinck acquired it, but he fully restored it, even installing a small theater for his actress wife, Renée Dehan. With the outbreak of war in 1940, they left for America and afterwards settled on the Côte d'Azur, where he died in 1949.

If Maeterlinck is remembered today, it is for his play *Pelléas and Mélisande*, popularized by the opera Debussy based on it, which Maeterlinck hated. But the Belgian-born Symbolist was one of the world's most respected poets and playwrights in the first decades of the twentieth century, greatly admired by such hard-to-please figures as Rainer Maria Rilke and Antonin Artaud, and winner of the Nobel Prize in Literature in 1911. However, post–World War II taste failed to respond to the subtle poetic moods he created.

After the Maeterlincks' departure the château fell back into ruin. It was used as a printing plant for *Combat* until the magazine folded in 1974, then was abandoned. Three years later, a young couple, the Aubin de Malicornes, bought it and did a masterful job of restoration. They receive visitors by appointment only.

The Near South

CHATEAUBRIAND'S VALLÉE-AUX-LOUPS IN CHÂTENAY-MALABRY

In the Middle Ages, the Valley of the Wolves was a primeval forest within easy horseback distance of Paris where lords came to hunt deer and wild boar. For the past two centuries it has been a peaceful valley, deeply marked by the eleven-year residence of François-René de Chateaubriand. His travels in America in 1791 and his life as a combative political figure during the Revolution, Empire, and Restoration are recounted by him in one of the greatest French autobiographies, *Mémoires d'outre-tombe* (*Memoirs from Beyond the Tomb*), which he began writing at the Vallée-aux-Loups:

> The trees which I have planted here are thriving; they are still so small that I provide them with shade when I stand between them and the sun. One day, giving this shade back to me, they will protect my old age as I have protected their youth. I have chosen them from the various climes in which I have wandered; they remind me of my travels and nourish other illusions in the depths of my heart.

These trees stand fifty feet high today, some shading the Tour Villéda, the charming little pavilion in which he wrote.

Chateaubriand was forced to retreat here in 1807 to avoid Napoléon's thunderbolts after comparing him to Nero in print, but he remained close enough to Paris for friends to visit. He described his dwelling as "a small country house, lying amid wooded hills." His additions respected its clean lines, even when he added porticos for the front and rear entrances. Appropriately for the writer considered the bridge between the Classical tradition in French literature and the new Romantic movement, one portico is Greek neoclassic, complete with caryatids, the other is Gothic.

The rooms have been restored in the spirit of the early nineteenth century, with etchings, paintings, and documents that shed light on the writer-diplomat-politician's public and private lives. But the most famous item in the house did not belong to Chateaubriand: it is the Empire settee on which his muse Juliette Récamier posed for Jacques-Louis David.

THE MAISON LITTÉRAIRE DE VICTOR HUGO IN BIÈVRES

While he was living at the Vallée-aux-Loups, Chateaubriand used to ride to the Château des Roches in Bièvres two miles away to attend the literary salon of his friend Bertin the Elder, the director of the prestigious *Journal des Débats*. But the house is best known as the place where Hugo, his wife, Adèle, and their five children spent their summers in the 1830s. Hugo enjoyed playing with the kids along the crystal-clear River Bièvre, and he wrote poetry on a shady little island or in the château. Bertin's daughter Louise, "The Good Fairy," as Hugo called her, was the accomplished musician who composed *La Esméralda*, an opera based on *The Hunchback of Notre-Dame*. She entertained the youngsters while Adèle went off for her trysts with Sainte-Beuve and Victor for his with Juliette Drouet. This early period in his affair with his longtime mistress inspired Hugo's cycle of love poems *La Tristesse d'Olympio*.

In 1991 the Château des Roches was refurbished in 1830s decor and given a new lease on life as the Maison Littéraire de Victor Hugo. Its rich collection of manuscripts, corrected page proofs, and other documents tell us far more about Hugo as a man of letters than does the Maison de Victor Hugo in Paris, which is devoted primarily to him as a public figure.

The Southeast

STÉPHANE MALLARMÉ'S COTTAGE IN VULAINES-SUR-SEINE

At the urging of his friend Edouard Manet, Mallarmé started looking for a house by the Seine, and in 1874 found just the thing: a charming little farmhouse by the Pont de Valvins in the village of Vulaines-sur-Seine, across the river from the Forest of Fontainebleau. "It is at Valvins," he said, "that I build enough energy and freshness of spirit each year." After his retirement from teaching in 1891, he and his wife lived here full-time until his death seven years later.

The property remained in the hands of his descendents, was damaged in a bombing during World War II, purchased by the Seine-et-Marne *département*, restored, and turned into a museum. In the tidy rooms on the ground floor are several objects that have become literary relics, including the wooden table trimmed in leather and copper around which Verlaine, Huysmans, Claudel, Gide, Wilde, Valéry, and so many other poets and men of letters gathered in his Paris apartment. The most famous poem in the museum's collection is "*Autre évential de mademoiselle Mallarmé*" ("Other Fan of Mademoiselle Mallarmé"), five brief, ethereal stanzas he wrote on the panels of one of his daughter Geneviève's fans.

The Far Southwest

THE MOULIN DE VILLENEUVE IN SAINT-ARNOULT-EN-YVELINES

The First Couple of the literary Left from the late 1920s on, Louis Aragon and Elsa Triolet bought the Moulin de Villeneuve in 1951, and lived in it until their deaths, hers at seventy-four in 1970, and his fifteen years later at eighty-five. The handsome white houses in the wooded twelve-acre park date from the eighteenth and nineteenth centuries, but the water mill on the River Remarde goes back to the twelfth century. Millers worked here well into the nineteenth century. Aragon and Triolet restored the old mill, and Aragon willed it to France.

The mill is the museum-home of this literary couple, appearing as it did when they lived in it—with books all over the place. One of the founders of Surrealism, Aragon wrote some of the movement's most brilliant works, including *Le Paysan de Paris*, published in 1926, one of a trilogy of great Surrealist explorations of Paris, alongside André Breton's *Nadja* and Philippe Soupault's *Last Nights of Paris*. Aragon joined the Communist party in 1927, and the next year met the Russian-born Elsa. From then on they were inseparable—from each other, from the Party, until the Soviet crackdown in Czechoslovakia in 1968, and from the written word. She won the 1944 Prix Goncourt for her novel *Le Premier accroc coûte 200 francs* (*The First Breach Costs 200 Francs*), awarded after the Liberation by a Goncourt committee eager to whitewash its complacency during the Occupation.

In a secluded corner of the Moulin de Villeneuve's grounds is the burial place of Aragon and Triolet, under a common gravestone beneath a beech tree which Elsa loved.

MARCEL PROUST'S MAISON DE TANTE LÉONIE AT ILLIERS-COMBRAY

Between the ages of age six and nine, Marcel Proust spent his Easter and summer holidays at the home of his Aunt Elisabeth (Dr. Proust's sister) and Uncle Jules Amiot in the village of Illiers, in the vicinity of Chartres. The city boy loved his escapes to the country, but they were cut short by his asthma attacks at age nine, which convinced his father to shift the family's vacations to the Normandy coast, where Proust could breathe pollen-free air from the sea. He returned only once, in September 1886, when he was fifteen, to attend his Aunt Elisabeth's funeral.

Proust's presence pervades the village. The local bakery sells souvenir boxes of *madeleines* with his picture on the lid. There are streets named for him and his

Marcel Proust's Maison de Tante Léonie

father. Signs point you to the *côté de chez* Swann or Guermantes. On the edge of town, along the tree-shaded rivulet of the Loir (the Vivonne in the novel) is the Pré Catelan, a delightful *jardin à l'anglaise* created by Proust's Uncle Jules, and donated to the community; it is the model for Swann's park in *Swann's Way*. And, of course, the Maison de Tante Léonie is the Musée Marcel Proust.

The house is much as it is described in the opening part of the novel, from the magic lantern of Geneviève de Brabant to the staircase the little narrator climbs all alone on the nights when M. Swann comes to call. Though she was neither ailing nor a widow, Aunt Elizabeth became the model for Tante Léonie, who rules her little domain from her sick bed by the window in her room upstairs. This room is where she gives the young narrator the *madeleine* dipped in tea, whose taste would later unleash a flood of memories in him:

> . . . All the flowers in our garden and in M. Swann's park, and the water lilies
> on the Vivonne and the good folk of the village and their little dwellings and
> the parish church and the whole of Combray and its surroundings, taking
> shape and solidity, sprang into being, town and gardens alike, from my cup
> of tea.

"La vraie vie, c'est la littérature," Proust wrote in *Le Temps Retrouvé* (*Time Regained*). In 1971, literature became real life, quite literally, when the town of Illiers changed its name to Illiers-Combray.

Acknowledgments

WITHOUT Joanne's boundless zeal for the project and remarkable gift for editing, I doubt very much that this mutual labor of love could have come to fruition.

To my guru and literary agent Bob Lescher's electrifyingly wise comments about the first material I sent him I owe the "eureka!" moment about what the book should do and resist trying to do. Among the army of people who have helped me along the way, I particularly thank René Demeestère and Phyllis Koshland for reading, correcting, and discussing the text with me time and again, and Evelyne Bloch-Dano, Noel Riley Fitch, Hazel Rowley, Beatrice Commengé, John Baxter, Christine Jordis, Georges Poisson, James Knowlson, Emily Emerson Le Moing, Trica Keaton, Velma Bury, and Simon Gallo for all the literary, biographical, and topographical references they gave me.

My old friend Bob Ellis has given me tremendous moral and intellectual support since my first tentative mulling-over of this idea, and his guidance about my *Writers in Paris* web site has been invaluable. Other close friends whose advice has helped me greatly along the way are Bernard and Catherine Rouault, Margaret O'Shea, Shelley Bradford-Bell, and C. D. B. Bryan, along with his friend and agent Carl Brandt. I thank Karl Orend for goading me into taking my first practical step on the book. And I am endlessly grateful to Jack Shoemaker, Roxanna Aliaga, Cheri Hickman, Patrick Barber, Holly McGuire, and the photography, map-making, and design teams at Counterpoint for creating the attractive and carefully edited book it has turned out to be.

My deepest thanks go to all the writers of all eras, whether in the book or not, who have helped make Paris the phenomenally rich and exciting city it is.

Photo Credits

PAGE	PHOTO	CREDIT
56	Chester Himes	Xavier University Library
57	Peter Orlovsky (in cap) and Allen Ginsberg in Paris, December 1957	Harold Chapman
58	Albert Camus in the late 1940s	Rue des Archives
62	Boris Vian at the 1949 Paris Jazz Festival	Rue des Archives/AGIP
63	Carrefour de l'Odéon, Rue Monsieur-le-Prince on the left, Rue de Condé on the right, and Rue de l'Odéon in the center, with the Théâtre de l'Odéon at the top of the street.	Courtesy of Bibliothèque Historique de la Ville de Paris
64	James Joyce and Sylvia Beach at Shakespeare and Company	Princeton University Library
67	The Marquis de Sade at twenty, his only known portrait from life, by Charles-Amédée-Philippe Van Loo	Suddeutsche Zeitung/Rue des Archives
69	Luxembourg Gardens	Courtesy of Bibliothèque Historique de la Ville de Paris
70	D'Artagnan and the Three Musketeers	Rue de Archives/The Granger Collection NYC
74	The Church of Saint-Sulpice and its Place	Courtesy of Bibliothèque Historique de la Ville de Paris
75	Djuna Barnes	Yale Collection of American Literature, Beinecke Rare Book and Manuscript Library
75	Jacques Casanova, portrait by Pietro Longhi	Rue des Archives
78	Café de Tournon, a refuge for many expatriates	David Burke
78	Joseph Roth	Rue des Archives/The Granger Collection NYC
81, 125	Ernest Hemingway	Rue des Archives
81	F. Scott Fitzgerald	Rue des Archives
85	Alfred Jarry, 1897 drawing by F. A. Cazals	Bibliothèque Nationale de France
87	The Quai Voltaire, Pont Royal, and Gare d'Orsay, early 20th century	Courtesy of Bibliothèque Historique de la Ville de Paris
89, 125	Charles Baudelaire, photograph by Carjat	Bibliothèque Nationale de France
89	Musée d'Orsay	Sophie Beogly, Musée d'Orsay, 2006
92	André Malraux in 1933, the manuscript of *Man's Fate* on the desk	Rene Dazy/Rue des Archives
92	Guillaume Apollinare after his head wound, photograph by Harlingue	Bibliothèque Nationale de France
93, 231	René de Chateaubriand	Bibliothèque Nationale de France
97	Edith Wharton, Christmas 1905	Yale Collection of American Literature, Beinecke Rare Book and Manuscript Library
98	Rodin Museum	David Burke
100	Eiffel Tower	Courtesy of Bibliothèque Historique de la Ville de Paris
102	The Dôme and the Boulevard du Montparnasse	Rue des Archives, Collection PVDE
106	August Strindberg	Bibliothèque Nationale de France
111	Ford Madox Ford, James Joyce, and Ezra Pound in the garden of Pound's house	Rue des Archives/The Granger Collection NYC

Index of Writers